Deep C#

Deep C#

Dive Into Modern C#

First Edition

Mike James

I/O Press
I Programmer Library

Mike James Deep C#: Dive Into Modern C#
1st Edition
ISBN Paperback: 978-1871962710

First Printing, 2021
Revision 0

Published by IO Press   www.iopress.info
In association with I Programmer   www.i-programmer.info

Preface

C# is a well-established language and, with its new open-source incarnation it has renewed vigor and a long-term future. It is now possible to treat C# as a single modern language with the ability to work cross-platform. It has gone from being a one-OS, i.e. Windows, language to something that works with Windows, Linux, Mac OS and more. However, it still has many features that make it an ideal choice for Windows development.

This book is what might be called a "deep dive" into various topics that are important or central to the language. Some of the dives aren't as deep as others – not all topics harbor the same degree of deepness and how deep you find something depends on how much you know already. If you are a C# super-expert, you might think that we are just getting our feet wet. However, my intention is to explain the topics at a level that will suit the majority of C# programmers. Not everything will be new to any given reader, but I hope that the motivation behind key concepts, which is so often ignored in the documentation, is new and thought-provoking.

Most of the chapters start off in the shallows and work their way towards deeper water. Each chapter is largely self-contained and this does entail some repetition and unfortunately there is still the need for some forward and backward references. If you encounter something that it is assumed you know about, but you don't, then look it up – none of the assumed ideas are deep.

While you can read the chapters in almost any order, there is a progression of ideas within each section. This book is not a cookbook, a language introduction or a reference, it is a general reader for the interested programmer. It is also focused on language aspects of C# and far less so on the technologies such ASP.NET, WPF or any of the framework libraries. These are comparatively easy when you have touched bottom with C#.

My thanks are due to my ever-diligent editors, Sue Gee and Kay Ewbank, for spotting errors and suggesting improvements.

Mike James
September 2021

To discover other titles by Mike James and to keep informed about forthcoming titles in the **I Programmer Library** visit the publisher's website:

www.iopress.info

The book's page is where you will find any errata or updates.

Table of Contents

Chapter 4
Structs & Classes 53

Chapter 5
Inheritance 65

Chapter 6
Interfaces & Multiple Inheritance 79

Chapter 14
Anonymous Methods, Lambdas & Closures 169

IV Async
Chapter 15
Threading, Tasks & Locking 189

Chapter 16
The Invoke Pattern 205

Chapter 1
Why C#?

C# is a logical modern language that has so many advantages that it is difficult to know where to begin – but if you are reading this book you probably don't need much convincing. Even so it is worth knowing where the language came from, how it developed and where it stands in the world today, if only to make the case to other programmers less well-informed.

The Politics

The language first appeared around 2000 as part of .NET, which was Microsoft's effort to modernize programming under Windows. It was the first major alternative to using C++, a very low-level language by comparison, and Visual Basic 6, a comparatively high-level one. Visual Basic 6 was, and still is, well-thought of by many but it was a language that had grown rather than been designed. C# was intended to provide a middle ground for programmers not wanting the intricacies of C++ nor the limitations of Visual Basic 6. At the same time a direct replacement for Visual Basic 6, Visual Basic .NET, was introduced but it satisfied no-one by being unlike its predecessor and not as logical or clean a language as C#.

This was a time when Microsoft really put effort into providing a programming environment that was special to Windows in order to attract programmers. The strategy worked, but internal divisions within Microsoft and later the turmoil of Windows 8 and Windows Phone resulted in a loss of focus. Eventually this led to Microsoft supporting languages from other sources and the loss of the idea that Windows needed its own homegrown language.

As a result in 2015 C# was open-sourced and adapted to work on any system, including Linux – the arch enemy of Windows. Much progress was lost in the effort to convert the .NET system to a fully cross-platform, but today we have a modern version of the language that will run on more than just Windows. It has to be admitted that there are still many areas of C# use where the available libraries make it "Windows-specific". For example, if you want to develop a good user interface then WPF (Windows Presentation Foundation) is a good choice, but it only runs under Windows. There are efforts to build cross-platform replacements for these facilities, but many think that these will always be second best to the Windows programming environment.

At the time of writing .NET and C# are alive and well and have a secure future, partly because Microsoft is not backing them as hard as it once did. The existence of a wider open source community is a reassurance that the C# programmer is no longer at the mercy of the volatile decisions of a company with a profit motive and lack of a wider vision.

Today C# is a language of the computer world but still with a Windows legacy.

What Is C#?

In its original incarnation C# was a more logical and hence easier to use C++, heavily influenced by Java. It was designed by Anders Hejlsberg who already had a string of successful language implementations to his credit. To date, C# is arguably his crowning achievement. The language implemented many of the concerns important at the time that were missing, or only partly implemented, in C++ and Java.

The key idea was that C# should be an object-oriented language – everything is an object – and it should be strongly typed so that type checking can detect simple errors at compile time. Its implementation was also important in achieving these goals. Rather than use the Java Virtual Machine (JVM) or compile to native code, C# compiled to the .NET intermediate language (IL) and was run in a managed way which ensured that memory could not be corrupted by bounds overruns or orphaned objects. All of this takes work and, as a result, C# programs are not as fast nor memory efficient as, say, the same program written in C, but they are in principle much safer.

Early versions of any language can afford to be pure and stick to their founding principles, but over time they tend to accumulate additional "nice" features. So it is with C#. At first the additions were intended to make up for omissions in the early versions. Many of these features were introduced with the benefit of seeing how they had been done in other languages and so tended to be more complete. For example, version 2 introduced generics, complete with covariance and contravariance to make type-safe programming more flexible. Facilities were improved to make them easier to use and more logical. For example, C# doesn't implement functions as objects, usually expressed as *functions are not first class objects in C#* so it provided a way to wrap a function in an object – a delegate – which is more or less the equivalent of the Java SAM (Single Abstract Method). Later it introduced anonymous methods and finally lambda functions to make functions easier to pass to other functions.

Other additions to the language have been influenced by external trends. In particular "functional programming" features have been added but always with an eye to type safety. For example, iterators, dynamic types, tuples, deconstruction, pattern matching and so on. This is enough to make some programmers say that C# is no longer a simple object-oriented, strongly typed language, but something more mixed with respect to programming paradigms. However, the backbone of C# is still its original approach.

How would C# be best described today?

C# is an object-oriented, strongly typed language with many of the features and facilities of other popular modern languages. Its primary development paradigm is object-oriented programming with conveniences imported from other approaches. It is multi-platform, but there is still a strong bias toward Windows development for desktop applications.

What Is C# For?

So should you use C# for a new project?

If you are creating anything running under Windows, as a desktop app or as a server, then C# is an excellent choice. It has library support for many Windows-only features that make creating sophisticated applications much easier. You also get the possibility of running the application cross-platform, but if you have used Windows-specific libraries you will have to find alternatives.

At the moment, Windows Forms and WPF, the two Windows GUI libraries, are not available for non-Windows systems and finding alternatives isn't easy. One possible is Avalonia, an open source XAML based GUI that works on Windows, Mac and Linux, with optional paid support. It is very similar to WPF, which was code-named Avalon before its release, but not directly compatible and there is no drag-and-drop editor. If you are able to restrict your attention to console applications then things are much simpler.

The alternative is to use ASP.NET which is a cross-platform web development system. This allows you to create applications which use HTML/CSS/JavaScript as their front ends. These are truly cross-platform, as long as you don't make use of any OS-specific libraries or facilities. The only problem is that they run in a browser and don't look native in any sense. You can hide the fact that the application is running in a browser by using a Web View component or a host like Electron which allows the application to render HTML.

If you are interested in cross-platform mobile development then there is MAUI (Multi-platform App UI). This is a project that brings Mono/Xamarin together with .NET. You can use it to create applications for Android, iOS, macOS and Windows. The only problem is that Linux is not supported, but there are efforts to add this to the open source project.

It is clear that the cross-platform uses of C# are still developing.

Working With C#

Although this isn't a book about project development, it is worth saying that the all-important development environment for C# is still Visual Studio, but this only runs under Windows. It is the development environment of choice for C# programmers as it supports a wide range of project types and it has drag-and-drop editors for both Windows Forms and WPF. If you want a quick-start, easy-to-use, IDE then this is your best choice. Perhaps its only downside is that it supports so many project types that it can be confusing.

If you are looking for a cross-platform solution then the similarly named Visual Studio Code is a good choice, but compared to Visual Studio it doesn't offer very much. With the addition of the C# extension you have a good code editor, but you have to manage the project structure yourself and there are no drag-and-drop editors and few features that allow you to configure a project.

Beyond these two Microsoft offerings there are a number of possibilities, each with their own drawbacks. Jetbrains has Rider which has a 30-day free trial, but again no UI editors. Eclipse has a plug in for C#, but its features are limited. Finally there is Xamarin's Visual Studio for the Mac which is good, but its future isn't clear.

A Brief History Of C#

There is no real need to know the history of C# unless you are forced to work on legacy code. If you are starting a new project, or one that can be modified to work with current versions, then you should use the latest version of C# and the .NET framework. You can mostly ignore the difficulties of converting between Microsoft's version of .NET and the open source version, which used to be called .NET Core. Simply use the latest version of the .NET framework unless you are forced to use an earlier version.

For interest and to help anyone working with legacy code, here's a timeline of major C# versions:

- 2002 - Version 1.0
  A very basic version of the language. It has all of the basic data structures, events and delegates.

- 2006 - Version 2.0
  The most important feature added was generics. It is also when nullable types were introduced.

- 2007 - Version 3.0
  This was when LINQ and lambda expressions were introduced along with extension methods and anonymous types. This is the point at which C# started to add functional programming features.

- 2010 - Version 4.0
  This version introduced minor additions including named arguments and improved interop. The inclusion of functional programming ideas continued with the ability to declare a variable as dynamic.

- 2012 - Version 5.0
  Async and await were new in this version and at last provided a simple, clean approach to writing asynchronous code.

- 2015 - Version 6.0
  Some minor additions including string interpolation.

- 2017 - Version 7.0
  More functional features were added including tuples and deconstruction and pattern matching.

- 2019 - Version 8.0
  Updated to make use of .NET Core, the open-source version of the .NET framework. It also introduced default interfaces, methods and extensions to pattern matching.

- 2020 - Version 9.0 2020
  Full supporting for .NET, the new name for .NET Core. The only major addition was the record type.

Outline Of This Book

This book is not a C# primer or a reference guide and you are expected already to know the basics of C# and have some idea of programming practices, in particular object orientation. The book is a look at some of the deeper ideas in the language. Hence it isn't complete and is more an exploration of the more interesting topics. Each section and chapter is relatively self-contained even when this results in some slight repetition and cross references.

It is divided into six sections

I. **Strong Typing & Type Safety**

    This is really the core philosophy of C# and yet it is rarely explained or discussed. In this section we look at what strong typing is and how it makes type safety possible. Along the way we look at the differences between value and reference and specifically class and struct. Inheritance is also a key part of type - without it type safety would be irrelevant and so we need to be sure that it is fully understood along with how multiple inheritance is implemented using interfaces.

II. **Casting & Generics**

    The problem with strong typing is that it limits how easy it is to do some things. The first solution to the problem is casting – stating the type of an object to override typing. A more sophisticated solution is to use generics and finally to allow dynamic typing.

III. **Functions**

    C# didn't take the option of making functions objects, instead it opted to use a wrapper class – the delegate – to convert functions into objects. Over time this idea has been developed to allow more and more functionality until we finally reach the pinnacle of the easy-to-use function - the lambda complete with closure.

IV. **Async**

    C# isn't a naturally asynchronous language in the sense that it isn't wedded to any particular UI framework, but it still needs to use asynchronous operations. The first approach to the problem was to use threads, then the task parallel library came along and finally the oh-so-easy to use async and await.

V. **Data - LINQ, XML, Regular Expressions**

All programming languages need to work with data and C# has some of the best data features around. LINQ is a general-purpose data query language built right into the core of C#. It provides a way to work with XML that is unique. In addition, C#'s regular expressions are more powerful than you might expect.

VI. **Unsafe & Interop**

Type safety and managed code is a big advantage, but there usually comes a time when you have to talk to legacy unmanaged code, often the operating system. To make this possible, C# provides the interop subsystem and, in the form of P/Invoke (Platform Invocation Services), this can be used to call operating system functions in DLLs or Linux libraries. If you are working under Windows then you can also interface to COM objects, which are still very important. Finally there is unsafe code which allows you use pointers and manage memory directly.

Postlude

C# is a modern, general-purpose language and it still has an edge when it comes to Windows programming. Its status as a cross-platform language is as good as any and improving all the time. If you can, it is worth using Visual Studio under Windows for program development as it provides the best environment for C# that is currently available. While there are many legacy versions of C# and the .NET framework, simply use the latest for new projects.

I Strong Typing & Type Safety

Prelude

This is really the core philosophy of C# and yet it is rarely explained or discussed. In this section we look at what strong typing is and how it makes type safety possible. Along the way we look at the differences between value and reference and specifically class and struct. Inheritance is also a key part of type - without it type safety would be irrelevant - and so we need to be sure that it fully understood. After that we see how multiple inheritance is implemented using interfaces.

Chapter 2

Strong Typing

C# is a language that started out in the style of Java with strong typing and very little extra. Over time it has added features in a careful and thoughtful way to include things that you might not associate with a strongly typed, "traditional" object-oriented language. For many this is what makes C# special. Today C# has late binding with dynamic typing. This provides the modern C# programmer with idioms that previously would have been thought out of the question. Dynamic typing goes directly against the static strong typing that is supposed to catch many errors at compile time that otherwise would only appear at runtime.

The worry is that by introducing such loose practice C# might become a mess by adopting models that go against its birthright of strict typing and object-oriented procedural code. What is interesting is the way that C# combines the best of both worlds - but see if you agree.

Strong Typing and Type Safety

Strong typing, which is a guiding principle for C#, is also the defacto default for most languages. The exceptions, Python and JavaScript for example, suffer much criticism for not being strongly typed and they also are subject to maintainers who slowly try to convert them into strongly typed languages in one way or another. As already mentioned, C# has been moving in the opposite direction. Starting out with nothing but strong types it has been slowly adding features that attempt to make it as easy to use as some of the dynamically typed languages. However, every modification to C# has tried to preserve its strong typing and type-safe approach. It is still a guiding principle and it is important to understand what it is all about and what its advantages and disadvantages are.

The first problem we have to overcome is that not everyone is very clear about what "strong typing" means. So the first thing to investigate is the nature of strong typing.

Strong typing is all about trying to detect a particular error at compile time. The error in question is calling a method, or using a property, of an object that it doesn't have. That is, strong typing will flag an error at compile time if `myObject.myMethod();` isn't possible because `myObject` doesn't have a `myMethod`. A type is defined by a bundle of properties and methods and when you claim that a variable is referencing a particular type then the system assumes that the type has exactly those properties and methods. So, when you write:

```
MyClass myObject=new MyClass();
```

`myObject` is assumed to have all of the properties and methods of `MyClass`.

If, after this, you write:

```
myObject.myMethod()
```

then the compiler can check that `MyClass` defines a function called `myMethod` at compile time and refuse to let the program run if it doesn't.

Strong typing is a bookkeeping method of making sure that you only use what you declare you have implemented.

What this means is that every variable has an assigned type, provided by its class definition, and it can only reference an object that has been created from that type definition. Of course, and you are probably so familiar with this idea that you don't notice it, we generally allow derived classes to stand in for a base class, or more generally any class that is lower in the inheritance chain.

So we are accustomed to the idea that there is nothing wrong with:

```
MyClassA myObjectA;
    . . .
myObjectA = myObjectB;
```

as long as `myObjectB` has inherited `MyClassA` somewhere in its inheritance chain.

Why is this permitted? The reason is that we can assume that any method or property that `MyClassA` has is present in `myObjectB`. This is sometimes expressed as the Liskov Substitution Principle which is informally *anywhere you can use a base class you can use a derived class*. Of course, this is nonsense as the derived class can override methods in the base class and if these are used in place of the base class methods then things can go wrong.

The Liskov principle is only true if we work to make it true. In particular, it is only true by default if the language specifies early binding, more of this later. This leads to the idea of being "type safe". An instruction is type safe if it is possible to use type to check at compile time that it will not cause a run-time error. If you want to determine that some feature of any language is type safe simply ask yourself if it is possible to determine at compile time that a run-time error is extremely unlikely on the basis of the types in use.

The strong typing bookkeeping allows derived types to be used in place of the base type simply because they have all of the properties of the base type.

Why is compile-time checking so important?

If you make a type error that isn't detected at compile time, it will most probably be detected at run time with a run-time exception. The reason that it is only *probably* detected is a matter of coverage. A syntactically correct program can cause a run-time error, but only if the inputs to the program cause it to exercise that part of the program where the error is located. You may run the program and never trigger the error, only for your first user to encounter it because they use the program differently to you. If you could guarantee to find all run-time errors on the first run there would be little difference between compile-time and run-time detection. This is the problem of "coverage".

It is often claimed that strong typing helps with entering the correct code in the first place via some sort of intelligent prompting. This is sometimes true, but it is often used to make up for poor documentation and the same facility can be implemented without having to enforce strong typing, or typing of any sort. The point is that the sort of errors that strong typing and type safety detect are very trivial – they have to be to be detected at compile time. It really does come down to determining that the object being used has the properties and methods you actually use.

Type safety is a very limited form of safety.

Static Typing and Binding

Even with strong typing we have a choice of how to implement it. We can opt to have a variable declared just once as one particular type that persists for the entire life of the program. That is, following:

```
string a;
```

you can be sure that wherever you see a in the program it references a string. Of course, things are not quite this simple as local variables can reuse the same name in another part of the program and there may well be a variable called a that references something that isn't a string. However, with these scope and lifetime issues taken into account, we can be sure that when a occurs in the program with its original meaning, i.e. it is in scope, then it is a string.

This is static typing and the alternative is dynamic typing where a variable can be declared to be a different type or more usually can acquire a new type implicitly by being assigned to that type. In this approach you can even dispense with the idea that a variable has a type as it can clearly be made to reference anything you like.

C# uses, mostly, static typing. This may seem like a small decision but it actually has far reaching consequences for the language. In particular static typing makes early binding the natural choice. The idea of binding is confusing and generally poorly defined. It basically is about when a variable acquires its reference or, more accurately, when its reference is determined. For simple cases early binding, i.e. binding at compile time, is not only obvious, it seems the only option. For example, if you write:

```
a="Hello World";
```

It is very obvious that a is a string and it references a string literal and this is determined at compile time. The variable a is early-bound to its reference.

It almost seems as if late binding is a silly idea – why would you ever put off binding a variable to its reference? Consider the case where we have two classes MyClassA and MyClassB that is derived from it. Both have a myMethod method, but MyClassB has overridden it and provides its own version of the method. Now consider what happens in:

```
MyClassA myObject;
myObject=anObject;
myObject.myMethod();
```

where anObject is either a MyClassA or a MyClassB. This is perfectly legal and type safe as MyClassA and MyClassB have a myMethod attribute. However, it raises the question of which of the versions of the method should be called?

If you use early binding then myObject.myMethod should be bound at compile time to the MyClassA version as this is the variable's declared type. If you use late binding then it could be either of the versions depending on what anObject is at run time.

Early binding only depends on the declared type of the variable. Late binding depends on the type of the object referenced at run time.

Notice that only the early binding version strictly satisfies the Liskov principle as only it guarantees that the method used is always the same, independent of the actual type of the object.

In C# early binding is the default but you can opt for late binding, see Virtual Functions in Chapter 4.

Type and Flow of Control - Signatures

Notice that early binding makes things more efficient. This applies to assignment, method parameters and return types, all of which can be compiled in and not dynamically determined at run time. This mostly applies to types derived from classes, structs or interfaces but it also applies to functions. The type of a function depends on its signature – the types of its parameters. Notice its return type isn't used.

Type determination can also affect the flow of control in a program, but static typing and early binding can only determine it at compile time. For example, consider the two overloaded methods defined within some object:

```
public string myMethod(int i){
        return "Integer";
}
public string myMethod(double f){
        return "Double";
}
```

Then, when you write:

```
MyObject.myMethod(X);
```

which method is called depends on the type of X. If X is an int, the first method is called and if it is a double, the second method is called.

You may well be used to the idea that overloaded methods are called according to signature, but you might not have realized how important this makes the determination of type as part of the flow of control in your program.

The method call `myMethod(X)` being resolved according to the signature of the call might be thought to be expressed by the equivalent code:

```
MyClass MyObject = new MyClass();
int X = 1;
if (X is int)
{
        MyObject.myMethodInt(X);
}
else if (X is double)
{
        MyObject.myMethodDouble(X);
}
```

but notice that this code actually determines the type of X at run time, not compile time. If X had in fact changed to a double before the `if`, `myMethodDouble` would be called. This is how it is done in late binding or dynamic typing.

If you examine   the code and remember that this is a static language, you can see that myMethodInt is always called - there is no possibility of anything else happening because X is always an int once it has been declared to be an int.

In this sense the whole if statement and testing is completely unnecessary and you might as well write:

```
int X = 1;
MyObject.myMethodInt(X);
```

In a statically typed language there is no way a variable can change the type it is assigned when it is declared. Thus static typing makes early binding possible for function overloading. However, even static typing is a little more subtle than this. The extra complexity comes, once again, from the idea that any type that derives from another type should be usable in place of the parent type. That is, if I declare a class as:

```
public class MyClassB:MyClassA
{
   ...
}
```

then, as already discussed, MyClassB can be used in place of MyClassA and generally treated as if it was of type MyClassA. For example, a method like:

```
public string myMethod(MyClassA obj) {
       return "MyClass";
}
```

can be called with a parameter of type MyClassA or MyClassB. So, from the point of view of method signatures, derived classes act like their parent classes. So what if we now overload myMethod with a specific version for MyClassB?

```
public string myMethod(MyClassB o){
       return "MyClassB";
}
```

Now if I call myMethod with a parameter of type MyClassB, which method will be called? The answer is, unsurprisingly the one with the signature that matches the parameter most closely. In this case the version of myMethod with the MyClassB parameter is called.

This is a general principle:

the method with the signature that most closely matches the types used in the signature is used.

Although this use of derived types in method calls is a little more complicated, notice that it uses the declared type of each variable and not what the variable actually references. Again, static typing simplifies the task. Consider what a late binding version of the "closest match" algorithm would require.

So, apart from the use of virtual methods, see later, all binding in C# is early binding and only the declared type of a variable can influence what a program does. As we will see, dynamic typing promotes the determination of type to something that can determine what happens at run time beyond the use of virtual.

Type and Flow of Control - Polymorphism

The second big use of type to determine the flow of control is polymorphism. The basic idea here is that every class defines methods that work with that class, even if they share the same name with other classes.

For example, suppose we had a non-object-oriented sort function. Then we would in practice need a number of such functions for each type that we wanted to sort, `SortInt`, `SortDouble`, `SortMyClass` and so on. Each function would accept a list of items of the appropriate type. If you wanted to sort a list of integers you would have to write:

```
SortInt(IntList);
```

The main motivation for introducing objects is to associate operations with the data that they operate on. So in an object-oriented world there would be just one sort function but it would be defined as part of the class that it sorted instances of.

So for example:

```
class ListofMyClass{
      MyClass[] sort(){ … sort algorithm ...};
}
```

Now you can write:

```
ListofMyClass list =  definition of a list of MyClass instances
list.sort();
```

It looks as though we have got rid of parameters, but of course we haven't as `list` is passed to the sort method as the default parameter `this`. This is how objects work – the instance, the receiver, is passed to methods as a default parameter and:

```
list.sort();
```

is best thought of as:

```
sort(list);
```

where the first parameter is named `this` by default.

You can say that this is all there is to objects…

This simple change means that objects use the method, i.e. function, that is appropriate to their type – obvious but this is what is generally called polymorphism and it is often said to be one of the pillars of object-oriented programming.

31

Polymorphism is often described as "if-less" computing because instead of having to write something like:

```
if ( MyObject is MyClassA)
{
        sortA(MyObject);
}
 else if (X is MyClassB)
{
        sortB(MyObject);
}
```

you can simply write:

```
MyObject.sort();
```

and expect the object-oriented mechanism to pick the correct method. To be more precise, if MyObject is MyClassA then it calls the sort defined in that class and if it is MyClassB it calls the sort defined in that class. Notice that, as C# is statically typed, this isn't quite as impressive as it looks as the decision is made at compile time. That is, the equivalent code is more like:

```
MyClassB MyObject:
sortB(MyObject);
```

No ifs were eliminated in this procedure as the correct function to call was always perfectly clear and unchanging.

Polymorphism is really only impressive if late binding is involved. For example, if we now assume that MyClassB is derived from MyClassA then we can write:

```
MyClassA myObject;
    .   .   .
myObject.myMethod();
```

If early binding is used then this is compiled into a call to myMethod defined in MyClassA, irrespective of what object myObject actually references. Only if myMethod is marked as virtual, see Chapter 5, is late binding used and then polymorphism is the same as:

```
if ( MyObject is MyClassA)
{
        call MyClassA version of myMethod
}
 else if (X is MyClassB)
{
        call MyClassB version of myMethod
}
```

You can see that early binding results in a fairly trivial form of polymorphism as which method is called is always known at compile time. If you want a decision to be made at run time, i.e. true polymorphism, then you have no choice but to use late binding.

Type and Flow of Control – Pattern Matching

Perhaps the ultimate expression of type affecting flow of control is in pattern matching. This idea is popular in functional programming where its key idea seems to be allowing conditionals to test a much wider range of things than simple value relationships. Pattern matching is a relatively recent introduction to C# and it is still evolving. Some are of the opinion that, as you could already do most of what it offers using existing features, it really isn't a good addition to the language.

You can use a pattern with the `is` or `switch` expressions. The former is simple:

```
expression is pattern
```

and it is true if the *expression* matches the pattern.

For more complex scenarios the `switch` expression is:

```
test expression switch {
    pattern case guard => expression,
    pattern case guard => expression,
    etc…
}
```

where the value of the `switch` expression is the *expression* corresponding to the first *pattern* that the *test expression* matches. If the *pattern* doesn't select the entity you want precisely enough you can add a *case guard*, which is a general logical expression that has to be true for the match to succeed.

The `switch` expression is very similar to the familiar `switch` statement:

```
switch (expression)
{
    case pattern:
            actions;
            break;
    case pattern:
            actions;
            break;

    .    .    .
    default:
            default actions;
}
```

but it only evaluates a single expression as its "case" action and the range of conditions that can be tested is limited. The `switch` statement can only use constant patterns and type patterns whereas the `switch` expression can use all of the possible patterns.

There are a range of different forms of pattern that can be used, but the two that are most relevant to type safety are the type and declaration patterns. The type pattern is seemingly simple - specify a type that the run time type of the expression has to match. For example:

```
object myObject = new MyClassA();
int myResult=myObject switch
{
        MyClassB => 1,
        MyClassA => 2,
        int => 3
};
Console.WriteLine(myResult);
```

In this case the result is 2 as myObject is a MyClassA. This looks simple, but there are a number of things to be aware of. The first is that if MyClassB is derived from MyClassA then you cannot test for MyClassA first. That is:

```
        MyClassA => 1,
        MyClassB => 2,
```

will give a compile time error. The reason is that testing for MyClassA matches all derived classes and so testing for MyClassB after it can never work. The second thing to note is that myObject has to be of type object to allow it to be all three types tested for. The compiler will use strong typing to detect match conditions that could never happen. That is:

```
MyClassA myObject = new MyClassA();
int myResult = myObject switch
{
        MyClassB => 1,
        MyClassA => 2,
        int => 3
};
Console.WriteLine(myResult);
```

gives a compile time error because you cannot set myObject to be an int. Thus pattern matching is implemented in a type-safe way.

What if you want to call myMethod on MyClassA and MyClassB? You can't do this without casting (see Chapter 8), for example:

```
int myResult=myObject switch
{
        MyClassB =>((MyClassB) myObject).myMethod(),
        MyClassA => ((MyClassA)myObject).myMethod(),
        int => 3
};
```

This "find a type – use a type" action is so common that there is a pattern that implements it directly – the declaration pattern. This allows you to declare a new variable for the expression to be cast to, for example:

```
object myObject = new MyClassA();
int myResult = myObject switch
{
        MyClassB myB => myB.myMethod(),
        MyClassA myA => myA.myMethod(),
        int myInt => myInt
};
Console.WriteLine(myResult);
```

This automatically casts the myObject to the correct type in the declared variable.

Pattern matching is a lot more sophisticated than this suggests. In addition to type and declaration patterns, you can also use constant and relational patterns to perform simple tests, for example:

```
int myObject = 10;
string myResult = myObject switch
{
        0 => "zero",
        >0 => "positive",
        _ => "negative"
};
Console.WriteLine(myResult);
```

The first pattern matches the constant 0, the second tests a relation and the final pattern is the discard pattern which matches anything. As switch expressions have to return a result, one of the matches has to succeed and the simplest way to do this is to include a discard pattern at the end, which always matches and ensures that the entire switch returns a result.

Perhaps the most sophisticated patterns are the property and positional patterns. The property pattern allows you to test individual properties in an object. The properties are specified as a comma-separated list in curly brackets, for example:

```
int myResult = myObject switch
{
        MyClassB {myProperty: >5} => expression,
        .      .      .
```

This only matches if the myObject.myProperty is greater than 5. Notice that this is type safe as myObject has to be of type MyClassB and the compiler checks that it has myProperty. You can nest the pattern in the sense that if myProperty is an object you can test its properties and so on.

```
MyClassB {myProperty: {A:0,B:>5} => expression,
```

This matches if myObject.myProperty.A is 0 and myObject.myProperty.B is greater than 5.

Positional patterns are very similar to property patterns, but they allow you to test on fields in tuples (see Chapter 4) or anything that has a `Deconstruct` method that will return a tuple, for example:

```
int A = 1;
int B = 2;
int C = 3;
int myResult = (A,B,C) switch
{
        (1,2,3) => expression,
        (>1,_,0) => expression,
            .       .       .
};
```

The first pattern matches if `A==1`, `B==2` and `C==3`. The second pattern matches if `A>1`, `B` is any value and `C==0`. The underscore is used as a discard pattern which matches anything. Also notice that `(A,B,C)` is a tuple and can be replaced by any object that has a `Deconstruct` method that will give a tuple.

The `var` pattern has nothing much to do with type apart from allowing you to declare a variable of the same type as the run time type of the expression. In most cases this means matching on the case guard. For example

```
int A = 1;
int B = 2;
int C = 3;
int myResult = (A, B, C) switch
{
        var myVar when A > B => myVar.A,
        var myVar when A < B => myVar.A
};
```

In this case `myVar` is the same type as the expression being tested, i.e. a tuple, and the case guard picks out what to do with it.

Finally, you can combine patterns using `and`, `or` and `not` to combine patterns in obvious ways.

Pattern matching is a new and powerful way to make use of type in its widest sense to determine the flow of control. It is type safe in that type declarations are used to detect when a pattern is unworkable or when you are trying to use a type as if it was another type. Pattern matching doesn't give you much in the way of new abilities, but it does give you the opportunity to write very dense and incomprehensible code. What seems neat and compact when you write it can often feel cryptic when you reread it.

Parameters, Type and Function Safety

One of the biggest attractions of using strong typing is its ability to seemingly make functions easier and safer to use. Strong typing stops you from trying to use methods and properties that clearly aren't available on the objects you are working with. The strange thing about this idea is that if you are writing the code then presumably you know what methods are available on the object you are using – so why is strong typing so well thought of?

The answer is that strong typing can help you move all of the uncertainty about objects and what they support to the boundaries of your code. Consider for a moment a simple function defined without type information:

```
add(a,b){return a+b}
```

The meaning of the function is clear, but what is the type of a, b and the return value? Clearly the intention of the, perhaps naive, programmer is that an operation "+" works for a and b and the result is also presumably the same type or at least an obvious type. You can see that the function definition represents a sort of boundary between the code in the function and the outside world of code that will make use of it. The function writer cannot rely on the function user to make sure that a and b are the right type. Of course, the function user needs to promise to use the function as intended.

Now compare this to a fully typed function:

```
int add(int a, int b){return a+b};
```

You can see that the boundary is protected and it is 100% clear that the function has to be used with integers and nothing but integers. This is the huge attraction of strong typing. It allows the compiler to check when the function is used that it is used correctly – it is type safe. For example:

```
int a = 1;
double b = 1.0;
int c = add(a,b);
```

will generate a compiler error because b isn't an int. This is an unfortunate example in a number of senses. The function refuses to add two numbers together, despite the fact that it makes perfect sense to do so. It might be that a better way to guard the entrance to a function isn't to rely on strong typing but to make sure that the methods and operations the function uses are appropriate for the data passed in.

There are more practical examples of similar difficulties, but the essential idea is that using strong typing you are using the class hierarchy to model the world in such a way that the only objects that have related methods are related by inheritance and, in general, this is difficult and sometimes illogical. It may be that we can fix the problem with int and double in the add function by making a general number class that both `int` and `double` inherit from, but this wouldn't solve the problem of "adding" strings as there is no logical way that a string can inherit from number. You can argue that the use of "+" for strings isn't the same as its use in numbers and hence the distinction is valid, but there are more subtle cases where this is harder to argue.

The real point is that constructing a class hierarchy that works from the point of view of type safety, but doesn't add strange and additional restrictions on what you can do, is very difficult. It is especially difficult if you don't have multiple inheritance, and statically strong typed languages tend not to because it introduces too many difficulties.

What is also clear is that as soon as you allow late binding, type safety is less useful. If you have a function:

```
void MyFunction(MyClassA myObject){
     myObject.myMethod();
};
```

then with late binding `myObject` could be any class derived from `MyClassA` and `myMethod` could have been overridden. While typing guarantees that `myObject` has a `myMethod` it doesn't say anything about what it actually does and hence it might not be safe to call in the context. That is with early binding `myMethod` will be that defined in `MyClassA` and you can be fairly sure what the code does. With late binding `myMethod` could be any of the overridden methods in the derived classes and what it does isn't clear.

Strong typing still give you some worthwhile guarantees in this situation – that the method accepts a particular set of typed parameters and returns a particular type of result - but nothing more.

Complications

Type safety is an idea that seems good and cost-free when you first start applying it to simple situations, but as things become more like the real world, problems start to arise. Mostly these problems are to do with having to write more code that you would need without strong typing. In an effort to fix these problems new features have been added to the language. They include generics (see Chapter 8), optional late binding and virtual methods (see Chapter 4), interfaces, pattern matching and variance.

How you view these features depends very much on how you view the advantages of strong static typing. There is no doubt that while they may solve problems, such problems only arise in complex situations and can be difficult to understand.

Postlude

So much is promised for type-safe code, but you have to see that in many senses it only solves a very simple problem – that the methods and properties that you use actually exist on the object you are working with. This is something worth having, but it can be achieved in many different ways. At the end of the day, code often has to determine the type of an object at run time and when this happens in a strongly typed language we have to resort to many complex techniques to make it work.

Chapter 3

Value & Reference

Value and reference are a fundamental division in the way C# treats data. It is important that you understand the differences and most importantly when to use a struct and when to use a class. These aren't just differences in efficiency, they affect the semantics too.

Value and Reference

As already discussed, see Chapter 2, C# is an object-oriented, strongly typed language. The "object-oriented" part of the definition simply means that, in principle at least, everything is derived from the object class. However, all object-oriented languages suffer from the need to treat some types of very simple values as something other than objects. The reason for this is mostly efficiency – do you really want to wrap a simple integer value in all the machinery needed to implement a full class? But there is also a fundamental difference in the way programmers think about simple data types and class-based types. C# tackles this distinction in a very reasonable way that combines efficiency, a natural approach and an object-oriented outlook.

Pointers Become References

C# defines two different types of variable, value and reference.

(There is also a pointer type which acts much like an untyped reference, but this needs special treatment - see Chapter 28)

A value type usually corresponds to the simplest of data types, i.e. an int or a float, and the data is stored on the stack or within the code itself. The amount of storage used by a value type depends on its exact type.

On the other hand a reference type is essentially a sophisticated pointer to the actual data and so always takes the same amount, usually eight bytes, of storage. A reference type is also stored on the stack but the object that it "points" at is allocated on the heap. You will notice the use of the terms "point" and "pointer" in connection with reference types and this isn't strictly correct even if it is easier to say than reference and references.

Pointers are variables that generally contain the raw address of another variable. This is a very low-level concept and can cause all sorts of problems and bad practices because it leads on to uncontrolled access to the machine's entire memory.

A reference type is a way of providing the same behavior, but in a controlled or managed way. Put simply:

references are safe - pointers are not!

However, despite all of the reservations, thinking about a reference as a sort of typed pointer does help understand how everything works and thinking about references as pointers, preferably some sort of abstract pointer which has nothing to do with an "address", is recommended - just don't admit to it in polite company!

Before we move on it is vital that you are 100% clear that you know what stack and heap storage is.

Heap and Stack

If you do know about heap and stack then skip to the next section.

When you declare a new variable the compiler has to generate code that allocates sufficient memory to store the data it is to hold.

The whole subject of memory allocation is a complicated and interesting one, but every programmer should know about the two very general approaches - the stack and the heap.

Stack-based memory is a natural match for the way that variables are allocated and created by a program constructed as a set of nested method or function calls, which most are. What happens is that when a method is called all of its local variables are created on the top of the stack - creating its so-called stack frame. While the method executes it has access to only its local variables, i.e. its entire environment is limited to the data on the stack frame. Exceptions to this local-only rule are global variables and objects but these are allocated on the heap. If the method calls another method then the new method creates its stack frame on the top of the stack. In this way each new method can allocate its own local variables in its own portion of the memory allocated to the stack.

The beauty of stack allocation is that to implement garbage disposal all that has to happen is that when each method terminates it simply clears the stack of its stack frame, i.e. it adjusts the stack pointer to point to the end of its stack frame, so returning the memory to use. Of course, when a method ends, control returns to the method that called it and it finds the stack in just the state it needs to access its own local variables.

In this way each method gets access to its local variables while it is running, without any need to keep track of where they are. The stack is also used to store parameters and return values passed between methods in a fairly obvious way.

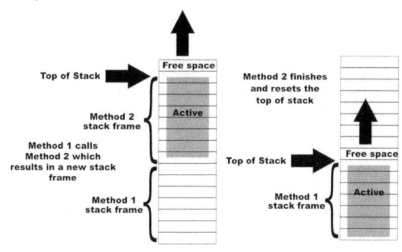

The stack in action

The stack works well for storing all manner of data that is created and destroyed following the pattern of method calls, but for global data and for very large or complex data we need something else.

The alternative is the "heap". This is a very descriptive name for an area of memory that is set aside simply for the purpose of storing global data. When a global object is created, by the use of new in C#, an area of the heap is allocated big enough to store it at its initial size and a reference to its location is returned - often to be stored in a local variable on the stack. However, unlike local variables which are created and destroyed along with the method they belong to, there is no clear signal that a global object is finished with. It doesn't necessarily become redundant when the local variable that it was initially created with goes out of scope because there could be many variables referencing it. So to deal with this problem a system-wide garbage collector is provided, which keeps track of what is stored on the heap and how many references there are to each item. When an object on the heap has no references to it then it is deallocated and the memory is recovered.

This the general idea of heap management, but in practice there are many subtle problems. For example, as the heap is used and released, it slowly becomes fragmented into small blocks of heap in use separating blocks of free space. The solution is to make the garbage collector consolidate memory every now and again.

It is generally better to adopt a throwaway approach to heap management. For example, if an object, a string say, needs to increase in size then, rather than try to open up some space to make the current allocation bigger, it is generally better to mark the current allocation as garbage ready for collection and allocate a whole new block of memory, even though this involves copying the existing object. This strange fact, that it is faster to create new storage rather than extend the existing, leads on to other ideas. For example, in most languages, including C#, strings are immutable. That is, once defined you cannot change a string. All you can do is apply operations that make new strings. You can think of immutability as a high-level concept motivated by philosophical considerations or just a good idea given the way storage allocation and deallocation behaves.

Storage on the stack fits in with the idea of local variables and the call and return pattern of methods. Storage on the heap gives rise to objects that are regarded as global, but with local references to them. When all of the references to an object are destroyed the object is no longer of any use and may be garbage collected.

Thinking About References

What you should have in mind is the idea that a value type stores its value and a reference type stores a "pointer" to its value.

Consider:

```
int a;
```

This declares and creates an integer variable which, in common with all value types, isn't initialized to a sensible value. However, for the sake of a simple explanation let's assume it is set to zero. C# enforces the rule that you can't make use of an uninitialized value type but nevertheless the integer variable exists and is ready to store something.

In contrast, if you declare a reference type, e.g. a `class`:

```
class Point
{
        public int x,y
}
```

you can then create a reference variable of the same type:

```
Point b;
```

This declares a reference type b which can reference an object of the type
Point, but at the moment no such object exists and the reference is set to its
default value null.

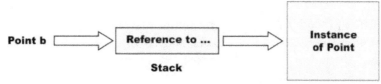

This way of thinking has a nice tidy symmetry, even if it is spoiled by C#'s
insistence on not letting you access an undefined variable - which is very
reasonable.

To create a Point object we need the additional step:

```
b = new Point();
```

Now we have a Point object created on the heap and b is set to reference or
"point" at it.

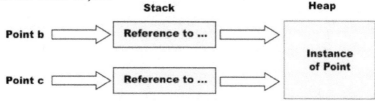

Notice that the reference variable b is just like the value variable a in that they
are both stored on the stack and both store immediate values - the difference
is that a's value is the data and b's value is a reference to the data.

Of course we often combine these two steps together to create the familiar
idiom:

```
Point b = new Point();
```

This often seems to the beginner as redundant because of the way it uses
"Point" twice.

The first use of Point declares a reference to a point object, i.e. b, and the "new
Point" part actually creates the point object. It doesn't take long for this to
seem so familiar that you don't give it a second thought.

Another important difference is that an object can correspond to multiple
reference variables. For example:

```
Point b = new Point();
Point c = b;
```

This creates a single Point object but two reference variables both of which
"point" at the same object.

Lifetimes

It is often said that an important difference between value and reference types is their life cycle. In fact, both types of variable have exactly the same behavior with respect to when they are created and destroyed. That is, a value or a reference type is destroyed as soon as the variable is clearly no longer accessible, i.e. goes out of scope. This means, for example, that a variable defined in a method is destroyed as soon as the function terminates. It is this behavior that makes local variables truly local to the method or block that they were declared in. Notice that there can be exceptions to this rule such as static variables which aren't destroyed until the application terminates. However, it is true to say that the vast majority of variables do behave in this way.

What is different between value and reference types is what happens to their data when the variable is destroyed. In the case of a value type variable, the variable and its data are one and the same and so when a value type variable is destroyed so is its data. However, a reference type variable only contains a reference to its data and while the variable and the reference it contains is destroyed, the object that it references isn't.

This is the source of the statement that value and reference variables have different lifetimes. They don't but the data associated with them can have.

Obviously we can't leave unwanted objects on the heap forever and this is where the system garbage collector comes in. This is a service that periodically scans the heap looking for objects that no longer have any references to them. An object with no references to it is clearly no longer required and using this fact the garbage collector eventually gets round to clearing up the heap.

Notice that this difference in lifetime is entirely to do with the way that things are stored. The value and reference variables are stored on the stack and this is naturally self-managing in the sense that when a method returns, all of its local variables are destroyed by the adjustment of the stack pointer. Anything stored on the heap has no such natural cleaning process and we have to implement a garbage collection system to determine when they are no longer required and when they should be removed.

How and when to tidy the heap is entirely a matter of efficiency. Garbage collect too often and you use up processor power when the is plenty of heap waiting to be used. Garbage collect too little and you risk bringing the application to a halt while the garbage collector has to work overtime freeing up memory by deleting objects and consolidating free space.

Defaults

What "value" does a variable have if it hasn't yet been assigned one?

This is just a question of default values. For numeric types the default value is zero. For strings and other reference types the answer is a little more complicated.

You can assign the default value to any type using:

```
default(type);
```

or, where the compiler can work out the type, just:

```
default;
```

The `default` operator or literal is very useful when used with generics, see Chapter 9. For a simple value type the default is produced by the default constructor and this is the value produced by a bit pattern of all zeros, in other words, zero cast to the appropriate type. For a reference type the default value is the special value `null` which means that the variable isn't referencing any object.

Sometimes variables are automatically initialized to their default value and sometimes they aren't. The rules for automatic initialization of variables seem strange at first. Any local variable in a method is not automatically initialized and if you try and use it you will see a compiler error telling you that you are trying to use an uninitialized variable. However, if the variable is a property of a class then it is initialized, as are the elements of an array. So if you write:

```
int i;
Console.WriteLine(i);
```

in a method then you will see a compile-time error message, but if you write;

```
class MyClassA
{
      int i;
      public void myMethod(T x)
      {
            Console.WriteLine(i);
```

everything works as the variable is automatically initialized. The difference comes down to:

variables allocated on the heap are initialized and variables allocated on the stack aren't.

The compiler is cleverer than you might think in determining if a variable is initialized or not. Consider the following:

```
Random R = new Random();
int i;
if (R.NextDouble() < 0.5)
{
    i = 0;
}
Console.WriteLine(i);
```

The variable is initialized roughly 50% of time, but the compiler still flags the use of the variable as uninitialized. If you add an `else` that initializes the variable then everything is fine and the compiler knows that all paths result in an initialized variable. You can spend many a happy hour trying to fool the compiler into thinking that a variable is initialized when it sometimes isn't!

Null

Modern C# has added the ability to change the way that nulls are handled for the better, see the next section. For reasons of backward compatibility, however, the original behavior is the default and this is described here.

The default value for a reference type is the special value `null` and as `string` is a reference type its default is `null` and not the null string. Historically nulls have been a big problem in programming because trying to call a method on a variable that is `null` results in a run-time error – that is `null` is not type safe. For example:

```
MyClassA myObject = null;
Console.WriteLine(myObject.myMethod());
```

doesn't produce a compile-time error, but it does produce a run-time exception. Traditionally this is a big problem as objects can be removed in ways that leave references to the object `null` and this isn't easy to find at compile time. In particular, setting all of the references to an object to `null` marks it as a candidate for garbage collection.

You can avoid this run-time error by testing for `null`:

```
MyClassA myObject = null;
if(myObject!=null) Console.WriteLine(myObject.myMethod());
```

You can make a reference look more obviously null safe using the null-conditional operators `?.` and `?[]`. The first returns `null` if a method or property doesn't exist and the second returns `null` if an array or index access doesn't exist.

For example:

```
MyClassA myObject = null;
Console.WriteLine(myObject?.myMethod());
```

works without a run-time exception and the value returned to the `WriteLine` method is `null`. Notice that if a non-conditional access to the method or property would have resulted in an exception for non-null `myObject` then the conditional access throws the same exception. That is, the null-conditional operators only protect you from exceptions caused by `myObject` being `null`. Obviously, if any reference fails in a chain of references, the remaining accesses are not evaluated. So, for example:

```
myObject?.A?.B?.C();
```

doesn't evaluate `B` or `C` if `A` is `null`.

While the null-conditional operator is equivalent to an `if` statement test for `null`, processing a chain is more difficult using ifs. We can go one step further than returning a `null` with the null-coalescing operator, `??`. For example, consider:

```
A ?? B
```

where `A` and `B` are expressions and the value is `A` if `A` is non-null and `B` if `A` is `null`. The

```
A ?? = B
```

operator works like the null-coalescing operator but it assigns the result of `B` if `A` is null.

You can use these operators on their own or in combination with one another. For example:

```
myObject??=new myClassA();
```

ensures that `myObject` isn't null and

```
int result=myObject?.myMethod() ?? 0
```

sets `result` to `0` if `myMethod` cannot be called.

Nullable versus NonNullableTypes

What has been described so far is the default behavior of references and it's not a very modern way to handle the null problem, but it is the way that C# first tackled the problem and hence, to avoid breaking existing code, it is the default. A much better idea than just allowing references to be nullable by default is to make them non-nullable by setting a compiler option. You can do this by adding `<Nullable>enable</Nullable>` inside a `<PropertyGroup>` element in your `.csproj` file.

49

Alternatively you can add #nullable enable at any point in your program. If you do this then all of your references become non-nullable and if you try to assign null to them the compiler will issue an error message:

```
#nullable enable
static void Main(string[] args)
{
        MyClassA myObject = null;
        Console.WriteLine(myObject.myMethod());
}
```

This generates a compile-time warning as myObject is a non-nullable and hence it is null safe.

Sometimes you need a nullable type even when playing by non-nullable rules. You can declare a nullable type using the ? operator in its declaration. For example:

```
MyClass? myObject;
```

declares myObject to be a reference to a MyClass object which, because of the logic of the program, could be null. If you change the previous example to:

```
#nullable enable
static void Main(string[] args)
{
        MyClassA? myObject = null;
        Console.WriteLine(myObject.myMethod());
}
```

you will find that you don't get a warning about assigning a null, but you do get a warning about possibly calling a method on a null object.

The non-nullable mechanism in C# isn't perfect because non-nullable types still have the ability to be set to null. The whole mechanism is implemented as compiler checks rather than anything deep in the language. It is also based on warnings rather than errors and so it is still up to you to take notice of the warnings. There are also a number of different settings for #nullable that turn on different levels of null checking and warning.

Overall you should use non-nullable types within your entire project. It's not a perfect fix for the problem, but it is better than nothing.

Nullable Value Types

Value types, by their very nature, aren't nullable. However, this raises the question of how to test for an exceptional value that indicates that the variable doesn't hold a legal value. In many cases you can use a default value, or some value that shouldn't occur as a signal that a value type doesn't currently have a valid value. For example;

```
int count = -1;
```

can be used to indicate that `count` doesn't currently hold a valid value. Such values are called "flags" or "sentinels" and finding a value that can work is often difficult. For example, if `count` was a temperature reading then `-1` could well occur. C# lets you define nullable value types to provide an indication of something exceptional without needing to use a value of the type. The way that this works conceptually is that the value type is extended to a struct that has a field used to indicate null. This means that nullable value types are not quite as efficient as non-nullable value types.

The syntax for nullable value types is the same as the new syntax for nullable reference types – you put ? after the type. For example:

```
int? a;
```

is a nullable `int` and you can assign `null` to it:

```
a = null;
```

and you can test that it is `null` using:

```
if(a == null){ . . . }
```

Nullable value types also work with the null coalescing operators ?? and = ??. You can assign a nullable type to a non-nullable but if the nullable is `null` an exception occurs. Operators produce `null` if any nullable is `null` except for the comparison operators which produce false unless both are `null`.

We also have two new methods that make working with nullable value types easier. `HasValue` is `true` if the nullable type is not `null` i.e. if it has a value. `Value` the value of the type if it is not `null` and throws an exception otherwise. However, rather than:

```
b = 0;
if(a.HasValue)b = a.Value;
```

it is probably better to write:

```
b = a?? 0
```

Postlude

The difference between stack and heap storage, local and global scope and reference and value types permeates all of computing. Even languages that do their best to hide the distinction are easier to understand when you know about the foundations. The way data is stored and handled explains so much about modern programming and there is unlikely to be a big change in programming languages until these basics are superseded. There is also a sense in which the reference type is the superior type. If everything is an object then every variable should be a reference type.

Chapter 4

Structs & Classes

Most languages have something like the C# struct – they may call it something different, often a "record", but the idea is the same. A struct is a collection of different data types with each data type beginning identified as a "field" – similar to a name and address card or record. C# has structs but they play a deeper role in the language being more like classes than the simple data structures they are in other languages.

Structs Are Value Types

Although value types are often introduced as "simple" types such as int or float, all value types are really just examples of struct which is generally thought of as a more complicated type with multiple values as fields.

The simple value types are structs, but they are also treated differently to avoid the overheads a genuine struct brings with it to make sure that your program runs efficiently. The fact that an int is a struct really only has an impact on your programs because this means that int inherits a set of simple standard methods from object. For example, it is perfectly OK to write:

```
int a;
string b = a.ToString();
```

In fact, int is just an alias for the System.Int32 struct and you could write:

```
System.Int32 a;
```

in place of int a, but it is usual not to. We will return to the issue of simple data types as objects later in this chapter because there is a little more to it.

It is reasonable to say that the most important division in the C# type system is the split into classes and structs (both descended from object). And the really big difference between the two is that class is a reference type whereas struct is a value type.

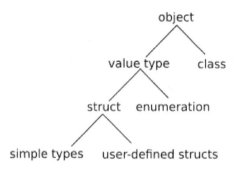

Structs are from value and classes are from reference

In many cases you have the choice of implementing something either as a class or a struct. For example consider a simple type designed to store the x,y coordinates of a point.

You can do this as a class:

```
class PointR
{
      public int x,y;
}
```

or as a struct:

```
struct PointV
{
      public int x,y;
}
```

Notice that the class is named with a trailing R for Reference and the struct with a trailing V for value.

The most important difference is due to the fact that a struct is a value type and a class is a reference type. That is, the class behaves as described earlier for general reference types and struct behaves like a general value type.

However, let's look at this more closely because a struct and a class look much more alike than say an int and a class and mistakes and misunderstandings are easy to make. The most immediate impact of this difference is that you don't have to use new when creating an instance of a struct. That is, you can create an instance of PointV using:

```
PointV a;
```

and this immediately creates a PointV object which you can use:

```
a.x = 10
```

The similar class, however, needs new to create an instance and:

```
PointR b;
```

creates only a reference variable. To make use of a PointR object you also have to use:

```
b = new PointR();
b.x = 20;
```

To make the difference even clearer, you can create other references to the same PointR object as in:

```
PointR c;
c = b;
```

Now c and b refer to the same PointR object and the same x value is changed by c.x = 30 or b.x = 30. In the case of a struct, and a PointV in particular, you cannot create multiple references to it and assignment creates a copy of the struct. That is:

```
PointV d;
d = a;
```

makes an independent copy of the struct a. Now assigning to d.x changes a different x to that assigned in a.x.

If you think you follow, try predicting the values in each of the fields of this admittedly complicated set of assignments:

```
PointV a;
a.x = 1;
a.y = 2

PointR b = new PointR();
b.x = 3;
b.y = 4;

PointV c;
PointR d;

c = a;
d = b;
c.x = 5;
d.x = 6;
```

The answer is:

```
a.x = 1,a.y = 2
b.x = 6,b.y = 4
c.x = 5,c.y = 2
d.x = 6,d.y = 4
```

because d is the same object as b, but c is a new object initialized to be the same as a.

The difference between the two types of behavior is usually expressed as value semantics versus reference semantics, i.e. is the variable the value or a reference to the value. The advice is that structs should be used for simple data types where value assignment seems natural and classes should be used for more advanced types where reference assignment is natural.

If you want to use a class to store data then C# has a predefined record class that makes it particularly easy, but a `record` is still a `class` and reference semantics apply.

Arrays

Value semantics also has another spin-off when it comes to arrays and indeed other complex data types. When you create an array you always use something closer to reference-type semantics as in:

```
int[] a = new int[10];
```

This creates 10 ints in a contiguous block of memory and this is very efficient. Now consider:

```
PointR[] b = new PointR[10];
```

This creates a contiguous block of 10 reference variables of type `PointR` all referencing nothing at all. That is, all you have created is an array of references to `null`.

To finish the array construction you have to use something like:

```
for(int i = 0;i<b.length;i++){
      b[i] = new PointR();
}
```

This, of course, is not as efficient because the 10 objects are created on the heap and have to be memory managed, but all object-oriented languages suffer from this type of problem. The good news is that C# treats arrays created using structs in the same way as simple types, i.e. using value semantics. For example:

```
PointV[] c = new PointV[10];
```

immediately creates an array of 10 `PointV` objects in a contiguous block of memory.

As long as you keep thinking of value types and reference types as being more or less the same, except that reference types don't automatically create the object they reference, you should follow and things should seem simple.

Structs versus Classes

Structs are so important and versatile that, before moving on, it is worth saying a few words that compares and contrasts them to classes while we are on the topic.

As you might expect of a value type, structs don't support inheritance – they inherit from objects, but that's the end of the inheritance hierarchy. They do support interfaces, however, more of which in Chapter 6. Also a struct can have methods, properties and constructors, but it can't have a destructor. Its default, i.e. parameter-less, constructor can't be changed and always initializes all its fields to the default value of 0 for a value type and to `null` for a reference type. You can add your own explicit constructor to initialize fields to specific values. Surprisingly, although you can create a struct without the use of `new`, you can write:

```
PointV a = new PointV();
```

It is important to realize that this way of creating a `struct` is no different from the point of view of value or reference semantics - a `struct` is always a value type.

There is a difference, however, and it is that the use of `new` calls the struct's default constructor which sets each field of the struct to its default value. If you don't use `new` then the fields are treated as undefined and the compiler displays an error message if you try to make use of any of the fields before they have been assigned to.

Simple Types

The simple data types, `int`, `char`, etc are clearly value types, but conceptually at least they are also examples of structs. Most of the time you can ignore this fact and just treat them as simple numbers or characters, but they do have methods. For example, `int` is just an alias for the `System.Int32 struct` which inherits from `object` and so it has a `ToString` method:

```
int a;
string b = a.ToString();
```

Each simple type also has methods of its own and even static methods. For example:

```
int I = int.MaxValue;
```

Of course, you can't inherit from a simple type and they have other special features such there being literals of the same type, e.g. 10, 233.34 and so on.

Simple types are structs in spirit only as the compiler takes care to make sure that they are implemented in an efficient manner. Notice that, as with a struct, you can opt to create a simple type using the new keyword. This doesn't have any effect other than to call the type's default constructor which results in it being initialized to its default value. So, for example:

```
int I;
int j;
I = j;
```

results in a compiler error because j isn't defined. However:

```
int I;
int j = new int();
I = j;
```

works perfectly because j is initialized to 0 by its constructor.

Value or Reference - Decide Early, Don't Change

You should by now understand the difference between a value and a reference type, but when do you use one in preference to another? In most cases this question is simply about using a class or a struct. The answer is nearly always that you should prefer a value type when the purpose is to store data and a reference type when some behavior has to be implemented. Whichever you choose, you need to be aware of the potential for trouble that any attempt at changing a value type to a reference type can produce. For example, suppose we initially design a program using a struct:

```
public struct MyStruct
{
        public int x;
}
```

We might very well use a method to do some computation involving a private instance of this struct:

```
private MyStruct MyData = new MyStruct();
public MyStruct doSum()
{
        return MyData;
}
```

In this example no computation is performed - the struct is simply returned. Now if some other part of your program uses this method it might well go on and perform further manipulations on the returned value:

```
MyStruct a = doSum();
a.x = 10;
```

In this case everything works as you would expect. The struct is treated using value semantics and the doSum returns a complete copy of the struct to create a completely separate entity in a. This means that storing 10 in the x field doesn't alter the value stored in MyData.

Now consider the seemingly small change from a `struct` to a `class`:

```
public class MyClass
{
        public int x;
}
```

The change to the `private` variable and the method are easy enough:

```
private MyClass MyData = new MyClass();
public MyClass doSum()
{
        return MyData;
}
```

However, if the client program performs the same manipulation:

```
MyClass a = doSum();
a.x = 10;
```

the result is very different. Now the object passed as the result is treated as a reference type and subject to reference semantics. This means that doSum passes back a reference to the, supposedly protected, Mydata object. Now when we store 10 in the x field, it is the field in the Mydata object which is changed.

Clearly changing from a value type to a reference type and vice versa is a potentially deep structural change to a program because it changes value semantics into reference semantics.

Alternative to Structs I – Tuple

Structs are often used to simply group items of data together and sometimes this grouping has little logical sense. For example, if you have a method which returns the maximum and minimum then you might well write something like:

```
public struct MaxMin
{
        public double Max;
        public double Min;
}

MaxMin FindMaxMin(double[] list){
        MaxMin result = new MaxMin();
        result.Min = 0.0;
        result.Max = 100.0;
                .    .    .
        return result;
}
```

The idea is that instead of using a pair of out parameters to return the result – not a good idea – we create a struct that holds all the results and return it. You can argue that a struct to hold the max and min is a reasonable expression of the relationship, but, if it is a one-off, defining a struct is overkill. This is where tuples come in.

A tuple, a value type, is a group of data types and it doesn't have to be formally defined and can be created on the fly. You do have to provide the type of each element, but this is all:

```
(double, double) result = (0.0, 100.0);
return result;
```

You can avoid having to specify the types that make up a tuple by using dynamic typing, see Chapter 11.

You can also name the fields if you want to:

```
(double min, double max) result = (0.0,100.0);
return result;
```

If you don't give them names, they are called item1, item2 and so on.

You can access the fields in the usual way:

```
result.item2
```

or:

```
result.max
```

You can also use a similar syntax for "deconstruction" to separate out the fields into variables. For example:

```
(double min,double max) = result;
```

separates the fields into two variables, min and max.

Tuples only have a small number of predefined methods supplied and you can't define new methods. You can also test tuples for equality or inequality and all that matters is that they have fields of the same type or that can be converted into that type and have the same values. The field names are irrelevant in a comparison.

Tuples are also mutable i.e. you can assign new values to the fields and they can be nested. For example:

```
(1,2,(3,4))
```

is a tuple with three elements, the third being a tuple with two elements.

Tuples are very useful as lightweight structs, but notice that you can use dynamic typing in the form of anonymous types to do almost the same thing, see Chapter 11.

Alternative to Structs II – Record

Just as struct has a value alternative, there is a reference alternative in the form of the record class. This is another way to group together data fields. You declare a record using the record keyword in place of class.

A record is primarily about defining data fields. You can do this in a number of ways. The simplest record declaration is:

```
public record Staff(string name, int age);
```

After this, you can define an instance using:

```
Staff me = new Staff("mike",18);
```

In this case the record has immutable fields and after initialization you can only read the fields. That is:

```
me.age += 1;
```

or

```
me.age=me.age+1;
```

will fail.

You can also define properties in the body of the definition:

```
public record Staff
{
    public string name { get; init; }
    public int age { get; set; }
}
```

The new init accessor is like set but it can only be used to set the value once. Using init gives you an immutable record. You can use set to produce a mutable record and you can use init in class-based properties. You can also use set in place of init to create a mutable record. After this definition:

```
me.age = 18;
me.name = "Mike";
```

is fine, but after this you can change age, but not name.

You can mix the two styles of definition:

```
public record Staff(string name,int age)
{
    public string name { get; init; } = name;
    public int age { get; set; } = age;
}
```

This is all good in the sense that it is a neater syntax for creating data-oriented classes, but what else does it provide?

The first is a value semantics test of equality. Two records are regarded as the same if their fields are of the same type and currently have the same values. This is achieved by the compiler auto-generating an override for the comparison methods – a `record` is still a reference type.

The compiler also generates an improved `ToString` method, which displays the `record` in a more readable format. For example:

```
Console.WriteLine(me);
```

produces:

```
Staff { name = Mike, age = 19 }
```

While this is not good enough for presentation, it can be handy for debugging.

A generated deconstruct method can also be used to transfer fields to local variables. For example:

```
string name;
int age;
me.Deconstruct(out name, out age);
```

Another useful feature is that a `record` plays a restricted role in inheritance. A `record` can inherit from another `record` but classes and records can't inter-inherit. Adding inheritance to a record is most likely an avoidable complication.

The big advantage of the `record` type is that it can be made immutable. The problem with using immutable data is that when you want to change something you have to make a copy. A copy method is automatically defined by the `with` expression, introduced for exactly this purpose and easier to use:

```
Staff you = me with { name = "harry" };
```

This creates a copy of the `me` record but with the name changed to `harry`. The `with` expression creates a completely new copy of the record then uses the object initializer to change any fields mentioned and then sets the variable to refer to the new object. You can only change properties that have an `init` or `set` assessor. Notice that:

```
me = me with { age = 21 };
```

is perfectly legal but now me references a completely new object with the age field set to 21.

Postlude

Structs are value types, but classes are reference types and never the twain shall meet. Well at least you should keep them well apart in your mind because they behave differently and they are for very different purposes. C#'s structs are more sophisticated than the same idea implemented in other languages and, partly to make up for this, we have two alternatives – the tuple and the record. Both are useful, but it is possible to become excessively addicted to the tuple as a way of temporarily packaging data into a single entity that can be passed around.

Chapter 5

Inheritance

Inheritance is a simple idea, until you try to make use of it. What's a virtual method? How do you use override and new? It's tricky when you look at the details. There are also all of the philosophical issues about what makes good maintainable code. In this chapter we look at the basics of inheritance and the subtle corners of the idea.

Simple Inheritance

C#'s inheritance mechanisms are particularly clean and easy, but let's make sure that we know how they work.

The fundamental class declaration in C# takes the form:

```
class name: baseclass
```

If you don't specify a base class then the default class called object is used.

Only a class can inherit and only from another class – structs always inherit from object and can't be used to create new structs or classes by inheritance. If you want to create a class that can't be used as a base class for a new class then simply add the sealed modifier to the start of the class definition – see Chapter 7.

Notice that C# only allows single inheritance which, by contrast to C++ and Python, is something of a relief! If you think that C++'s ability to create classes from more than one base class is a good idea then you haven't seen some of the stranger things that can happen when this powerful facility gets out of hand. The preferred approach to multiple inheritance is to make use of interfaces which define the type of what is to be inherited without supplying an implementation. There is no doubt that single inheritance is safer and can do everything that multiple inheritance can if you are prepared to approach it in the right way and do some additional work.

Variable Type and Object Type

As we have already seen, when you create an instance of a class you first create a reference variable of the correct type. For example:

```
class MyClassA {};
MyClassA MyA;
```

doesn't create an instance of MyClassA - only a reference variable capable of pointing to an object of type MyClassA. You have to be careful how you phrase such 'pointing to an object' because C# doesn't have pointers as such.

After declaring a reference variable you can set it to point to, or reference, a new instance of the class using:

```
MyA = new MyClassA();
```
or putting this together:

```
MyClassA MyA = new MyClassA();
```
Notice that there are two things going on here – the type of the variable making the reference and the type of the object it references. In a simple world these would always be the same.

If you now create a class that inherits from MyClassA:

```
Class MyClassB:MyClassA;
```
then any instance of MyClassB starts out with all of the methods defined in the definition of MyClassA. This is what inheritance is all about - code reuse. If class MyClassA has a show method then so now does class MyClassB and without you having to write a single line of code.

Notice that this means that class MyClassB has two types of method - those that are defined as part of MyClassA and those that are defined within it.

If you simply want to use the inherited methods of class MyClassB you can simply use them as if they were "native" to MyClassB.

For example:

```
MyClassB MyB = new MyClassB();
MyB.show();
```
results in the show method defined in class MyClassA being called.

There is one small complication - what if the methods of class MyClassB need to call the methods defined in class MyClassA? One of the advantages of single inheritance is that if you want to call the base class's methods you can do so with a single keyword base because you don't have to specify which base class is to be used as there is only one. For example, if MyClassB inherits a method "show" from MyClassA then MyClassB can call the method using:

```
base.show();
```

In practice you can omit base as long as there is no ambiguity, i.e. if MyClassB doesn't have a show method.

Inherited Constructors

A special case of using the methods of the base class is the inherited constructor. A constructor is a function that creates the class and optionally initializes it. Beginners are often worried by the idea that the constructor has to "create" the class and they think that there is something they have to do to make it happen. In practice you don't have to do anything to create an instance of the class. The system does it all for you and the constructor returns a reference to a new object with all of the properties the class defines initialized to their default values. However, if you want those properties to be initialized to something then you might have to write some code in the constructor.

If you want to provide different types of initialization then you can define a number of alternative constructors, each with its own unique signature. Which constructor is used is determined by the signature of the call. All classes have one constructor with no parameters, either explicitly defined or automatically generated, which is used as the default constructor in situations where you don't explicitly specify a constructor.

If a class inherits from another class then the base class default constructor is automatically called before the child class's own default constructor. If the base class also inherits from another class its constructor is called first and so on until we reach the first class in the inheritance chain.

If a class defines an explicit constructor and inherits from another class, the explicit constructor must call one of the base class's constructors. If the base class only has constructors that use parameters, the child class has to call one of them using the base keyword.

For example, suppose MyClassA has a constructor of the form:

MyClassA(int n)

then to call it you would write:

```
class MyClassB: MyClassA
{
        public MyClassC:base(7)
        {
                rest of constructor
        }
}
```

In this case the MyClassB constructor calls the MyClassA(int n) constructor as MyClassA(7) before continuing with its own instructions.

Notice that the `this` keyword can nearly always be used to make clear that the version of something to be used is the class's own version and `base` can be used to indicate that the, possibly hidden, base class's version should be used. In most cases you don't have to use `this` and `base` because the compiler can work out what you mean, but it is a good idea to be explicit whenever clarity warrants it.

Changing Types - Casting

As we already know, inheritance results in a type hierarchy of base classes and derived classes. We also know, see Chapter 2, that it is assumed that any derived class can stand in for its base classes, i.e. the classes it inherits from. This is such an established idea that we don't think twice about the way that a variable can be used to reference any object of its type or derived from its type. So, in:

```
Class MyClassA{};
Class MyClassB:MyClassA{};
```

MyClassB inherits from MyClassA. Following on with:

```
MyClassA MyA;
MyClassB MyB;
MyA = new MyClassB();
```

you can see that you can use a reference to a base class to reference a derived class without any change in syntax.

This is called downcasting because the variable is supposed to reference a class higher up in the hierarchy but it actually references an object lower in the hierarchy.

It is also true that a variable of a derived type can reference a base type, but in this case we do need some extra syntax. For example:

```
MyB = (MyClassB) MyA;
```

In this case we need an explicit typecast expression, or just cast, to indicate the conversion, i.e. `(MyClassB)`. Typecasts are simply types written in parentheses in front of a variable and they have the effect of changing the type of the object for the duration of the expression.

This is usually called upcasting because the variable is supposed to reference a class lower in the hierarchy than the object being assigned to it.

Upcasting may be legal but what does it mean?

The only sense that:

```
MyB = (MyClassB) MyA;
```

can possibly make is if MyA actually references an object of type MyClassB i.e. it has been downcast earlier. Only then can we make use of methods that are only defined on a type MyClassB object. That is:

```
MyB = (MyClassB) MyA;
MyB.MethodB();
```

only works if the object we are using, i.e. what MyA references, really is a type MyClassB object. If it isn't then we are trying to call a method that doesn't exist and the result is a run-time error.

You can see that upcasting isn't type safe as you cannot easily work out whether what is being cast is of the correct type. For example:

```
Random R = new Random();
MyClassB myObject;
if (R.NextDouble() > 0.5)
{
        myObject = new MyClassB();
}
else
{
        myObject = (MyClassB) new MyClassA();
 }
Console.WriteLine(myObject.myProperty);
```

This program generates no compile-time errors or warnings, but 50% of the time it fails because trying to cast an object of type MyClassA to a type MyClassB doesn't work. In this case the random input is a stand-in for a variability injected into the program by the rest of the world in a real program.

Is and As

There are two operators that can help avoid run-time exceptions when casting. The is operator can be used to test the type of the reference before applying a cast. For example:

```
if (MyAnything is MyClassB)
{
        MyClassB MyB = (MyClassB)MyAnything;
};
```

This is the basic form of the is but as well as a type it can also test for a more general pattern – see Pattern Matching in Chapter 2.

The **as** operator is an alternative way of writing a cast but with the difference that if it fails the reference is to null. For example:

```
MyClassB MyB =  MyAnything as MyClassB;
```

never throws an exception but you have to make sure that you don't end up using a null reference because it didn't actually work.

Notice that you can use **as** to write a cast method call more neatly:

```
(MyAnything as MyClassB).MethodB()
```

but notice that you will generate a run-time error if the cast fails and **MethodB** doesn't exist. To avoid this you can use the null conditional operator:

```
(MyAnything as MyClassB)?.MethodB()
```

Now the result is a null if the method call fails.

Always use as in place of explicit casting.

Overriding and Abstract Class

Inheritance is complicated by the fact that inherited methods can be overridden. That is, not only can you add completely new methods and properties to a derived class, but you can define methods which replace inherited methods.

There is a sense in which the ability to override methods is where things start to go wrong – or at least get complicated. If the purpose of object-oriented code is code reuse, why inherit some code only to override it with something different? In an extreme case you could even override every single method that was inherited – what does that mean for code reuse?

In case you think that overriding every method is unlikely, you need to recall that an **abstract class** can have method definitions that have no implementation details and have to be overridden. As the abstract class definition is incomplete, you can't actually create an instance of the class – it exists purely to be inherited. For example:

```
abstract class MyClassA {

      abstract public void myMethod1();

      public void myMethod2()
      {
            Console.WriteLine("implemented");
      }
};
```

In this case you can see that there are two methods, myMethod1, which is abstract and has no implementation, and myMethod2 which has.

When you use `MyClassA` as a base class you have to override `myMethod1` so as to provide an implementation:

```
class MyClassB : MyClassA {
      public override void myMethod1()
      {
              throw new NotImplementedException();
      }
}
```

The method as shown is automatically generated by Visual Studio, which is a help, but you still have to do the work implementing the abstract methods.

So what are abstract classes all about?

Clearly as a class can be 100% abstract it isn't about code reuse. Code reuse may have been the initial motivation for object-oriented programming, but clearly other considerations have taken over. The considerations in question are of course the role of classes and inheritance. An abstract class is designed to be inherited and nothing else – you can't instantiate it. The only reason for using a class that has to be inherited is to determine the basic set of methods, complete with signatures, that a class has to have. The abstract class is a promise that any class that inherits it has these methods.

Why doesn't the abstract class provide default implementations for all its methods? There is nothing stopping you from doing this, but often class hierarchies start with a base class that is so general that no sensible implementation is possible. The most quoted example is a class called `Animal` with a method call `sound`. The idea that each animal that inherits from `Animal` has to override `sound` to the sound they they actually make but `Animal` is so general no such implementation is reasonable.

You can see that the rationale here has clearly moved from code reuse to that of type safety.

An abstract class is all about making it clear what methods a derived class can safely be assumed to have.

Overriding as part of the use and implementation of inheritance seems natural enough and completely general not just for abstract classes. Even in copy-and-paste code reuse some modification of what is copied seems inevitable. However, just as in copy-and-paste code reuse, code modification spoils the benefits of inheritance. Now we can no longer assume that a modification to the code in a base class is inherited by a derived class – overriding is a break in the chain of inheritance. The derived class has the method in name and signature but it just isn't the method that was in the base class.

Inheritance with overriding simply promises that a derived class will have a defined set of methods with a given signature, not that what they do is in anyway consistent or interchangeable.

Overriding – Virtual and Late Binding

At first sight, overriding a method seems easy and simple and the possibility that there could be any complications seems unlikely. However, there are complications and C# provides facilities which allow you to say how to handle these complications. In particular it provides both late and early binding options for overriding. In this section we look at late binding.

If you have a class that inherits from a base class and an inherited method doesn't do the job it needs to in its new class, then override it with a new method. The base class carries on using its original method and the derived class uses its new method - what could go wrong?

The first thing to notice is that now if you use the derived class as a base class for another class it is the new method and not the original base class method that is inherited. That is, once a method is overridden in a class the modified version is passed down to other derived classes – it replaces the base class method in the inheritance hierarchy. This is sometimes what you want and sometimes not. The only reasonable solution is to override the method again to get the behavior you want. Notice that while you can use base.myMethod() to call the method in the immediate base class, you cannot use expressions like base.base.myMethod() to call methods in an earlier base class.

The biggest complication in using overriding is what to do about casting. As explained earlier, we can use a variable of a base type to reference an object of a derived type – a downcast. However, this causes ambiguity over which method to call if an inherited method has been overridden.

For example, we have seen in earlier chapters that, if MyClassB inherits myMethod from MyClassA and overrides it:

```
MyClassA MyA;
MyClassB MyB;
MyB = new MyClassB();
MyA = MyB;
MyA.myMethod();
```

which version of myMethod is used?

Novice programmers expect to get MyClassB's version of the method, i.e. the new one and the one that belongs to the instance being used, but they would be wrong. By default you actually get MyClassA's version of the method, i.e. the reference variable's type determines what version of a method is actually called.

As explained more in Chapter 11 this is an example of early binding, i.e. the method used is bound to the call at compile time and it has to be determined by the type of the variable not the type of the object the variable references at run time.

If you want to use the, apparently more reasonable, late binding so that the method called depends on the type of the object referenced at run time, you have to explicitly ask for it using the virtual keyword. For example:

```
class MyClassA
{
        public virtual void myMethod()
        {
                Console.WriteLine("implemented A");
        }
}
```

Now when MyClassB inherits from MyClassA it can override the method in the usual way:

```
class MyClassB:MyClassA
{
        public override void myMethod()
        {
                Console.WriteLine("implemented B");
        }
}
```

Notice that you need the modifier override to override a virtual method. The two keywords work together like parentheses. The existing method has to be declared virtual and the new method has to be declared override. Miss out either of the declarations and you will generate a compiler warning. If you run the program then leaving out virtual but using override produces a run-time error. Leaving out override and using virtual instead works, but produces early binding.

With virtual and override in place the example:

```
MyClassA MyA;
MyClassB MyB;
MyB=new MyClassB();
MyA=MyB;
MyA.myMethod();
```

produces the message implemented B as MyClassB's method is called and without it it produces implemented A.

To be more accurate, without it you also get another compiler warning. To override a method using early binding you have to use the new keyword and this is described in the next section.

Notice that whichever method runs, it runs in the context of its defining class. That is, if myMethod refers to properties or methods then these are the ones defined in the class the method is defined in, either MyClassA or MyClassB. So if myMethod in class MyClassB references a property that doesn't exist in class MyClassA it accesses that property in MyClassB even when run with a MyClassA reference i.e. as if it was a MyClassA. You cannot reference that property directly but the method can access it.

For example, if we change the definition of `MyClassB` to:

```
public class MyClassB : MyClassA
{
    public int myProperty=42;
    public override int myMethod()
    {
        Console.WriteLine("MethodB "+myProperty.ToString());
        return 2;
    }
}
```

You can see that now the overridden `myMethod` now accesses a field that only exists in `MyClassB`. If you now run:

```
MyClassA MyA = new MyClassB();
MyA.myMethod();
```

You will see 42 printed but if you try to access the property directly:

```
MyA.myProperty=43;
```

you will see a compile-time error as `MyClassA` doesn't have a `myProperty`.

Hiding Methods With new

If you don't declare a method as `virtual` then overriding using early binding isn't quite as simple as in C++ and other languages. C# doesn't really have a default overriding method. You can just leave out any additional keywords and redefine the method in the derived class but if you do this you will get a compiler warning. It works but it isn't the correct way to do the job.

That is, if you declare a class and a method as:

```
class MyClassA
{
    public void myMethod()
    {
        Console.WriteLine("implemented A");
    }
}
```

Now when `MyClassB` inherits from `MyClassA` it can override the method in the usual way:

```
class MyClassB:MyClassA
{
    public void myMethod()
    {
        Console.WriteLine("implemented B");
    }
}
```

This works and results in early binding and it is what in other languages would be the default way to override a method, but it generates a warning. The reason is that C# expects you to use the new keyword if you are redefining an inherited function:

```
class MyClassB:MyClassA
{
      public new void myMethod()
      {
            Console.WriteLine("implemented B");
      }
}
```

This also works, but without generating a warning.

In the C# documentation this use of new is said to "hide" the inherited method. What this means is that the new definition is used in preference to the old one wherever it is in scope, i.e. wherever its definition applies.

This appears to work just like overriding a non-virtual method, but there are some subtleties. For example, after:

```
MyClassA MyA;
MyA = new MyClassB();
MyA.myMethod();
```

MyClassA's original version of method is called as you would expect with late binding. However, the subtle part is that nothing changes even if the original method was declared as virtual – you still get early binding. In other words, the use of new kills virtual inheritance. If you derive a class MyClassC from MyClassB and use override on a new version of the method then virtual inheritance works again. This can be confusing.

The final twist is that the effect of new depends on whether or not the method is accessible. For example, if you declare the new method as private it only overrides the inherited method within the class – when used outside the class the inherited method is once again called.

Finally, why is the new keyword needed and why is only a warning generated when you forget to use it? The reason is that you might very well create a MyClassB that inherits from MyClassA and give it a new method called myMethod. This method doesn't need either new or override because it isn't hiding or overriding an inherited method – it really is new. Everything is fine, but suppose that later on class MyClassA is modified independently of MyClassB and it has a myMethod function added to it. Now there is a name collision between MyClassB.myMethod and MyClassA.myMethod. By default, MyClassB always uses its own myMethod, which is presumably what its programmer would have wanted since they couldn't have guessed that the owner of MyClassA would add a myMethod. Of course, when the owner of class

`MyClassB` recompiles the code they will be greeted with a warning that lets them know about the change. They can then either add `new` or `override` as appropriate.

To Summarize

- ◆ For early binding there is no need to add anything to the base class declaration of the method and the overriding method should be declared `new`. Early binding occurs even if the base class method is declared `virtual`.

- ◆ For late binding the base class method should be declared `virtual` and the overriding method has to be declared `override`.

Late or Early

The C# handling of overriding might seem over-complex. Many other languages simply make late binding the default. This is simple, but doesn't give you any flexibility.

So which should you use, early or late binding? The first thing to say is that if you don't use any downcasts, you might think that you are safe from considerations of when binding happens. This is true, but just because you don't use downcasts now it doesn't mean that you or someone else won't write code that uses your classes in this way.

There is also an issue of efficiency. Early binding means that the compiler can generate code that has the reference to the method fully determined. Late binding involves determining which method to call at run time and this takes more time. Efficiency is the reason that early binding was used in C++ and probably the reason it is the default in C#, but this should be of no consideration in a modern system unless you are calling a method a huge number of times.

From a purist standpoint, early binding is to be preferred as it is the only option that fits in well with the mantra that anywhere you can use a base class you can use a derived class. The problem here is that this is far less useful in the real world. For instance, it doesn't allow polymorphism to be implemented. The method call depends on the type of the variable and not the type of the referenced object and so the same method is always called. When you add to the fact that any sort of overriding tends to weaken the same mantra of "derived classes can be used anywhere a base class can" then you have to admit that things are not clear-cut. Some methods are better early bound and some late bound. The key is that the subset of inherited methods in the derived class has to work properly in the environment of the base class and this might need early binding or it might need late binding.

Postlude

Inheritance is simple when you restrict it to code reuse. Unless, that is, you allow overriding existing methods as well as adding new methods. If you allow overriding then you have to make a choice about which version of the method is called – early or late binding. This is a complication that can be difficult to understand and even more difficult to keep under control. This complication is entirely due to enforcing strong typing. In a language that doesn't assign a type to variables, only to objects, then the only possibility is late binding.

Today inheritance is only partly about code reuse and abstract classes can be used to ensure that derived classes have a particular set of methods. This allows us to implement, rather than inherit the implementations of, those methods.

Chapter 6

Interfaces & Multiple Inheritance

In the previous chapter we discovered that code reuse is no longer the main concern of object-oriented programming – type safety is. With this in mind the idea of an interface becomes very obvious as a way of ensuring type safety and even allowing a form of multiple inheritance.

One problem with C#'s implementation of the interface idea is that, while it started out simple and with a single clear objective, over time features have been added which make it more confusing. When to use an interface is no longer as clear as it was as now an interface is much more like an abstract class. Many of the extensions to the basic interface idea introduced are practically useful, but theoretically muddled. The concept of interface has slowly been drifting back toward that of class, but with seemingly arbitrary restrictions on what you can do. It can be confusing, but there is reason behind it all.

The Basic Interface

Superficially an interface is like a class in that it can be inherited. The C# syntax is even very similar. For example, to define an interface with a single method you would write:

```
public interface IMyInterface
{
        void myMethod(int value);
}
```

An interface can only define methods, properties, indexers and events, but not raw fields, and in it purest form it contains no implementation of any of these. IMyInterface looks like a class and indeed it can be inherited.

For example:

```
public class MyClass:IMyInterface{}
```

This looks a lot like simple inheritance, but, and this is the important difference, `MyClass` doesn't have to inherit any implementation details from `IMyInterface`. That is, if you try to create a `MyClass` object without doing anything about `IMyInterface`:

```
MyClass MyObject = new MyClass();
```

you will see a compile-time error.

You can't create `MyObject` unless you write some code that implements all of the methods defined in the interface. That is, to make the previous example work you would have to define `MyClass` as:

```
public class MyClass:IMyInterface{
      void IMyInterface.myMethod(int value)
      {
             code that does something
      }
}
```

You don't have to specify the interface method as `IMyInterface.myMethod` if there isn't any chance of a name clash, but it's a good habit to get into.

In this case it looks as if `myMethod` is being overridden by a new definition provided by `IMyInterface.myMethod`. This isn't really true as there is no implementation of `myMethod` provided for you to override.

To be clear:

- **A class that inherits from an interface doesn't usually inherit any methods, only method declarations.**

The reason for "usually" will be explained later, see default implementations.

What good does this do?

An interface is very similar to the idea of a pure abstract class. If you declare a class as `abstract` then any methods that are also declared as `abstract` don't have definitions and have to be overridden by any class that inherits the abstract class – unless it too is declared to be `abstract`. An abstract class can't be used to create objects and it only becomes "non-abstract" when all of the abstract methods have been overridden.

You can see that abstract classes allow the definition of an inheritance chain that adds more implementation code at each step. The role of an abstract class is to represent the most abstract object in the hierarchy, perhaps so abstract that implementations of the methods it defines wouldn't be useful but would be for derived classes.

An interface is like an abstract class but it doesn't fit into the usual class and type hierarchy. The intended use of an interface is to ensure that all classes that inherit from it have the methods that it declares. If a class doesn't implement all of the interface methods exactly then the class doesn't compile. You can think of it as a template for a class and its use is to ensure that classes present a uniform and enforced set of methods that can be used with confidence by other objects. Used in this way it is a central part of most modern programming methodologies.

The interface is a promise that the class has a set of methods and hence it is about type safety and not code reuse.

Multiple Inheritance

One big difference, and the important difference, between `class` and `Interface` inheritance is that interfaces support multiple inheritance.

You can make a class implement two interface specifications using:

```
public class MyClass:IMyInterface1,IMyInterface2
```

This looks like multiple inheritance. However, as nothing but the method definitions are inherited, it isn't nearly so dangerous or, of course, as useful.

Some other facts worth knowing about interfaces are that a `struct` can inherit an `Interface` and an `Interface` can inherit from other interfaces. Of course, an `Interface` that inherits from another set of interfaces doesn't have to implement anything and it simply serves to extend or add to the base interfaces. When an interface is inherited you have to implement all of the methods defined in all of the inherited interfaces.

So why, if it is "dangerous" to inherit multiple classes, is it safer to inherit multiple interfaces? The problem with inheriting from more than one class is that you run the risk of inheriting a method and its implementation more than once, the so-called "diamond problem". To be exact, the problem is whether there are multiple inherited implementations or a method which is used when the method is called on the derived class. Different languages solve the problem in different ways, but essentially you can either insist that the user implements any multiply defined methods or you need some rule that selects which method is used. C# solves the problem by not allowing multiple class inheritance, only multiple interface inheritance. In this case all that is inherited is the definition so you have to implement it and implementing it means that there is no conflict. This form of interface inheritance is the same as having class multiple inheritance, but insists that any method clash is resolved by implementing the method.

This account is only correct if interfaces don't provide their own implementation and in modern C# they can. This is a topic we need to return to, but first we need to look at how interfaces are used as types.

Interfaces As Type

A class determines what methods an object has. An interface determines what methods an object has. Class determines a type hierarchy, so why shouldn't we use interfaces in the same way? The answer is that we can. If you create a variable using an interface as a type then it can be used to reference any object that inherits the interface. However, you can only access the methods defined in the interface.

For example:

```
public interface IMyInterface
{
        int myMethod();
}
class MyClassA:IMyInterface {
        public int myMethod()
        {
                return 42;
        }

        public void myMethod1()
        {
                Console.WriteLine("implemented A");
        }
}

IMyInterface myObject = new MyClassA();
Console.WriteLine(myObject.myMethod());
```

You can see that IMyInterface is just a single method, myMethod, which is implemented by class MyClassA. In the main program, notice that myObject is declared to be of type IMyInterface and is made to reference an object of type MyClassA. You can use myObject to call myMethod, but that is all as it is the only thing defined in the interface. This looks a lot like an upcast and that's exactly what it is, with IMyInterface being regarded as a base type for MyClassA.

Our type hierarchy dogma is now extended to include interfaces as well as classes. The principle that any derived class can be used in place of a base class now includes any class that is derived from an interface can be used as that interface type. Of course, the big difference is that you can't instantiate an interface only inherit it, but the idea and the motivation is the same, type safety.

You may be wondering what advantage there is in using an interface as a type. After all, the class that inherits the interface has all of the methods it defines. In other words if myMethod is defined by `IMyInterface` you can use:

```
IMyInterface myObject = new MyClassA();
Console.WriteLine(myObject.myMethod());
```

or

```
MyClassA myObject = new MyClassA();
Console.WriteLine(myObject.myMethod());
```

Where there is something to be gained is when you are defining input parameters. If you define a function as:

```
void myFunction(IMyInterface a){};
```

then the parameter a can be any class that inherits from and implements `IMyInterface` and this "short circuits" the inheritance hierarchy. Notice that you cannot use any of the methods of the class beyond those of the interface and in this sense exactly what the class is that is passed to the function is irrelevant.

Also notice that interfaces play by the same rules as the class hierarchy. That is, if an interface inherits another then a variable of the base type can reference an object that implements the derived type, for example:

```
public interface IMyInterfaceA
{
        int myMethodA();
}
public interface IMyInterfaceB:IMyInterfaceA
{
        int myMethodB();
}
```

A class that implements `IMyInterfaceB` has to implement both methods:

```
class MyClassA:IMyInterfaceB {
        public int myMethodA()
        {
                throw new NotImplementedException();
        }

        public int myMethodB()
        {
                throw new NotImplementedException();
        }
}
```

If you use a variable of type `MyClassA` then you can use both methods. If you use a variable of type `MyInterfaceB` then you can use both methods.

However, if you use:

```
IMyInterfaceA myObject = new MyClassA();
```

i.e. a variable of type `MyInterfaceA` then everything works but you can only use `myMethodA`.

The interface hierarchy works in the same way as the class hierarchy.

The Diamond Problem – Explicit Implementation

The big problem with multiple inheritance of any kind is the diamond problem. It's name comes from the shape of the inheritance diagram you get if you draw it out.

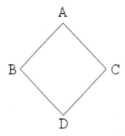

At its most general, it is what happens if A is inherited by B and C and then D inherits from both B and C. In this case D gets two copies of A.

Equally problematic, however, is what is to happen if B and C have the same method complete with the same signature? This is a problem that can easily happen with interfaces but the solution in this case is trivial – as the inheriting class has to implement the method this new implementation becomes the defining one.

However, what if this isn't what you want? Suppose that a class inherits from two interfaces, `IMyInterfaceA` and `IMyInterfaceB`, both with `myMethod` with the same signature and suppose also that `myMethod` does different things in each interface – one is say equality of value and the other equality of reference. Then providing a single implementation which does for both isn't going to work. The solution C# adopts it to allow you to define both versions of the method, but as members of the interface types rather than of the class.

For example:

```
class MyClassA : IMyInterfaceA, IMyInterfaceB
{
        int IMyInterfaceA.myMethod()
        {
                throw new NotImplementedException();
        }

        int IMyInterfaceB.myMethod()
        {
                throw new NotImplementedException();
        }
}
```

This is called an explicit interface implementation. Now there is no myMethod defined within class MyClassA, only two different interface methods:

```
MyClassA myObject = new MyClassA();
Console.WriteLine((myObject as IMyInterfaceA).myMethod());
Console.WriteLine((myObject as IMyInterfaceB).myMethod());
```

Having to cast to an interface type before you can use the correct method isn't elegant or convenient, but it does allow you to pass the class to a function that is expecting an object with that particular method implemented.

You don't have to use an explicit implementation for all of the identical methods inherited from different interfaces, you can provide a class implementation which is used if the class isn't cast to the interface type.

Default Methods

Interfaces are so practically useful that inevitably they have evolved to include more features. C# interfaces allow you to define default implementations for methods. Although they are called "default" this doesn't really reflect how they work or how they are used. They are not simply default implementation of methods in the interface that are used only if the class doesn't provide an overriding implementation and this can be misleading.

A default implementation is created by filling in the code for any method in an interface.

For example:

```
public interface IMyInterfaceA
{
        int myMethodA() {
                return 42;
        }
}
```

In this case the interface has a single fully-defined method. Now we can create a class that inherits this interface:

```
class MyClassA:IMyInterfaceA {
}
```

After this you will not be prompted to implement the interface. You are only prompted to implement the interface if it has declarations without implementation. If you think that myMethodA is a "default" method then you might expect:

```
MyClassA myObject = new MyClassA();
Console.WriteLine(myObject.myMethodA());
```

to work. It doesn't.

A default method is not a member of the class that inherits an interface, it is a member of the interface type and you have to use it as if it was an explicit implementation, see the previous section. This means that if you want to call the method you need to use something like:

```
IMyInterfaceA myObject = new MyClassA();
Console.WriteLine(myObject.myMethodA());
```

or, using a cast, see Chapter 8:

```
MyClassA myObject = new MyClassA();
Console.WriteLine(((IMyInterfaceA) myObject).myMethodA());
```

or, using a safe cast:

```
MyClassA myObject = new MyClassA();
Console.WriteLine((myObject as IMyInterfaceA).myMethodA());
```

Notice that there is no question of having to override the default method in the class as it doesn't inherit it. You can simply provide an implementation that is used if you try to call the method via the class:

```
class MyClassA:IMyInterfaceA {
        public int myMethodA() {
                return 43;
        }
}
```

Now you can call either method according to the type of the variable referencing the class:

```
MyClassA myObject = new MyClassA();
Console.WriteLine(myObject.myMethodA());
Console.WriteLine(( myObject as IMyInterfaceA).myMethodA());
```

The first `WriteLine` calls the class default method and the second calls the interface version of the method.

At the moment in C# you can't easily use a default interface method as a default for a class method of the same name. This was part of the original intent and the proposal was to extend the meaning of base to include an inherited interface so that the default method could be called from an inheriting class, but this causes problems similar to the diamond problem. You can call a default method within a class by simply casting `this`:

```
public interface IMyInterfaceA
{
        int myMethod()
        {
                return 42;
        }
}
class MyClassA : IMyInterfaceA
{
        public int myMethodA()
        {
                return((this as IMyInterfaceA).myMethod());
        }
}
```

This looks promising as a way of implementing `myMethod` directly on class `MyClassA` by delegation, but if you change the name of `myMethodA` in the class to `myMethod` you will find that there is a stack overflow:

```
public int myMethod()
{
    return((this as IMyInterfaceA).myMethod());
}
```

The compiler translates the call to recursion which overflows the stack.

Currently the suggested use of default interface methods is not to implement default class methods but to extend an interface in a backward-compatible way. Suppose you already have an interface and you need to add a method, then adding it as a default method means that classes that already use the interface do not have to be modified and any classes which want to use the new method simply have to add the cast to the interface.

87

What Can An Interface Do?

In modern C# an interface can include definitions of:
- Constants
- Operators
- Static constructors
- Nested types
- Static fields
- Methods
- Properties
- Indexers
- Events

None of these member declarations typically contain a body being just a declaration ready to be implemented by the inheriting class. As already discussed, beginning with C# 8.0, an interface member may declare a body as a default implementation although these are not inherited by the class and so don't really complicate the overall picture.

This is a long list of things that can be in an interface and it begs the question of what is left out and why?

The key idea is that an interface cannot contain anything that would determine the state of an instance. This comes down to not allowing any instance fields, either directly or indirectly. As the documentation says, static fields are permitted but instance fields are not. As it also points out this seems a contradiction as properties are allowed, but if you look into a little further, even though auto-implemented properties might look as if they are implemented, they aren't. That is:

```
public string Name {get; set;}
```

doesn't implement a string property complete with backing field - it is up to the class to implement it. It simply states that an inheriting class has to have a read/write Name property.

What is the theoretical justification for not allowing instance entities? The answer is that an interface should only provide a definition of what entities the class should implement and not an implementation of those entities. Allowing instance variables would be breaking this idea by fixing the data types, and hence representation, used. This seems to be a very weak justification given the range of entities that can be represented and the introduction of default methods. A better reason is that it is better to use properties complete with get/set and backing variables than simple fields – which is of course what you should do if you need an interface with properties. Alternatively, you could use an abstract class if you can live with the limitations of single inheritance.

Currently C# interfaces are at their best when used as simply as possible.

Postlude

Inheritance for code reuse really does need to be multiple inheritance, but it is a difficult tool to work with due to the diamond problem among others. C#'s single inheritance is tempered by the use of interfaces which, despite having default methods, don't help much with code reuse. What they do is to allow type safety with multiple inheritance but without the need to worry about selecting between multiple inherited implementations. The use of interfaces as types makes the type hierarchy less of a strict hierarchy.

Chapter 7

Controlling Inheritance

Inheritance, both class and interface, is a great idea, but it is a powerful technique that can be misused. C# provides the tools to keep inheritance under control or to turn it off completely if you want to.

Most C# programmers are well aware that it is an object-oriented language and one of the pillars of the object-oriented method is inheritance as a way of making software reuse easy. However, the idea goes beyond simply software reuse, as raw objects can provide reuse without the need for inheritance just by being a prototype for other objects as in languages such as JavaScript. Class and interface inheritance gives you the opportunity to control how others will use the code you produce but this is a tricky business.

Class As The Unit Of Software

If you create a class then the code you have implemented is a template for as many instances of the class as you care to create. This is software reuse in action and you benefit from it whenever you use any class library.

Inheritance is a cornerstone of the object-oriented method but not everyone is of the opinion that it is a good idea. Some see it as a contrived and a dangerous approach to building software. The problem is that if you modify a base class how can you be sure that the change doesn't break the derived classes in ways that are complex and difficult to fix? This is also sometimes expressed by referring to the "coupling" between classes. For a good design, classes should be loosely coupled, i.e. have a low dependency on each other's working, and clearly inheritance involves very tight coupling between the base and derived classes. However, the nature of this coupling is very precise and not really in the same category as classes that just happen to use each other's internal workings.

As a result of these views, inheritance is often treated with caution, if not downright avoidance. Many programmers believe that inheritance is difficult to control and that there are better ways to work. Interface inheritance, introduced in the previous chapter, is one such method – where a class inherits an interface which the programmer then has to implement.

If this sounds a lot like an invitation to return to copy-and-paste inheritance you wouldn't be far from the truth. The whole point of interface inheritance is that it isn't inheritance at all – it stops the propagation of changes down a chain of derived classes. Each class that implements the interface has the same set of methods and this is useful, especially when writing generic methods, but there is still the problem of maintaining multiple implementations of each interface to contend with. Interface inheritance is about type safety not code reuse.

Similarly containment, or delegation, where a class is extended by being wrapped in an outer class, has its advantages, but brings with it duplication of code and a partial reinstatement of the inheritance chain. That is, if the contained class is changed then the containing class can break. C# almost has a simple mechanism for delegation if interface default methods really are default methods.

Encapsulation

If you want to extend software and make use of code that has already been written, you have to accept the fact that change to the base code can result in the derived code not working. So basically the problem is in finding ways of controlling inheritance and the current situation is confused and difficult. There are some simple ideas, such as dividing the workings of a class into external and internal and making sure that only the external details are available for use – the principle of encapsulation – but this doesn't specify what should be inherited.

Are the internal workings of a class fair game for reuse in a derived class?

The best answer is, "sometimes". There are cases where the internal workings are important enough to the functioning of the class that not allowing derived classes access to them would defeat the point of inheritance. There are also cases where an internal facility shouldn't be reused by inheritance – but it is very difficult to find convincing examples that aren't just poor design or coding. Even more draconian is the idea that inheritance should be prohibited completely – an easy option in C#. Finally after finding ways of disabling inheritance we have the idea of the extension method, which was introduced in C# 3.0 to allow class reuse and extension without inheritance. Extension methods are so easy to use and so attractive that they are often used to make up for the inability to extend the workings of a class via inheritance.

When reading about the practicalities of inheritance control you need to keep in mind that there are many strong opinions about how things should be done, but very little theoretical or practical evidence that this is indeed the case.

Access Modifiers

As you can't do much with object-oriented programming without mastering access modifiers you probably know about them already. However, it is still worth gathering the basic ideas here. There are four access modifiers you can use to control which classes have access to properties and methods of another class:

- `public` – access is allowed by any code, no matter what class or assembly it belongs to
- `internal` – as public, but restricted to code in the same assembly
- `protected` – access is allowed by code in the same class or a derived class
- `private` – as protected, but restricted to code in the same class. This is the default.

There is also the combined modifier:

- `protected internal` – access is allowed to any code in the same assembly or by any derived class in another assembly.

It is important to realize that `private` and `protected` are not code security measures. A `private` or `protected` method can be decompiled just as easily as a `public` method and reflection (when the code is running with full trust) can be used to call a `private` or `protected` method from any code. This confusion between security and design is a general problem in considering any mechanism of inheritance control. It is tempting to always deny access to any code that you somehow feel is proprietary and belongs to you, even if it actually doesn't succeed in denying access and only makes it more difficult to get further value from your work.

This is about all there is to know about basic access modifiers, together with the simple fact that no derived class can have a freer access modifier than its base class. If this wasn't the case what was supposed to be private could become public via a derived class.

As far as encapsulation is concerned, the use of the modifiers is simple enough. Any property or method that is part of the class's interface with the outside world should be declared `public`. Public types can be accessed by the outside world and by classes derived from the class that they are declared in. Any internal mechanism that is strictly to be hidden from the outside world should be declared as either `protected` or `private`.

Protected versus Private

The big problem is when should you use `protected` and when `private`? The answer is often based on the question – do you want a programmer working on a class derived from your class to have access to its inner workings? This is a difficult question. Why would you refuse the use of a method, say, to the "end user" of a class but not to a programmer who is creating a new class from your class? You might feel that a programmer who is capable of creating a new class is probably more technically capable of treating your method correctly, but this assumption may be unfounded. In most cases the reason why you make a resource protected is because you, the implementer of the class, wants to derive new classes from it. After all, if you can't trust yourself to use resources you have created, who can you trust? However, if you do this, notice that you also allow other programmers to do the same. It is also probably unreasonable to extend this privilege to yourself on the grounds that you can be trusted. In a few months' time, the code in question may look as alien to you as it does to another programmer.

The decision about which code should be protected and which kept private should really relate to the code and not the coder. Public methods should define the external world's view of the class - they should define the way the class is used. In the same way, private and protected methods should define the inner workings of the class. They are the resources that the class uses to get the job done. To decide which should be `private` and which `protected` the important question is which of the methods are general tools that a derived class might also need to use as part of its extended implementation. In most cases any resource that a base class uses is probably needed by a class that extends it and so `protected` is most often appropriate – even if `private` is the default.

A simple example should make the situation clearer especially with reference to inheritance. Consider the class:

```
public class MyClassA
{
        public void myMethod1()
        {
                Console.WriteLine("Method1");
        }
}
```

and a derived class:

```
public class MyClassB:MyClassA
{
      public new void myMethod1()
      {
            base.myMethod1();
            Console.WriteLine("Method2");
      }
}
```

where the overriding method in the derived class can both override and access the base class method.

Let's consider the changes that adopting different levels of protection for myMethod1 of MyClassA brings about.

If you change the myMethod1 of MyClassA to protected everything still works as before. Then the overriding method can even remain public and this means that although code outside of the classes can't call myMethod1 directly on an instance of MyClassA it can call it via an instance of MyClassB.

If you change myMethod1 in MyClassA to private, the call in the MyClassB version of the method to the base class myMethod1 no longer works. The derived class has no access to the parent's private resources. However, the derived class can create a method with the same name and there is no need for the new modifier as nothing is being overridden, i.e. the class doesn't inherit a myMethod1 from the base class.

If you change the MyClassA myMethod1 to virtual then it cannot be private as the whole point of a virtual method is to allow derived classes to override it dynamically. However, you can make the method virtual protected and the derived class can either use the override or new modifier on its method.

If it uses the override modifier then the overriding method cannot be public. It can only be protected as private is ruled out because the method is once again virtual. The reason that the protection level cannot change is that the compiler cannot work out if, at run time, a reference to MyClassA such as:

```
MyClassA myObj;
```

is going to be referencing an object of type MyClassA or of type MyClassB.

Now consider the method call:

```
myObj.myMethod1();
```

If myMethod1 is virtual then which method will be called depends on the run time type of myObj and, if the protection levels were different, the compiler would not be able to work out at compile time if the method was or was not accessible.

Notice that if the method isn't declared as virtual then this problem doesn't arise because early binding means that, no matter what class myObj references, the method defined in MyClassA is called – because that's the declared type of myObj. For this reason if you declare the derived class's method as new then it can be public, private or protected. Once again, this is reasonable as the new modifier "kills" the virtual inheritance, i.e. it works as if the MyClassA method wasn't declared as virtual.

Sealed Pros and Cons

If you are considering inheritance there is another access modifier, sealed. If you apply the sealed modifier to a class then the class cannot be used as a base class for a new class. Many programmers think that sealed is a great idea because they don't want to make a gift of their class to use as the basis for something new – but software reuse is the basis of the object-oriented method and using sealed breaks this. Just like private and protected, sealed is not a code security measure. It is fair enough to decompile a sealed class. For example, if you define two classes as:

```
public sealed class MyClassA
{
        void myMethod1(){}
}
public class MyClassB : MyClassA
{
}
```

you will see a compile-time error saying that you cannot derive from a sealed type.

Many, perhaps most, of the classes that make up the .NET framework are sealed and this is a mistake as it causes many a programmer to have to reinvent the wheel when a derived class would be the simplest way of creating something that does the job. Notice that you can add new behavior to any class using extension methods but this isn't as powerful or elegant as using inheritance.

The only good reason for using sealed is if the class you have just created contains something low-level that would most likely break a class that extended them – however, it is difficult to find any really convincing example. Even so some programmers, and the .NET design team in particular, take the attitude that all of their public classes should be marked as sealed.

You could then ask why C# supports inheritance at all if every class has inheritance turned off? Indeed, as already discussed, many programmers are of the opinion that inheritance is not the best way to reuse code. Interface inheritance and composition, for example, are design alternatives to inheritance that are simpler to manage.

It is also argued that allowing classes that are in the framework to be extended is inviting misuse and hence bugs that would bring the entire system into disrepute. The effort needed to create classes that can be safely extended by inheritance in a manner that stops the inexperienced from doing damage is just too much. Far better to have a library of code that can be used in a narrow, well-defined, way with a high degree of confidence that the code does exactly what it claims to.

Another reason for sealing a class is that it permits the compiler to perform optimizations by making all of the methods non-virtual. As there can be no derived classes all method calls can be made early bound and this is type safe and more efficient.

So using `sealed` as a default option is easy, safe and rewarding to the class implementer, but not as much to the class consumer.

On the other hand if the code doesn't quite do what you want, it isn't quite complete, and adding some additional methods and properties would make it just right then to discover that the class is sealed is annoying. The only solutions to the problem involve a lot of work. You can recreate the code for the base class and then extend it – a task that is relatively easy if you have the source code of the base class. Even if you are able to implement a copy-and-paste version of source code inheritance, you have made the system more error-prone by there being two copies of essentially the same code.

The Static Class

There is also another variation on class that cannot be inherited – the static class. Classes can have static constructors as well as instance constructors. All you have to do is put static in front of the constructor definition and it is used to initialize any static fields the class may have. If you also create a private constructor for the class then no instances can be created and you have a pure static class – the ultimate singleton object which cannot be instantiated nor inherited.

For example:

```
class MyClassA
{
      static public int value;
      static MyClassA() {
            value = (new Random()).Next(1,7);
      }
      private MyClassA() { }
}
```

In this case `MyClassA` has a static constructor which assigns a random value to its only static field and a private constructor which means you cannot instantiate it. That is

```
class MyClassB:MyClassA
```

and

```
MyClassA MyA=new MyClassA();
```

generate compile-time errors. Notice that the static constructor is called just once at the start of the program and:

```
Console.WriteLine(MyClassA.value);
```

displays the same random number.

Sealed Methods

There is a less well-known use of the `sealed` modifier. You can use `sealed` on a method that overrides a `virtual` method. This stops the chain of overriding of virtual methods at the first derived class that applies `sealed`. For example, given the class:

```
public class MyClassA
{
      public virtual void myMethod1()
      {
            Console.WriteLine("Method1");
      }
}
```

then a derived class can override the `virtual` method:

```
public class MyClassB:MyClassA
{
      public sealed override void myMethod1()
      {
            Console.WriteLine("Method1");
      }
}
```

but, as the sealed modifier has been applied, a class derived from MyClassB cannot override myMethod1. Of course, if you want to stop the chain of specifically virtual overriding at the first class, i.e. MyClassA, simply don't declare the method as virtual.

The Delegation Pattern

A better approach is to use object composition or containment. Recently composition came into the spotlight as a good alternative to inheritance and you would often read the quote *"prefer composition to inheritance"*. The truth of the matter is that composition in C# isn't easy and, if you can, you should use class or interface inheritance.

To use composition, simply create the object that needs to be extended as an object property of a new class and then provide methods that mirror the methods of the contained class and which simply call the methods of the contained class. Because the containing class's methods call the contained class's methods to get things done this is also called the delegation pattern. For example, if you have the class:

```
public sealed class MyClassA
{
        public void myMethod1()
        {
                Console.WriteLine("Method1");
        }
}
```

then it can be extended using containment:

```
public class MyClassB
{
        private MyClassA MyContained= new MyClassA();
        void myMethod1()
        {
                MyContained.myMethod1();
        }
}
```

In a more complex case you would have to add methods and properties corresponding to all of the methods and properties exposed as public by the contained class and this could be a lot of work.

The simplest way to pass on a method call to a contained instance is to use a lambda expression, see Chapter 14:

```
public void myMethod1() => MyContained.myMethod1();
```

You can also make use of a constructor to create the contained class and this opens up the possibility of dynamically selecting the class to be contained. There is also the lazy way of achieving containment by allowing the contained object to be `public`, for example:

```
public class MyClassB
{
        public MyClassA MyContained = new MyClassA();
}
```

With this change you no longer have to implement methods and properties to re-expose the members of the contained class, you simply have to use a double-qualified name as in:

```
MyClassB myObj = new MyClassB();
myObj.MyContained.myMethod1();
```

The obvious disadvantage of this approach is that it results in unwieldy names and if you really want to create a new class that looks and behaves in a similar way to an existing class then simply making the contained class `public` isn't good enough.

All of this seems like a lot of trouble to go to just to defeat the effects of `sealed` but there is sometimes little choice.

Nested Classes

A nested class is another way to control the visibility and access to a class. To create a nested class you simply declare the class in the usual way but within the definition of another class, for example:

```
public  class MyClassA
{
        public class MyNestedClass
        {
                public void myMethod2()
                {
                        Console.WriteLine("Method2");
                }
        }
}
```

MyNestedClass is declared within MyClassA and so is nested within MyClassA.

Compare this to the simpler idea of creating an instance of a `class` as a member of a `class`, e.g:

```
public  class MyClassA
{
        public MyClassB myobj=new MyClassB();
                etc.
```

This isn't a nested class, just an instance of `MyClassB` that is a member of `MyClassA`. Notice that both classes are declared as `public` and this isn't good practice, but let's follow the example a little further to see how it works.

If we also declare a method within `MyClassA` it can make use of the nested class in the usual way:

```
public void myMethod1()
{
        MyNestedClass myObj1 = new MyNestedClass();
        myObj1.myMethod2();
        Console.WriteLine("Method1");
}
}
```

Any code within `MyClassA` can create and use objects of type `MyNestedClass`. If you move outside of `MyClassA` then your code can create objects of type `MyClassA` which in turn use objects of `MyNestedClass`, for example:

```
MyClassA myob2 = new MyClassA();
myob2.myMethod1();
```

However, `MyNestedClass` isn't directly accessible from code outside of `MyClassA`. As the nested class is `public` it can be accessed using a qualified name. For example, to create an instance of `MyNestedClass` outside of `MyClassA` you would use:

```
MyClassA.MyNestedClass myobj3 = new MyClassA.MyNestedClass();
```

and you could then access the object's methods and properties in the usual way:

```
myobj3.myMethod2();
```

This use of nested classes to create types with qualified names isn't usual and most programmers, and the Microsoft recommendations, say that this isn't a good use. Also notice that nested classes are just a special case of nested types where a type, a `struct` say, is declared within a `class`.

In most cases nested classes are used as a way of hiding the implementation of a `class`. Normally classes cannot use the `private` or `protected` type modifier, but nested classes can. What this means is that, if you declare the nested class to be `private` or `protected`, it is no longer accessible to code outside of the containing class, even if you use a qualified name. However, it is accessible from within the containing class. In short, the whole of a nested class is `private` or `protected` according to its declaration.

A nested class also has access to all of the members of the outer containing class, but a reference to the instance of the containing class isn't provided automatically. That is, `this` within the containing class refers to the instance of the containing class and `this` within the nested class refers to the instance of the nested class, not the containing class. The nested class has its own `this`.

To allow the nested class access to the containing class, you have to pass it a reference to the instance, for example:

```
public  class MyClassA
{
        protected class MyNestedClass
        {
                private MyClassA that;
                public MyNestedClass(MyClassA outerthis)
                {
                        that= outerthis;
                }
        }
```

Now when the nested class is created the container passes a reference to its current instance:

```
MyNestedClass myObj1 = new MyNestedClass(this);
```

The inner class can use the variable name that to access members of the container class including private and protected members. This is the C# equivalent of the Java inner class where the instance of the nested class is bound to an instance of the containing class.

Clearly the intended use for a nested class is to allow the creation of classes, and types in general, that are only to be used within another class. Hence the reason why public nested classes are generally thought to be bad practice.

Extension Methods

If you don't have access to the source code of a class and the class is sealed, or you are of the opinion that inheritance is bad and dangerous, what can you do to add functionality without recreating or containing the class? Currently the only answer is to use an extension method.

An extension method is a static method declared within a static class that has a special "pointer" to an instance of the class it extends. The name of the static class has nothing much to do with the extension method's name and use. So, for example, you could create a general class to be used to hold all the extension methods in your project:

```
public static class MyExtensions
{
```

If you want to add a method called MyExtension to MyClassA the declaration needed is:

```
        public static void MyExtension(this MyClassA myinstance)
        {
                myinstance.myMethod1();
        }
}
```

The first parameter specification of all extensions has the same form. The `this MyClassA` part, indicates the type that the method is added to and the actual parameter, `myinstance`, is set to a reference to the instance of `MyClassA` that the method has been invoked on. That is, `myinstance` can be used like `this` in a regular class method and hence it gives access to all of the members of the class.

To use the extension method you simply invoke the method as if it was a regular method defined as part of the class:

```
MyClassA myobj2 = new MyClassA();
myobj2.MyExtension();
```

At this point it looks as if the extension method is exactly the solution we have been looking for. It even allows you to add methods to classes that have been sealed and so provides a way of extending the .NET base class library and fundamental types such as `int` or `string`. However, there are some restrictions on the way that an extension method works and behaves.

The first restriction is that an extension method only has access to the public types of the class it extends. In particular, an extension method cannot access private or protected members. An extension method is no more privileged that any code external to the class. In addition you can't override a class method by an extension method. If you attempt to give an extension method the same name and signature as a class method then the class method is always used in preference. Notice that no warning is given of the name conflict. This means that extension methods really are only able to extend the behavior of a class and not modify it. This makes extension safer than inheritance and overriding.

Extension methods are, however, inherited. If you create a `MyClassB` which inherits from `MyClassA` then a `MyClassB` object will have all of the extension methods of `MyClassA`. This inheritance isn't virtual and hence polymorphism isn't supported. The availability of an extension method depends on the declared type of a reference and not on the type of the instance it actually references. This means that extension method calls are early bound and type checked at compile time.

For example, if `MyClassB` inherits from `MyClassA` and both declare an extension method `MyExtension` then `MyClassA` will use its version and `MyClassB` its version. Notice that there is no need to use `new` or `override` to redefine extension methods in derived classes. The rule is that the extension method used by a class is the one that matches its type most accurately. Such matching is done at compile time. For example:

```
MyClassA myobj1;
myobj1= new MyClassB();
myobj1.MyExtension();
```

results in the extension method for `MyClassA` being called, even though the reference is to an instance of `MyClassB`.

Postlude

Inheritance is a powerful idea and it can be misused more easily than used to good effect. The problems usually arise when inheritance chains are long and ad hoc, but long inheritance chains are usually an indication that either the principles of object design are not being used or that the situation is truly complex.

Your choices are to either to attempt to control inheritance piecemeal with access modifiers or forbid it completely using `sealed`. If you choose not to use inheritance then you need to be aware that the alternatives, containment or extension methods, that you are almost certain to be attracted to, carry their own problems and increase your workload. Whatever you do, make sure you understand the technology you opt for.

II Casting & Generics

Prelude

The problem with strong typing is that it limits how easy it is to do certain things. The first solution to the problem is casting – overtly stating the type of an object to override variable typing. A more sophisticated solution is to use generics and, going one step further, to allow dynamic typing.

Chapter 8

Casting - The Escape From Strong Typing

Casting is one of the most confusing aspects of any modern language and it often makes beginners think hard. But if you know **why** you are doing it, then the **how** makes a lot more sense. We have encountered casting earlier in the context of strong typing but there is more to it.

Casting

Casting, stating the type of an object to override variable typing, is an odd business that has found its way into many modern languages via C and C++. Both Java and C# make use of it to allow programmers to escape the confines of strong typing without being able to create anything too unsafe. The big problem is that it confuses two aspects of dealing with variables – type and representation.

Type is simply a system of classification that is used by strongly-typed languages to determine what sort of data a variable can store or reference. Type conversion can just mean changing the classification of an object or variable, or it can mean changing the actual representation of the data, for example from integer to floating point.

In an ideal world we wouldn't need to convert or even mix types – an integer would always be combined with other integers and why would you ever want to convert an integer to a floating point number? Of course, if you want to write useful programs you have to allow a certain interplay between data types and this is where casting as conversion comes in.

Originally, in C, casting was all about type conversion and this is how it is usually introduced, but in fact there is more to it as there are some very confused semantics behind a simple piece of syntax – just write the type name in brackets in front of the variable you want to convert – but does this mean passive type conversion or active representation conversion?

What is worse is that most books on C# don't venture very deeply into the idea beyond presenting the basic idea that casting is just type conversion. It's actually more tricky, so let's start simple with casting value types and then look at the more interesting reference type casting.

Type Conversion

The simplest use of a cast is to convert from one numeric type to another and this is where active representation conversion first enters the picture. When the cast is safe from the point of view of representation then the compiler will do the job implicitly for you.

For example:

```
int MyInt;
long MyLong;
MyLong = MyInt;
```

is fine as the compiler can always store a 32-bit integer in a 64-bit integer.

This is an example of a "widening" cast in the sense that the conversion is from a smaller or narrower type to a bigger or wider type. Here "bigger" and "smaller" refer both to the amount of memory the data takes to store but also, and more abstractly, the range of data that they can store. A narrower type can, in principle, always be represented by a wider type but usually only a sub-range of a wider type can be represented by a narrower type. The terminology is commonly used but isn't precise.

The key idea is that:

A wider data type can always be used in place of a narrower data type because it can represent everything the narrower type can.

As in this case the required conversion is from a narrower to a wider type the compiler assumes that you intended to write:

```
MyLong = (long)MyInt;
```

However, if the implied cast could be unsafe then the compiler insists that you write out your intentions explicitly. For example, for a wider to a narrower cast:

```
MyInt = MyLong;
```

the compiler will, quite rightly, generate a compile-time error because you can't always convert a 64-bit integer into a 32-bit integer.

The fact that you can't always do it doesn't mean that it is always wrong. If you really mean it then you can write:

```
MyInt = (int)MyLong;
```

and the compiler will perform the type conversion by generating the necessary IL (intermediate language) to convert a 32-bit integer into a 64-bit integer. Notice that there is no natural way to do this conversion and in practice C# simply moves the low 32 bits of the long value into the int.

Notice that casting only works in this way for numeric data. A beginner might suspect that if:

```
MyInt = (int)MyLong;
```

works then so should:

```
MyString=(string)MyInt;
```

but of course it doesn't. Why it doesn't is something we could argue about for a long time. If you are going to use casting to perform a change of representation for numeric values, why not for strings and other data-based objects? Instead, for most active type conversions, you have to use a method:

```
string MyString=MyInt.ToString();
```

There are, of course, a number of versions of the `ToString()` method that allow you to control the format of the conversion and this makes it more flexible than the cast syntax.

Convert

So the next question is – are there other conversion methods? The answer is yes, but you have to use the `Convert` class. So while you can't write:

```
MyInt = MyLong.ToInt32();
```

you can write:

```
MyInt = Convert.ToInt32(MyLong);
```

Unlike the simple cast, the method throws an exception if the long is too big to fit into the int.

If you want to convert a single or a double to an int then things are even more confusing as there are two ways which give different answers:

```
double MyDouble = 2.6;
MyInt = (int)MyDouble;
MyInt = Convert.ToInt32(MyDouble);
```

The cast truncates to give 2 but the `ToInt32` rounds to give 3.

Of course, if you want to take control of type conversion you can always use the `Math` class as in:

```
Math.Round(MyDouble);
Math.Truncate(MyDouble);
```

and there are overloaded methods that will give you control of how the rounding is to be performed. Notice, however, that neither method actually performs a type conversion so you will still need a cast as in:

```
MyInt = (int) Math.Round(MyDouble);
MyInt = (int) Math.Truncate(MyDouble);
```

Of course you could also use `Convert`.

Upcasting and Downcasting

We have already encountered the ideas of upcasting and downcasting, but it is worth going over again briefly in the light of casting in general.

Originally casting may have been about changing data representation, but today it is mostly about changing the type label on a variable, not the active conversion of representations. You can view its involvement with data format conversion of value types as an accident due to the need for some consistency. Indeed, C# modeled its casting on C++ just at the point where C++ was attempting to put its house in order by adding some constructs that removed the need to use casts at all.

Casting acquired its wider meaning when we moved to strongly typed object oriented languages that supported inheritance. This gives rise to an inheritance hierarchy which it is natural to interpret as a type hierarchy. There is a sense in which a base class is smaller than a derived class in the same way that an int is "smaller" than a long. That is you can use a long anywhere that an int can be used simply because a long can represent every number than an int can.

This notion of "x can be used anywhere y can" generalizes to the wider type hierarchy only in this case x is "derived class" and y is "base class".

That is, as we have seen in previous chapters:

```
class MyClassA;
class MyClassB : MyClassA;
```

then

```
MyClassA myA = new MyClassB();
```

is valid and myA can be treated as if it was referencing an object of type MyClassA even though it is actually referencing an object of type MyClassB.

As MyClassB has all of the methods and properties of MyClassA this is always safe to do and so the cast is automatic – this is like a widening cast for value types but the analogy is far from perfect. If you want to make it look more like a cast, you can write:

```
MyClassA myA = (MyClassA) new MyClassB();
```

If you try this, however, you will most likely find that there is a warning that a cast is unnecessary but it does make it clear that a MyClassB is being treated as a MyClassA object, an upcast, just as an int is treated as a long in the earlier example.

Downcasting works in the same way, but it isn't always safe. Its type safety depends on the class being referenced actually being of the correct type, and it is again like a narrowing cast for value types but the analogy is not exact. For example, after:

```
MyClassA myA = (MyClassA) new MyClassB();
```

it is obvious that myA is actually referencing a MyClassB object, but the rules of strong typing means that you can only use the methods defined in MyClassA. Suppose you know that myA is referencing a MyClassB object and want to use its methods, what can you do? The answer is you can downcast to MyClassB as in:

```
MyClassB myB= (MyClassB) myA;
```

and now you can use myB as if it referenced a MyClassB object – because that is what it is.

If you want to avoid having to involve another variable and just want to use MyClassB methods, you can write the cast as:

```
((ClassB) myA).MyMethodB();
```

The extra parentheses are necessary because of the precedence of the operations. You can also make use of the as operator:

```
(myA as MyClassB).MyMethodB();
```

A downcast is not always safe. If myA turns out to be a type that isn't a MyClassB object or derive from MyClassB then a run-time error occurs.

Generic Algorithms

Having made clear what up- and downcasting are, why do we need them?

What downcasting allows you to do is to use a reference to a class without really knowing exactly what it is. The most extreme example of downcasting is to use an object reference for any class you want to work with, for example:

```
object MyAnything = new MyClassB();
((ClassB)MyAnything).methodB();
```

Why might this be useful?

The answer is that you can now write code that will work with any type using nothing but object references. In short, you can write generic algorithms.

For example, if we define a sort method that works with objects:

```
public object[] MySort(object[] array)
{
        //do the sort
        return array;
}
```

then, if we declare an array of custom objects:

```
MyClass[] testdata = new MyClass[10];
```

we can sort the array using:

```
MyClass[] resultdata = (MyClass[]) MySort((object[])testdata);
```

There is an upcast to `object []` in the call and a downcast to `MyClass[]` in the return – and this is the first time we notice the connection between input parameters and upcasting and outputs and downcasting. This really does mean that the method can sort any type we care to throw at it – assuming it knows how to order the type, i.e. to know when `MyClass[i]` is greater or smaller than `MyClass[j]`.

You can usually provide an order relation to a class by giving it a `Compare` method. In addition, you can make the sort method safer by writing it so that it only works with arrays of classes that implement an `ICompare` interface using introspection. There are lots of useful examples to be found in the framework in facilities introduced before generics, see the next chapter.

This is an extreme example of using casting to implement generic algorithms. In many cases the function will accept a base class and work with it and all its derived classes courtesy of upcasting. For example:

```
public base[] MyFunction(base[] array)
{
        //do the sort
        return array;
}
```

enables you to pass any object of the base class or a derived class. `MyFunction` can only make use of methods that the base class has unless it uses a downcast to the appropriate derived class and then the problem is making sure that that it is working with the correct derived class. The result of the function is returned as an array of base types and usually this would have to be downcast to the type of the object passed into the function. Of course, any mistakes in downcasting result in run-time errors because they cannot be picked up at compile time. Put simply, this approach to writing generic algorithms is not type safe.

If you abandon strong typing by using casts then this is the sort of problem you have to live with. The alternative approach is to use generics as outlined in the next chapter. While generics are type safe the disadvantage is that they achieve this by being very restrictive and ultimately very complicated.

Casting and Overriding

You need to be aware that considerations of virtual versus non-virtual inheritance also come into play with both up- and downcasting. If a method is defined to be virtual then it is late bound. If a method isn't virtual, or if the override uses the new modifier, then it is early bound.

For upcasting the way that this works has already been described in Chapter 5. If MyClassB inherits MyMethod from MyClassA and overrides it then:

```
ClassA myA = new MyClassB();
myA.MyMethod();
```

will call the method defined on MyClassB if it was declared virtual and the method defined on MyClassA if it wasn't declared virtual or if new was used in the MyClassB override.

The same considerations apply to downcasting, but things are a little bit more complicated because, as already mentioned, a downcast usually involves an earlier upcast. The downcast is always early bound, but any upcast is late or early bound depending on the way the methods are declared. An example should make this clear.

Suppose we have three classes which form an inheritance chain and each of the methods is non-virtual and hence early bound:

```
class MyClassA
{
        public void MyMethod()
        {
                Console.WriteLine("A");
        }
}
class MyClassB : MyClassA {
        public new void MyMethod()
        {
                Console.WriteLine("B");
        }
};
class MyClassC : MyClassB {
        public new void MyMethod()
        {
                Console.WriteLine("C");
        }
};
```

Now we can implement a downcast:

```
MyClassA myA = (MyClassA) new MyClassC();
((MyClassB) myA).MyMethod();
```

Notice that myA is in fact a `MyClassC`, but the downcast is to a `MyClassB`. However, as early binding is used, we see the `MyClassB` method print B. The declared type of myA is `MyClassB` when the method is called.

If you now make the `MyClassA` `MyMethod` virtual and that of `MyClassB` override you will see no change and the `MyClassB` method is called – early binding is still used.

Finally, if you also change the `MyClassC` implementation of `MyMethod` to override then it is the `MyClassC` `MyMethod` that is called – late binding is used for the final upcast and you see C printed.

It can be subtle, but it is logical.

Arrays of Value Types

The earlier example of a sorting method brings us to an interesting problem in casting that isn't much discussed. This isn't a theoretical point but a practical decision made to make the language more efficient. When it happens it can leave you puzzled for some time.

You might think that the previous example of sorting objects would work with:

```
int[] testdata = new int[] { 1, 2, 3 };
int[] result =  MySort((object[])testdata);
```

After all, there is nothing wrong with the cast and the system should box the integer value type automatically into a reference type that can be cast to object. However, to avoid you unthinkingly writing this and causing the inefficient boxing of many integers this is not allowed and you will see the error message:

```
Cannot convert from type int[] to object[]
```

This leads some programmers to conclude that you can't cast arrays. You can cast arrays as long as they have the same number of dimensions, but you can't cast value arrays to an array of reference types because it is a very time consuming process.

There seems to be no better way around this problem than to convert the value type array to an array of reference types by way of iteration – even if this fact is hidden by the way it is written. For example, you can use the Array static class and its Copy method, which will perform a cast on each element during the copy:

```
int[] testdata = new int[] { 1, 2, 3 };
object[] obtestdata =  new object[testdata.Length];
Array.Copy(testdata,obtestdata,testdata.Length);
object[] result =  MySort(obtestdata);
```

114

Notice that the array sizes have to match and that you can't cast the object[] back to int[] for the same reason, i.e. unboxing is inefficient.

You can also use the newer generic method that is part of the Array static object to write the whole thing without using intermediate arrays:

```
object[] result = MySort(
     Array.ConvertAll<int,object>(testdata,
                    delegate(int i){return(object)i;}));
```

but you still have to also do the conversion from object[] to int[].

No matter how you approach this problem, it is messy due to the syntax having to change for a method that works by upcasting to object when you move from reference to value variables. Part of a better solution is provided by custom casts.

Custom Casts

You can write methods that will be called when a cast is performed to your class. However, you can't define a custom cast to or from the base class. In fact, apart from making conversions to and from value types, it is difficult to see what sort of custom casts you could possibly create. For example, if you want to allow MyClassB to be custom cast to an int you might add something like:

```
class MyClassB{
       public int Value=42;
       public static explicit operator int(ClassB MyB)
       {
              return MyB.Value;
       }
}
```

This simply returns the value stored in an instance variable, but in practice you could return something more complicated. All cast operators have be declared static but you can choose between explicit and implicit for the style of the cast. An explicit custom cast has to always be written as a case but an implicit cast can be left to the compiler to work out.

Following this definition you can write code like:

```
ClassB MyB = new MyClassB();
int v = (int)MyB;
```

There is the argument that if you want to do a custom type conversion like this then it would be clearer to define a ToInt method rather than a custom cast, but you can decide which suits your approach.

The Cast System

Now that we have looked in detail at casting, you can begin to see what it is really all about. Casting is really to do with introducing a little organized freedom into the type system so that object-oriented programming is more flexible. That is, the primary purpose of a cast is to change the type of an object, not to change its representation. Without this facility there are a lot of things that would be much more difficult to do.

It is arguable that casting really shouldn't be involved in an active type conversion because it confuses the issue. If you want to be "pure" it might be better to implement all active type conversion as methods. To demonstrate how confusing this can be, consider the following example where an object reference is downcast to an int (this is also an example of explicit boxing):

```
object MyAnything;
int MyIntA = 3;
MyAnything = MyIntA;
```

To convert back to an int (or to unbox the int) all you have to use is a simple cast:

```
int MyIntB = (int) MyAnything;
```

This works, but what about:

```
long MyLong = (long) MyAnything;
```

This looks as if it is the same sort of cast, but it doesn't work because it is attempting two sorts of type conversion in one go. You can't downcast MyAnything to an int and perform the active widening conversion needed to go from an int to a long in one go. The reason is that the boxed int can only be unboxed to an int and not to another type. The correct way to do it is the rather ugly:

```
long MyLong = (long) (int) MyAnything;
```

First the explicit downcast/unboxing and then the explicit widening cast are needed to make it all work.

Variance and Casting

You may not have noticed, but the role of input and output parameters forces on them a particular type of behavior when it comes to casting. This is usually called "variance" and is something that is generally introduced as part of generics. However variance is also part of casting.

To see the difference between input and output consider three classes, MyClassA, MyClassB and MyClassC, where MyClassC inherits from MyClassB which inherits from MyClassA.

Now consider a function that has MyClassB as its input parameter:

```
myFunction(MyClassB parameter)
```

An input parameter is something that is going to be worked on by the method assuming that it is a `MyClassB` object and so it could be substituted by a derived class, i.e. a bigger object such as a `MyClassC` object for example.

So you can downcast the `MyClassB` parameter and call the function with anything derived from `MyClassC`, but you cannot use `MyClassA` because it might not have all of the methods of a `MyClassB` object. This ability to accept a bigger object but not a smaller one, i.e you can only downcast the parameter, is often referred to as "contravariance".

Now consider the situation with respect to a return value of type `MyClassB`, i.e.

```
MyClassB myFunction();
```

In this case the calling program receives a `MyClassB` object as the result and can safely use it as a `MyClassA` object by upcasting from the result, but clearly you can't use it as a `MyClassC` object by downcasting. That is, the return parameter can be safely upcast to a smaller object and this in turn is referred to as "covariance".

That is if the input and output are of type MyClassB then

- an input parameter can be downcast
- an output parameter can be upcast

or

```
     output      input
MyClassA ← MyClassB ← MyClassC
```

So in the current jargon input parameters are contravariant, output parameters are covariant and in/out parameters are invariant because they can't be safely cast in either direction at all. The reason for this terminology and the idea is explained in more detail in Chapter 10.

Postlude

When you realize how confused the use of casting is in C# and most modern languages you can't help but be unhappy about it. If you want to put some order into your use of casting then use it only for passive type conversions and for any active type conversion that involves manipulation of the representation of a type. If your real purpose is to provide active type conversion for your classes, then see the `TypeConverter` class and the `IConvertible` interface in the C# documentation.

Keep in mind that generics provide a good way of avoiding the use of casts, but that there are times when casting provides a more powerful solution to the same problem.

Chapter 9

Generics

Generics are an essential part of any modern language. C# has generics that are easy to understand, but using them can be more taxing.

Why Generics?

We start out programming not really worrying too much about type and then it becomes central to everything we do. Everything has a type and when you write code it works with a specific set of types. However, some algorithms are the same no matter what type they work with. For example, a sorting algorithm doesn't really care what it is sorting as long as it has a way to decide if one element is bigger than another. Yet in a strongly-typed language you have to write a sort routine for each type you want to sort. Of course, this isn't what happens. If you want to do something in a type-independent way then you can give up strong typing and work with object and upcasting.

We have already seen that this has problems in an earlier chapter where we discovered that an array of value types cannot be cast to an array of objects due to the cost of conversion. An even bigger problem is that object has very few methods and generally you can't do very much. For example, object doesn't have a compare method so writing a generic sort function using upcasting isn't going to work.

As object does have an Equals method we can write a Find function which will return true if a target is in an array of almost any type:

```
Boolean Find(object[] a, object Target)
{
    Boolean result = false;
    foreach (object x in a)
    {
        if (x.Equals(Target))
        {
            result = true;
            break;
        }
    }
    return result;
}
```

You can call Find to test for equality (of reference) between any two objects of any almost any type. The "almost" is necessary because there is a problem with value types not being automatically boxed to objects, see the previous chapter. If you keep away from simple value types then the function works as written.

For example:

```
MyClassA myA1 = new MyClassA();
MyClassA myA2 = new MyClassA();
MyClassA myA3 = new MyClassA();

MyClassA[] classes   = {myA1, myA2, myA3};

Boolean result = Find<MyClassA>(classes, new MyClassA());
Console.WriteLine(result);
```

prints false. Notice that the equals method tests not for equality of value but equality of reference. That is, our function tests to see if the target element of the array references the same object. This is not the test of equality you might want when comparing objects, but it is all that is possible if you restrict your attention to object.

Notice that if the actual type passed to the function has redefined the equals method to be more appropriate to the type, it will only be called if the method is virtual and the derived class uses override.

As explained in the previous chapter, if you have a base type that has all of the properties you need to use then you can write a function that accepts the base class and use casting to make the function process any derived type. The problem here is working out what the actual type of something passed as an object really is. The limited range of methods available for the top of the type hierarchy, and the difficulty of determining the actual type are also problems that you will encounter with generics and not just casting.

Generics is a purpose-built solution for writing general algorithms that work on a range of types in a type-safe way. However, it is worth pointing out that generics doesn't offer much more than working with variables that reference object and often imposes restrictions which have to be overcome to implement what you want. It is not the perfect solution to implementing type-free algorithms.

Simple Value Types

You might be surprised that if you try:

```
string[] test = { "A", "B", "C" };
Boolean result = Find(test, "B");
```

you will find that the answer is true.

If you think about this for a moment it is an incorrect result if you believe that the literal "B" is a different string object to the "B" stored in the array. This behavior is because the C# compiler goes to great lengths to avoid storing the same string literal more than once. A compiler optimization, called "interning", checks to see if the string literal already exists and if it does it reuses it and hence the equality of reference. Notice that this is a compiler optimization and not part of the language definition, and certainly nothing to do with the type hierarchy, and so the result you get does depend on the compiler you use. This is a good reason to be very careful when using reference equality on anything but classes.

Basic Generics

The basic idea of generics is very simple – it extends the idea of a parameter to include specifying type. That is, it allows type parameters in class, interface and method definitions. To make use of such generic declarations you have to supply real types for the type parameters at the time they are used.

A type parameter is defined by being enclosed in **< >** used as brackets and can be used anywhere a type specification can be used – class, interface, functions, etc. So, for example, the function to find an element in an array can be re-written as a generic function with the use of a single type parameter:

```
Boolean Find<T>(T[] a, T Target)
{
    Boolean result = false;
    foreach (T x in a)
    {
        if (x.Equals(Target))
        {
            result = true;
            break;
        }
    }
    return result;
}
```

The <T> at the start declares the type parameter. You don't have to use T as the name of the type parameter and you can have as many type parameters as you like. Within the function definition, the type parameter is just used as T without angle brackets. Following this we can call the generic function:

```
MyClassA myA1 = new MyClassA();
MyClassA myA2 = new MyClassA();
MyClassA myA3 = new MyClassA();
MyClassA[] classes   = { myA1, myA2,myA3 };

Boolean result = Find<MyClassA>(classes, myA2);
Console.WriteLine(result);
```

which will work no matter what type the array is. This time it also works with int types as no conversion to another type is involved.

Class, delegate and interface generic declarations work in the same way – add a type parameter in angle brackets at the start of the declaration and use the parameter as if it was a type in the body of the declaration. For example:

```
class MyClassA<T>
{
      public void myMethod(T a)
      {
            Console.WriteLine(a);
      }
}
```

declares a class with a single type parameter and a method that accepts a single parameter of that type. You would use this class in the obvious way:

```
MyClassA<string> myObject = new MyClassA<string>();
myObject.myMethod("Hello Generic World");
```

Notice that this is different to:

```
class MyClassA<T>
{
      public void myMethod<T>(T a)
      {
            Console.WriteLine(a);
      }
}
```

where in this case the <T> in the function definition isn't the same as the <T> in the class definition. You can call this method with its own type parameter:

```
MyClassA<string> myObject = new MyClassA<string>();
myObject.myMethod<int>(42);
```

As the compiler will try and infer the types in the call:

```
myObject.myMethod("Hello");
```

this looks as if it works and it looks like it might be using the class type parameter. This is a common error.

You can specify the type at the class level and at the method level.

Now we come to the big restriction inherent in using a generic. As the type parameter is unknown at the time of declaring the class, interface or function, you can't use any of its methods other than the ones supported by `object`. So, for example, if you try to write:

```
static T add<T>(T a,T b)
{
        return a+b;
}
```

the result is an error message saying the system can't work out what a+b is for type T. That is, when you are writing a generic, <T> is the same as object. This isn't unreasonable as, without knowing what T is, how can the system determine at compile time how to implement the + operator? In this sense working with simple generics is no better than working with the base type object as a way of creating generic algorithms.

Generic Inheritance

You can include a base class and interfaces within the class definition and these can also be generic. That is, apart from the use of the type parameter, the class declaration is standard. The same is true for a generic interface. However, things are a little more complicated due to the need to provide values for the type parameters use in inherited classes and interfaces. For example, if you create a generic interface:

```
public interface IMyInterfaceA<T>
{
        void MyMethod(T a) {}
}
```

then you would inherit it in a generic class using:

```
class MyClassA<T>: IMyInterfaceA<T>
{
        public void MyMethod(T a)
        {
                throw new NotImplementedException();
        }
}
```

It looks as if there are two definitions of the type parameter T but there is only one. When you use <T> sometimes it is a definition of the parameter and sometimes it is a use of the parameter. When you write:

```
MyClassA<int>{}
```

the type parameter T has the value int and the effective class declaration is:

```
class MyClassA<int>: IMyInterfaceA<int>
{
```

You don't have to use T and:

```
class MyClassA<T1> : IMyInterfaceA<T1>
```

works just as well.

If you want the inherited interface or class to have a different type then you can use:

```
class MyClassA<T1,T2> : IMyInterfaceA<T2>
```

and now creating an instance is something like:

```
MyClassA<int,double> myA = new MyClassA<int,double>();
```

You can also specify a type in the class definition:

```
class MyClassA<T>: ImyInterfaceA<double>
```

and in this case IMyInterface is set to double no matter what T is.

Run Time Type

Some languages, Java for example, implement generics by using "type erasure". This essentially converts anything passed as a generic type to the most general type – object in the case of C#. The idea is that generics are compiled to the implementation you would create by casting everything to object and then forgetting what the original type was.

C# doesn't do this, i.e. it doesn't use type erasure. What this means is that anything passed as a generic type still retains its type and you can use this at run time. What happens is that when you use a generic type <T> in a definition, the compiler treats it as an unknown type and restricts method calls to the properties of object, but at run time the type is exactly as it would have been if generics had not been used. For example, in C# you can write:

```
typeof(T).Name
```

and see the name of the type the type parameter has been set to. This doesn't work in languages that use type erasure.

You can make use of the type to extend what generic functions can do using casting. The only problem is that the compiler will not let you cast T to anything other than object. However, once you have cast it to object you can cast it to anything you want. There is a sense in which the refusal to cast T to anything other than object is a way to make sure that you really know what you are doing, for example:

```
class MyClassA<T>  {
      public T add(T a, T b)
      {
            Console.WriteLine(typeof(T).Name);
            if (typeof(T).Name == "Int32")
            {
                return (T)(object)((int)(object)a + (int)(object)b);
            }
      return default(T);
      }
}
```

You can see that we test for the actual type of T and then cast to int to use the addition operator.

Returning generic types is something of a problem as you can't create an instance of the type when you don't what it is and similarly you can't directly initialize a variable without knowing its type and this is one of the problems that default solves.

This is also an ideal use of pattern matching, see Chapter 2:

```
class MyClassA<T>
{
      public T add(T a, T b)
      {
         T result = default(T) switch
         {
                int => (T)(object)((int)(object)a + (int)(object)b),
                 _  => default(T)
         };
         return result;
      }
}
```

Notice the use of default(T) to create a temporary object of type T so that the switch can test it and to return a default value of type T. This is a standard approach to testing generic type specifications in switch statements.

There is no suggestion that this is a good way to program using generics. The purpose is to make sure that you understand that the type of a generic parameter is not erased and you can work with it. It also reveals the way generics are essentially a way of using object to work with any type.

Generic Properties

You can define generic properties using the same syntax:

```
class MyClassA<T>
{
        public T MyProperty { get; set; }
}
```

This works because assignment is defined for any type and hence the default get and set work:

```
MyClassA<int> myObject = new MyClassA<int>();
myObject.MyProperty = 42;
Console.WriteLine( myObject.MyProperty);
```

The problems begin when you try to make the get or set process the value as this requires you either to restrict your operations to what works with object or to find the type and cast. To manually implement the get and set, complete with backing variable you would use:

```
class MyClassA<T>
{
        private T _value;
        public T MyProperty
        {
                get
                {
                        return _value;
                }
                set
                {
                        _value = value;
                }
        }
}
```

Supplying Generic Actions

So how can generics implement anything useful if you cannot apply any type-specific actions to generic entities?

One very general answer is to use specific implementations of a generic function type that performs the operation you require on those specific types. For example, you can't use a+b when the types are unknown unless you go to a lot of trouble casting. Alternatively you can define a generic function that has the appropriate signature and then implement a version for each type you want to work with.

For example, a generic delegate with the correct signature for an addition function is:

```
public delegate T Addmethod<T> (T x,T y)
```

this simply says that `Addmethod` is a delegate that accepts two parameters of type `T` and returns a value of type `T`. Using this we can now define a generic addition function:

```
public T Add<T>(T a, T b, Addmethod<T> add)
{
        T c = add(a, b);
        return c;
}
```

Notice that the third parameter is a function that takes two parameters of type `T` and returns a `T`. All of this is fine as no knowledge of the type `T` is used in this – it works for any type. So now we just need to call `Add` with the correct parameters, integers say, To do this we need a function that adds two integers together to pass as the third parameter:

```
int Addints(int x, int y)
{
    return x + y;
}
```

Notice that the function you pass is not a generic – it has a definite type, even at compile time.

Now we can call `Add`:

```
Console.WriteLine(Add<int>(2,3, Addints));
```

This works and the only downside is that you need to define a function that has the correct signature for each of the types that you want to use e.g. `Addfloat`, `AddDouble`, `AddString`, `AddMyClass`, and so on. This sounds almost as bad as having to write complete functions for each type, which is what you have to do if you are not using casting or generics. In practice it isn't so bad because usually the specific functions perform small actions such as comparing two objects or "adding" them and the full generic routine is much larger. In short, generic actions allow you to implement complex type-independent algorithms using generics while isolating the type-dependent parts of the program into strongly-typed functions.

It is something of a chore to have to package the type specific operation in a delegate each time you want to use the generic method, but lambda expressions make it less painful as you can create the action on the fly:

```
Console.WriteLine(Add<int>(2,3, (a, b) => a+b));
```

Notice that there is no need to specify the type of `a` and `b` or the return type as they can be deduced from the generic function definition.

Arrays and Generic Actions

The idea of a generic action may seem to be ad-hoc, but it is useful enough to have found its way into the framework. Before generics were introduced, the Array.Sort function was implemented using interfaces and how this works is also worth knowing.

The C# array sort function can sort any array type because it accepts a definition of an order relation between objects. To define the order relation used in the sort you need to implement an object with an IComparer interface. This defines a Compare method that returns −1, 0, or 1 depending on the result of the compare – less than, equal or greater than respectively:

```
private class CMyCompare : IComparer
{
        int IComparer.Compare(Object x, Object y)
        {
```

The problem now is that we have to do the comparison between x and y but this is difficult without knowing what types they are.

The simplest solution is to cast to the type that you know is stored in the array and then use the type's CompareTo method:

```
private class CMyCompare : IComparer
{
        int IComparer.Compare(Object x, Object y)
        {
                return (((int)y).CompareTo((int)x));
        }
}
```

This, of course, is just the "use an object as a reference to anything" approach to writing type neutral functions. This is really only useful if you are working with your own classes and can implement your own CompareTo method. Notice that this also supposes that we create an implementation of IComparer for each type we want to use the sort routine with.

With a suitable object we can sort the array into descending order using:

```
Array.Sort(A, new CMyCompare());
```

The wider point being made is that without using generics this is the only way the job can be done. You need an interface to define the form of the function to be used and you have to cast to actually do the work that makes use of the nature of the objects actually being passed. This clearly isn't type safe at compile time as the casts cannot be checked, but it can be made type safe at run time by adding code to make sure the objects are of a type you can work with.

The more recent generic sort methods are much safer, for example:

```
public static void Sort<T> (T[] array,Comparison<T> comparison)
```

This uses the generic `Comparison` delegate to supply the order relation used in the sort:

```
public delegate int Comparison<T> (T x,T y)
```

To implement the same sort all we have to do is write a comparison function:

```
public int MyCompare(int x, int y)
{
      return y.CompareTo(x);
}
```

Now, as long as we select the generic sort, i.e. `Sort<T>`, we hardly have to make any changes:

```
Array.Sort<int>(A, MyCompare);
```

This is, of course, the same approach demonstrated in the previous section with the sum function.

Along with the generic versions of `Sort`, other useful generic methods exist including `Find`, `FindAll`, `FindIndex`, `FindLast`, `FindLastIndex`, `LastIndexOf`, `TrueForAll`, and `ConvertAll`. Once you have seen how the `Find` method works the rest are easy to understand. The `Find` method returns the array element that satisfies a condition, it is defined as:

```
public static T Find<T> (T[] array,Predicate<T> match)
```

The `Predicate` delegate function is defined as:

```
public delegate bool Predicate<T> (T obj)
```

From these you can probably work out how to use `Find` correctly. For example, to pick out the first negative value in the array we first need a suitable predicate with the correct generic signature:

```
public bool MyLess(int x)
{
      return (x < 0);
}
```

Notice that this implies that `T` is `int`.

Now we can return the first negative value in the array using:

```
int result=Array.Find(A, MyLess);
```

If having to introduce an explicit method, e.g. `MyLess`, is something you would rather avoid then you could use an anonymous `delegate`:

```
int result = Array.Find(A,delegate(int x) { return (x < 0); });
```

The same thing works for all of the generic methods, for example:

```
Array.Sort(A, delegate(int x, int y)
                {return (((int)y).CompareTo((int)x)); });
```

Notice that there are some generic methods that need you to specify the types because the compiler cannot work them out from the context. For example, the very useful ConvertAll, which was used in Chapter 8, can be used to implement custom conversion from one array type to another. For example, to convert from Int32 to Int64 you would write:

```
public Int64 MyConvert(Int32 input)
{
        return (Int64)input;
}
```

So far nothing new, but to call the ConvertAll method you need to write:

```
Int64[] B = Array.ConvertAll<Int32, Int64>(A, MyConvert);
```

You can't drop the <Int32,Int64> type definition because it's just too difficult for the compiler to work out.

Postlude

Generics are a better way to write generic algorithms that make use of the object type and casting. In fact, generics are just syntactic sugar wrapping the use of object and casting. C# even implements generics in a way that preserves type at run time and this allows you to use real time type determination to extend what can be done with a generic approach. However, things aren't quite as simple as they seem at first. Formalizing the use of object in a generic style has consequences when we try to extend the idea to make it more useful.

Chapter 10
Advanced Generics

A better title for this chapter would be "Evolving Generics" because the whole idea is still being developed. Trying to find a way of writing generic algorithms, i.e. ones that work for a range of types, isn't a simple problem if you want type safety. Recall that type safety requires you to be certain that the type that you are working with is correct for the operations you are using at compile time. We have already discovered that basic generics are a type safe way of creating algorithms that require almost nothing from their working type, so much so that it is equivalent to working with object and not using any casts. The question to be answered is how can we extend generics to make it more flexible while allowing the widest range of types possible to be covered?

As it stands, generics achieves type safety by being very restrictive. This said it should be noted that it allows a great many standard generic algorithms to be implemented and, when supplemented by generic actions, nearly anything is possible. However, as it stands it doesn't even capture the freedoms that the basic hierarchical typing rules allow. In basic generics <T> can be any type and hence to be type safe we have no choice but to treat it as if it was object. By applying some additional conditions on <T>, we can assume more about the type and this is where generic constraints enter the picture.

Once we have a generic facility that is this sophisticated we also have to consider how this affects the whole type system and, in particular, what is type safe and this is where variance has to be considered.

Generic Constraints

The problem is that when we use a type parameter like T it can be any type. This is the advantage of generics, but it means that, if we want to use any operations on a particular type we have to implement specific functions that work with the type.

The reason we can't call specific methods on a generic type is that the compiler has no idea what the type is at run time. We can relax this by applying generic constraints to the type parameter which limits what sort of types are allowable. Knowing that the type parameter must be a particular type, or a subtype of that type, we can allow methods to be used, secure in the knowledge that the methods will exist at run time.

Generic constraints are the great hope for turning generics into something really useful. In practice, they often fail to make things simple, or even possible, because of the nature of the inheritance hierarchy. In many ways generic constraints are just another way of using a base type to process derived types and they suffer from all the same problems.

All of the constraints are generally "upper bounds" on the inheritance hierarchy, but some are more specific. You can follow the type parameter with a `where` type specifier:

`<T>`   where T: *constraint list*

If there are multiple type parameters then use one `where` per parameter:

`<T,U>` where T: *constraint list* where U: *constraint list*

The constraint can be any of:

Type	T has to be
struct	a non-nullable value type
class	a reference type
notnull	non-nullable
unmanaged	an unmanaged type-free
new()	a parameterless constructor
baseclass	*baseclass* or a derived type
interface	the *interface* itself or an implementation of it
U	*U*, another type parameter, or a derived type

You can apply multiple constraints by using a comma separated list.

It is worth pointing out that adding a constraint has two purposes. The first is that the compiler will generate an error message if you use a type that doesn't satisfy the constraint. The second is that you can make use of the methods of the type implied by the constraint within the generic code.

The most commonly used constraint is the name of a base class. In this case the type parameter has to be either the specified base class or a class derived from it. This allows the compiler to infer that an object described by the type parameter can have any of the methods of the base class and so these can be used in the generic.

For example:

```
int MyFunction<T>(T a) where T: MyClassA
{
    . . .
```

defines a function that accepts an object of type `MyClassA` as a parameter or anything derived from it. Notice that this is exactly the same as:

```
int MyFunction(MyClassA a)
```

since a derived class can be used in place of a base class.

Also notice that constraints have the same problem as using a base class as a type. If the base class doesn't implement the methods you want to use then you can't make use of them. For example, you still can't implement a generic `add` function because there is no top-level class that all numbers derive from and:

```
T add<T>(T a, T b) where T: struct
{
    return a+b;
}
```

doesn't work because `struct` doesn't define an addition operation. Even with constraints you are still at the mercy of the way the class hierarchy is constructed for what you can easily implement as a generic.

As well as a single base class constraint you can also specify multiple constraints using `where`, for example:

```
int add<T>(T a, T b) where T :struct, Icomparable<T>
{
            return a.CompareTo(b);
}
```

In this case `T` has to be a value type and also implement the `IComparable` interface. All of the usual number classes satisfy this constraint. With the constraint in place we can use the `CompareTo` method return the maximum, say. Also notice that `IComparable` is itself a generic interface and this form of constraint would be difficult to implement in any other way.

Notice that it isn't so much that creating generic numeric routines is difficult, it is more a way of illustrating that the form of the class hierarchy is all-important. This is a completely general problem. If you want to write a generic that works with all of the derived classes of an upper bound then the class that forms the upper bound has to have all of the methods you want to use. The basic idea of constraints is that you specify as much as you can about the type you are using and the compiler will let you use whatever methods are available on a type that just satisfies the constraint. This provides compile time type checking and hence type safety.

Covariance and Contravariance

This is one of the most complicated of the generic topics and is made more complicated by the use of some advanced sounding terminology. However, it isn't as difficult as many explanations and examples would have you believe. Even so, many users, and even designers of generic classes, don't have to understand what is going on at first. So come back and read this when you need to and once you have a good grasp of inheritance.

The first thing to understand is that inputs behave differently to outputs.

We have already looked at this idea in the context of the inheritance hierarchy, but it becomes particularly important once we introduce generics.

If you recall, derived classes are "bigger" than base classes because they have everything that the base class has, and possibly some additional methods and properties. You can think of this as defining a partial order on the classes. So, if class B is derived from class A you can write A>B, indicating that A is higher in the class hierarchy than B, even though B potentially has actually more methods than A. This is confusing, but it is widely used.

This is the Liskov Substitution principle, and it is more of an ideal than a principle or a practical reality. In the real world it is very easy to construct derived classes that override methods in such a way that they cannot be use in place of their base class. The Liskov Substitution principle can't be a law of nature. Instead it is something you have to work at ensuring is true. You can extend the idea and say that any entity B that can be used anywhere A can satisfies A>B, even if A isn't in any proper sense a base entity for B.

Now consider the following function:

```
MyClassB MyFunction1(MyClassA a){
        do something with a MyClassA
        create myObjectB an instance of MyClassB
        return myObjectB
}
```

You can see that the function is associated with two types – `MyClassA` is its input type and `MyClassB` is its output type.

Let's focus first on the input type. Consider two functions that you assume you know nothing about beyond the declarations:

```
void MyFunction1(MyClassA a)
```

and:

```
void MyFunction2(MyClassB a)
```

and ask yourself can you pass in a `MyClassB` into `MyFunction1`? The answer is yes because, whatever the function does, the properties it uses are all present for `MyClassB`. Now ask if you can pass in a `MyClassA` into `MyFunction2`? The answer is clearly no as `MyFunction2` could well use methods that `MyClassA` doesn't have. So as we can use `MyClassB` in place of `MyClassA` and this means we can only use `MyFunction1` in place of `MyFunction2`.

We clearly have the conclusion that

`MyClassA > MyClassB`

implies:

`MyFunction1(MyClassA a)< MyFunction2(MyClassB a)`

This is called contravariance and, in general, we say that if A>B means that G(A)<G(B) where G is a type that involves the classes A and B, then the relationship is contravariant.

Put in even simpler language, if you construct a new type involving an existing type then it is contravariant if the construction reverses the "use in place of" relationship. Inputs are generally contravariant for the reasons outlined above. In physics and mathematics inputs are generally contravariant and this is where the nomenclature comes from.

Now consider the same argument but for output. Consider:

`MyClassA MyFunction1(){}`

and:

`MyClassB MyFunction2(){}`

For `MyFunction1` the return type is `MyClassA` and function `MyFunction2` returns a `MyClassB`. If you use a call to `MyFunction1` in some of your code then you can safely replace the call by one to `MyFunction2`. The reason is, of course that `MyFunction2` returns a `MyClassB`, which has everything a `MyClassA` has and so your code will continue to work. However, if you use `MyFunction2` in your code then you are are assuming that you get a `MyClassB` as a result and so you cannot replace its use by a call to `MyFunction1`, which only returns a `MyClassA`, which might not have methods you use.

This means that `MyFunction1`>`MyFunction2` because `MyFunction2` can be used anywhere `MyFunction1` can. In this case we have

`MyClassA > MyClassB`

which implies

`MyClassA MyFunction1() > MyClassB MyFunction2().`

This is an example of covariance and in simple terms means if you construct a new type involving an existing type, then it is covariant if the construction follows the same "use in place of" relationship. In general, outputs are covariant. As in the case of contravariance, the terminology comes from physics and mathematics where outputs are generally covariant.

Notice that you come to this conclusion without any mention of generics. However, by the same reasoning if you have a pair of generic functions:

```
T1 MyFunction1<T1>(T1 a);
```

and:

```
T2 MyFunction2<T2>(T2 a);
```

then if:

```
T1>T2
```

we have:

```
MyFunction1<MyFunction2
```

with regard to parameter type and:

```
MyFunction1>MyFunction2
```

with regard to the output type.

Generic functions are contravariant in input types and covariant in output types.

General Variance

Now that we have looked at the way that a change to a function affects its type, we can generalize the idea of covariance and contravariance to any situation, not just where functions are involved. Suppose we have two types, A and B, and we have a modification, or transformation, G that we can make to both of them to give new types, G(A) and G(B).

- If G is a covariant transformation we have A>B implies G(A)>G(B). Outputs are covariant.

- If G is a contravariant transformation we have A>B implies G(A)<G(B). Inputs are contravariant.

- It is also possible that neither relationship applies. That is, A>B doesn't imply anything about the relationship between G(A) and G(B). In this case G is referred to as invariant, which isn't a good name.

In our example we had two transformations G1, which converted the type into the input parameter – a contravariant transform, and G2, which converted the type into the return result – a covariant transform.

It can be very difficult to keep all of this in your head when reasoning about particular data types, arrays for example, but eventually you get used to it.

Why is any of this important? On one level it isn't as you can quite happily reason about what you can access and what you might not be able to access as you write code at a very basic and simple level. However, the ideas of co- and contravariance is an automatic way of determining what is or is not type safe and the compiler can flag errors based on these behaviors.

Notice that, as before, type safety is really only a guide to what might or might not go wrong. Going back to the case of the two functions, MyFunction1 and MyFunction2, we conclude that we cannot use MyFunction1 with a return type of MyClassA as the code may use methods of the MyClassB object that MyClassA doesn't have. Of course, if the code doesn't make use of these methods in the derived class then it all works. It's not obviously safe at compile time, but it throws no exceptions at run time.

Similarly, if you use MyFunction2 in place of MyFunction1 then this is type safe in that MyClassB has everything MyClassA has, but if you are using virtual inheritance, the MyClassB overrides are used and these might not be appropriate and a run-time error might occur.

You can think up other ways in which type safety doesn't guarantee anything at run time. However, it does make it harder to make such errors.

Covariant and Contravariant Generics

What else is a generic declaration other than a transformation from a type T to another type G(T)? For example Array<T> converts an Int into Array<Int>.

Next we come to the question of whether an array, considered as a transformation on the type of its element, is covariant, contravariant or invariant. After all, it has to be one of these three. Put in its most practical terms, given that int is a derived class of object, int[] could be a derived class of object[], which would make it covariant. Alternatively, the array could be a superclass of object[], which would make it contravariant, or it could have no relationship with object[], which would make it invariant.

As already said, you have to answer this question, even if you don't use the academic-sounding terms taken from category theory and physics. In Java and most other languages, including C#, arrays are covariant. This works well when array use fits in with the idea that outputs are covariant. For example, consider this code, which is perfectly acceptable as arrays are treated as covariant:

```
object[] a;
string[] b = { "A", "B", "C" };
a = b;
```

This assignment is safe as long as you only use the variable a to access the array and not store anything new in it. That is, a[i] is treated as object and you can use any of the methods that object has, and the underlying int certainly has these. However, if you assign to an element of a then things are potentially more risky. You can assign any object you like as all objects are derived from object. This leaves our int array in something of a potential mess.

Consider what happens if we assign an int to an element and then try and access it as if it was a string:

```
a[0] = 1;
Console.WriteLine(b[0].Length);
```

The result is a run-time exception and there is no easy way that this could be picked up at compile time. This is clearly not a good idea from the strong typing point of view. You can also come to the conclusion that treating the array as contravariant isn't a good idea either. In this case the problem arises when you try and access an element of an array and treat it like a derived class of String only to discover that it is just a String. As in C# an array is covariant this error would be detected at compile time. Notice that you can't actually do this as String is a sealed class and hence it can't have any derived classes, but the principle holds.

Another important thing to notice is that generic classes are always invariant. That is, a class instantiated with one type has no relationship with a class instantiated with another type.

Controlling Variance – in and out

You can see that arrays are problematic when it comes to variance, but we can make things a little better. The idea is that if a type is used only as an input then it is safe to treat the generic as contravariant. If it is only used as an output then it can be used covariantly and if it is both you have no choice but to treat the generic as invariant.

C# provides two modifiers, in and out, which allow you to mark type parameters as contravariant or covariant. You can only use type variance modifiers on interfaces and delegates, but this is often enough. The out modifier means that the type parameter can only be used as an output, i.e. as a result and not as a parameter, and the in modifier means that it can only be used as a parameter. If this isn't the case then the compiler will display an error message – which is one of the main advantages of using in and out.

First an example of a covariant interface, i.e. one that uses out:

```
interface ICovariant<out T>
{
        T myMethod();
}
```

You can use this interface to define a class::

```
class MyClassA<T> : ICovariant<T>
{
        T[] Array;
        public MyClassA(T[] array) {
                Array = array;
        }
        public T myMethod()
        {
                return Array[1];
        }
}
```

Notice the class also has T as a type parameter, but this is not marked as out. This allows us to use a constructor to create an array of type T. The method inherited from the interface returns a single element of the array which is, of course, correctly of type T.

As usual, it is the interface which is covariant not the class which is invariant. So, to see the covariance in action, we need to use the interface as a type:

```
string[] array = { "A", "B", "C" };
MyClassA<string>();
ICovariant<string> a = new MyClassA<string>(array);
ICovariant<object> b;
b = a;
```

The assignment of a to b is valid and everything works, but of course you can only use b as if it was an object and not a string and hence it is type safe. If you remove the out from the interface definition you will find that it generates a compiler error.

An example involving contravariance is simpler. As before we need an interface:

```
interface IContravariant<in T>
{
        void myMethod(T x);
}
```

We need a class to implement this interface:

```
class MyClassA<T> : IContravariant<T>
{
        public void myMethod(T x)
        {
                Console.WriteLine(x);
        }
}
```

As before the class is invariant and the interface is contravariant, so:

```
IContravariant<object> a = new MyClassA<object>();
IContravariant<string> b;
b = a;
b.myMethod("Hello Contravariant");
```

works as intended and the string is passed into the method, but treated as an object within the method. If you remove the in from the interface definition the compiler will give you an error message.

It is not often that in and out are useful in generics and to an extent if you find that you need to use them you should probably look at your design and see if it can be simplified to eliminate the need for such behavior.

Postlude

Do we really need generics? In an object-oriented language with strong typing the answer, surprisingly, is "no". Generics as generally implemented don't give you much over and above using a base class as the type of a parameter or a return value coupled with a careful, run-time checked, use of casting.

 Generics go some way to detecting errors at compile time, but they do so by limiting what you can do at run time. This is sometimes a good trade-off, but the complexities introduced by generics are a high price to pay. Generics can make your programs easier to understand and more robust, but only if you put some effort into keeping their use simple and clear.

There are many situations where your first choice might be to use generics – your second choice might be better.

Chapter 11

Anonymous & Dynamic Typing

Strong typing is a key idea in C#, but over time new features have been introduced to make the language as easy to use as other, less strongly-typed languages. As always, the way that C# has done this is to try to preserve type safety at all times. For example, dynamic typing in C# isn't quite the same as in other languages and we need to look at it in some detail. But before we look at dynamic typing we need to take a look at a related feature with which it is often confused - anonymous typing.

First, recall that in early C# you always had to determine the type of the result of an expression and use an appropriate type or supertype to store it and this determination had to be made at compile time. That is, C# was a statically-typed language. Even now, the compiler always looks at an expression, determines the type of the expression and makes sure that this is compatible with the "assignment" variable. What has been relaxed is the need for a variable to have a fixed and unvarying type.

Anonymous Typing

The most type-free statement you could write in C# 2.0 and earlier was something like:

```
object x = MyFunc();
```

which worked no matter what type `MyFunc` returned. However, you couldn't do anything with the returned object unless you cast it to a more appropriate type. That is, in most object-oriented languages the topmost class in the hierarchy, usually called `object`, can be used as a reference to any subclass and in this sense using it is a way to make the language less type-dependent.

In C# 3.0 the anonymous type was introduced as an alternative to using `object` and the potential confusion began. An anonymous type is strongly and statically typed in that the compiler works out its type at compile time and then applies all the usual strong typing rules. The only complication here is that if the type implied by the code doesn't actually exist as a named type the compiler will also generate a suitable name and type.

That is, anonymous typing is still early binding in action and everything that happens is fixed at compile time.

Let's start off with the simplest anonymous type. For example, given the function:

```
public int MyFunc() {
      return 1;
}
```

the statement:

```
var x = MyFunc();
```

allows the compiler to deduce that the variable must be an int. So after this you can use:

```
x = 2;
```

However, the statements:

```
string i;
i = x;
```

will still result in a compile-time type error as x is an int and i is a string. Anonymous types are still strongly typed at run time and their type is deduced at compile time, i.e. they are static types that the compiler infers from the code.

A slightly more complicated situation is where the type is created "on the fly":

```
var x = new {
            name = "Mike",
            Address = "AnyTown"
          };
```

In this case the new type doesn't have a name and so the compiler creates one something along the lines of "AnonymousType#1".

Now you can use statements like:

```
string i;
i = x.name;
```

as, not only has the type of the structure been determined, so has the type of each of its fields.

A subtle point that is important not to miss is that an anonymous type created in this way is read-only so you can't assign to any of its fields and any attempts to do so will be picked up by the compiler. Notice that this is different from the behavior when the inferred type already exists, unless otherwise restricted to be read-only.

For example, if you first declare as `public` the structure previously created on the fly:

```
public struct MyAdd {
      public string name;
      public string Address;
}
```

and change the function to read:

```
public MyAdd MyFunc(){
      return new MyAdd {
                  name = "Mike",
                  Address = "MyTown"
            };
}
```

then you can write:

```
string i;
var x = MyFunc();
x.name="new name";
i = x.name;
```

If you need even more proof that an anonymous type is strongly typed, just notice the fact that the type and its fields are included in Intellisense prompting as you work with the code at design time!

It really is that simple. If you declare two anonymous types that have an identical field structure then the compiler is smart enough to notice that it needs to create only a single new type name, but as the resulting objects are read-only you still can't use assignment.

There are some restrictions on how you can use anonymously-typed variables, but they are all fairly obvious and reasonable. In particular, the anonymous variable has to be local, i.e have method scope. This means that you can still use them within `for`, `foreach` and `using` statements. Of course it has to be mentioned that anonymous types were introduced mainly to make LINQ look easier to use, but you can still use LINQ, which we return to in Chapter 19 and indeed everything in C#, without ever using the `var` statement.

Anonymous types are entirely a convenience and in no way a necessity as, if the compiler can deduce the type of a variable at compile time, so can you.

Dynamic Typing

The other end of the spectrum from static typing is dynamic typing. In true dynamic typing a variable really can change its type at run time. This doesn't have to be the abandonment of type checking, just a move to type checking at run rather than compile time. C# hasn't quite adopted the "duck typing" approach that makes languages such as JavaScript, Ruby and Python so easy to use, as it is still attempting to play within the strong typing rules it started out with.

The best way of thinking about dynamic type is as a sort of formal way to use a general object type which which allows you access to the methods and properties of the actual data type in use without the need to cast. For example, suppose we have a class:

```
public class MyClass {
       public int MyProperty;
       public int MyMethod() {
              return 1;
       }
}
```

If we now create an instance using an object reference type:

```
object MyObject = new MyClass();
```

then trying to access any of the methods or properties of the object will fail for obvious reasons – an `object` type doesn't have the methods and properties of a `MyClass` type. However, if you use a cast to `MyClass` then you can access all of the properties and methods as if `MyObject` was of type `MyClass`. That is:

```
((MyClass) MyObject).MyMethod();
```

works perfectly.

In this sense using `object` and casting has long been the C# programmer's way of implementing dynamic typing. In this sense dynamic typing is nothing new to the language. However, you must have had the thought, *"why do I need to cast the object to the correct type – either the method call works or doesn't work at run-time"*. Apart from making it easier to discover the programmer's intention, the cast does absolutely nothing to protect you from an error at compile time – any problems only become apparent at run time.

With the `dynamic` type introduced in C# 4.0, which only resolves to a method or property at run time, you can indeed "drop the cast". The above code in C# can be written:

```
dynamic MyObject = new MyClass();
MyObject.MyMethod();
```

You can mix dynamic and anonymous as in:

```
dynamic MyObject = new MyClass();
var i = MyObject.MyMethod();
```

and the compiler correctly works out that i should be an `int`, suggesting that it isn't completely blind to the type stored in `MyObject`. Notice that as `dynamic` is a valid static type name it is perfectly possible that an anonymous type will resolve to `dynamic`.

You can swap from dynamic to fully static simply by making appropriate assignments. For example:

```
dynamic j = 1;
int i = j;
```

first creates a dynamic variable, an int, which is then converted to a strongly-typed int. You can also force a conversion using a cast but, as always, if it can't be done the result is a run-time exception.

Notice that `dynamic` really is dynamic in the sense that the determination of its type at run time isn't a one-off. A dynamic type can change its type as many times as necessary, for example:

```
dynamic i;
i = 1;
i = i + 1;
i = "mike";
i = i + 1;
```

When 1 is assigned to it i becomes an `int`, and i+1 is an integer expression which evaluates to 2. Assigning the string "mike" to i changes its run-time type to `string` and now i+1 concatenates the string "1", which is implicitly cast from an int to give "mike1".

Notice that there is nothing new going on here as everything works just as it would if the variable i was first declared as an `int` and then declared as a `string`. Of course, you can't change the type of a static type at compile time and this is what is new.

The guiding principle that has been used in implementing the `dynamic` type is that what happens should correspond to what happens if the dynamic type was known at compile rather than run time. So to work out how a dynamic type behaves simply imagine that you know its type at compile time and what happens in this case should be what happens to the dynamic type.

Late or Early?

Whenever you change something in a language, no matter how small or innocent the change is, the ripples spread out and reach parts of the language that you might never have guessed at. For example, with dynamic typing late binding is the rule, even if the method in use isn't `virtual`. Consider the following class with two overloaded versions of the same method:

```
public class MyClassA{
      public string MyMethod(int i){
            return "Integer";
      }
      public string MyMethod(double f){
            return "Double"; }
      }
}
```

If we now call the method but with a random type, i.e. the type of the object is selected randomly, something that was impossible to do before the introduction of `dynamic`, as in:

```
Random R = new Random();
MyClassA MyObject = new MyClassA();
dynamic i;
if(R.NextDouble()<.5){
      i = 1;
}else{
      i=1.0;
}
string result=MyObject.MyMethod(i);
```

then which `MyMethod` is actually called is determined at run time according to the type of i which is discovered using reflection. If i is a double then `MyMethod(double f)` is called and if it is an int then `MyMethod(int i)` is called.

This should be the behavior you expect from your understanding of the way that dynamic types work, but notice that this means that the late binding is being used in a situation where you might have expected the usual early binding. That is, it fits into the principle that what should happen should be the same as if the type of the dynamic variable was known at compile time.

Overloading and Overriding

Things can be slightly more complicated in that we can mix method overloading with overriding in a derived class, but the guiding principle still applies. For example, suppose we have a derived class which overrides a non-virtual method in the original MyClassA:

```
public class MyClassB:MyClass{
        public new string MyMethod(double f){
                return "ClassB Double";
        }
}
```

As the method isn't virtual you would expect early binding to be used based on the compile type type of the object. However, we have already noted that using a dynamic parameter forces late binding. So which is it? That is, if we now change the creation of MyObject in the previous example to read:

```
MyClassA MyObject = new MyClassB();
```

which method will be used for a double, that of MyClassA or of MyClassB?

At compile time the type of MyObject is MyClassA, even if at run time it actually refers to a MyClassB object and so, by the usual early binding rules, it should be the MyClassA methods that are used. This is indeed what happens, even though which MyClassB method is called isn't determined until run time.

Thus the method call is early bound to the class type but late bound according to the signature of the call.

However, if you change the method declarations to virtual and override, late binding is used on them both and the MyClassB double method is called. This is ruthlessly logical and, if you stop to think about it, is what really should happen in each case.

There are a number of other interesting but fairly esoteric "features" of dynamic, but one worth mentioning is accessibility. Currently all methods and properties have to be public to be dynamically accessible. This isn't a huge problem, but it means that you can't call private methods from within a class using dynamic parameters, even though without the dynamic parameters the call would be perfectly legal. Similarly you can't use extension methods dynamically – the information to implement them isn't available at run time. Anonymous functions can't appear as arguments to a dynamic method call for the same reason. This makes it difficult to use LINQ queries over dynamic objects, which is strange given that LINQ was, and is, a major motivation for C# becoming more dynamic.

Beyond Plain .NET Objects

How the method invocation or property access is handled depends on the type of object that the dynamic type references. You might think that the only possibility is the plain old .NET object, but part of the reason for introducing dynamic is to make externally derived objects easier to work with.

In the case of a standard .NET object, reflection is used to dispatch the operation. This is more sophisticated than you might imagine because any dynamic objects passed as parameters are resolved using reflection and then the resulting signature combined with reflection is used to make the call to the appropriate method. Moving beyond plain .NET objects, a new class of dynamic objects can customize how they behave by implementing the IDynamicObject interface. In this case the task of working out which method or property is needed is handed off to the object itself to work out using any method that suits. This is the key to building truly dynamic object models that can respond in sophisticated ways.

A very big advantage of dynamic types comes when you start to think about C#'s relationship with external and non-native objects, COM objects in particular. In this case a dynamic type is resolved using the COM IDispatch interface and this in turn means that you can use COM objects "raw", i.e. without a Primary Interop Assembly (PIA). As many COM objects make extensive use of the variant type, which can store any of a number of standard data types, being able to use dynamic types in place of variants is a big simplification. For example, consider the standard difficulty encountered in using the Office COM object model:

```
((Excel.Range)excel.Cells[1,1]).Value= "some string"
```

The cast has to be included because the PIA uses object types to represent variants. Using dynamic types in place of objects makes it possible to dispense with the cast and allow the run time system to work out what is legal:

```
excel.Cells[1,1].Value= "some string"
```

Not using the PIA and driving the COM interface raw also means that you can hope to achieve a more efficient and lightweight program.

There are other minor enhancements to the way COM objects are dealt with that go together with dynamic types to make the whole thing easier to use. For example, COM objects often pass parameters using pointers which result in the use of ref parameters in the corresponding C# methods. This can force you to create temporary variables to avoid any changes to a variable that you regard as logically being passed by value. Now the compiler will do the job for you by converting the value parameter to a temporary copy and passing this by reference. The overall result is pass-by-value semantics for parameters that are passed as pointers.

Postlude

Dynamic typing seems to be mostly harmless and it does improve the way that you can write code that relies on determining type at run time rather than compile time. It is a big change in philosophy, but it doesn't go as far as introducing a truly dynamic approach to type. Even if you regard it as an attempt to work with other systems that are less strict about type, it is still a change that makes C# less pure and more ad-hoc.

III Functions

Prelude

C# didn't take the option of making functions objects, instead it opted to use a wrapper class – the delegate – to convert functions into objects. Over time, this idea has been developed to allow more and more functionality until we finally reach the pinnacle of the easy-to-use function, the lambda complete with closure.

Delegates are C#'s original way of allowing you to work with functions as if they were first-class objects. The aim may be simple, but the need to define a type and then an instance of the type can be confusing. Let's see if we can make it all seem logical.

Delegates are at the core of a number of different .NET facilities, events in particular. It's long been a truism that the way to get work done is to delegate, but what are C# delegates all about? First we have to understand the nature of the problem that delegates are designed to solve.

First-Class Functions

In many languages functions are treated in the same way as objects. In JavaScript, for example, functions are objects. This is often expressed by saying the functions are first-class objects or they are first-class functions.

Why should this matter? The simple answer is that sometimes you want to pass a function as an argument to a method call. There are other things you might want to do with a first-class function, including having a reference to it or having an array of such functions, but if we concentrate on the most common usage, passing functions to methods, then we have the key idea. For example, suppose you have a sorting routine, you might want to pass in a function that determines what A>B means, i.e. return true if A is greater than B and false otherwise, where A and B are objects of some type.

This seems like a reasonable thing to do, but notice that in C# and in other object-oriented languages there are no "disembodied" functions. All functions are methods that belong to some class or instance of a class. This make things a little more complicated because now you cannot simply create a function called myOrder and pass it into a method because myOrder has to be a method of some class or object.

You might think of defining something like:

```
class Compare{
      public myOrder(){};
}
```

and now you could try to pass an instance of the object:

```
Compare myCompare = new Compare();
myData.Sort(myCompare.myOrder);
```

That is, you are trying to pass `myCompare.myOrder` to the `Sort` method.

This is an approach that could be made to work, but C# is strongly typed and every parameter in a method has to have a type. What type is `Compare.myOrder`? It's a method of a type and not a type in its own right and trying to make it a type will quickly become very messy.

A different alternative is to demand that every time you want to pass a function you have to pass an object that has that function as a method. This is what Java does, for example. In this case we don't have a problem with types:

```
Compare myCompare = new Compare();
myData.Sort(myCompare);
```

However, within the `Sort` method the `myOrder` function has to be called as:

```
myCompare.myOrder();
```

In other words, to pass a function you have to pass an entire object which wraps the function. Of course, the one advantage of this method is that, in principle, you could pass a whole set of functions in one go, but this doesn't make up for the inconvenience of the approach when you are trying to pass just one function.

As any Java programmer will tell you, this approach is workable but very verbose. You have to define a class for every function you want to pass and create an instance to pass every time you want to pass it. It is the original method that Java used to implement event handling and over time new facilities such as anonymous classes and eventually lambdas have been added to the language to make this cumbersome method easier to use.

The C# Approach

The overall C# approach to allowing functions to be first-class entities has developed over time as well. Initially delegates were used as a way of wrapping a function in an object in a way that is superficially similar to Java's approach but with some special advantages. C# delegates also acquired features that made them easier to use - anonymous methods and finally lambdas. However, it is important that you fully understand the original idea of delegates and how to use them, so let's look at how it works and some of the more interesting ways that you can put it to work. The relationship of delegates to events is covered in the next chapter.

Delegate Basics

What is initially confusing is that to create a delegate you first have to create a type and then create an instance of the type. That is, a delegate is a user-defined reference type that encapsulates a method. Consider, for example, how to encapsulate the simple example method:

```
public int hello(int param1){
        MessageBox.Show("Hello delegate World"+param1.ToString());
        return(++param1);
}
```

All this does is display the current value of `param1` and then return an incremented value.

First, we need to define a delegate type that matches its signature, including the return type:

```
delegate int HelloType(int param);
```

This delegate type defines the methods that it can encapsulate. Notice that it is only the function's signature and return type that specifies the delegate type. The `HelloType` delegate can wrap any function that has the specified signature and return.

Next, we have to create an instance of the type and supply it with the `hello` method to encapsulate:

```
HelloType HelloInst = new HelloType(hello);
```

If you prefer you can use the overloaded assignment operator:

```
HelloType HelloInst = hello;
```

to create an instance.

Now we can run the original `hello` method by calling it directly in the usual way:

```
int i = hello(2);
```

or by using the delegate's invoke method:

```
int i = HelloInst.Invoke(2);
```

or by calling the delegate instance as if it was the `hello` method:

```
int i = HelloInst(2);
```

This last form is just a convenience as it implicitly uses the `Invoke` method.

Notice that the default use of the `Invoke` method makes the delegate instance look like a function object. That is `HelloInst` is an object but `HelloInst(2)` looks like a function call.

Of course, there are a few slightly hidden details in these examples which are obvious to experts, but often confuse the beginner. The first is that the method being wrapped is still a method belonging to some object and not a "disembodied" function. When the delegate is used to wrap the method the method has to be accessible from wherever the delegate is being declared. In the example above there is the implicit assumption that all of the code is defined within the same class.

A more elaborate and complete example would create the hello method within a new class:

```
public class Greetings
{
   public int hello(int param1)
   {
        MessageBox.Show("Hello delegate World"+ param1.ToString());
        return (++param1);
   }
}
```

and then within the class that wants to make use of the method you can make use of the delegate type to wrap the method instance:

```
delegate int HelloType(int param);
private void button1_Click(object sender, EventArgs e)
{
        Greetings g = new Greetings();
        HelloType HelloInst = new HelloType(g.hello);
        int i = HelloInst(2);
}
```

Another subtle point is that Invoke uses the same thread to run the delegate and in this case you need to be aware of any potential "cross-threading" problems that might arise. This also means that the invocation is synchronous and the calling code will wait until the delegate returns. You can invoke the delegate asynchronously using a thread from the thread pool using BeginInvoke or you could create a thread manually to run the delegate.

To summarize:

To wrap a method belonging to an instance of a class you have to first define a new delegate type with a specific signature and return type, then you wrap the method in an instance of the delegate type.

Delegate Patterns

Why would you use a delegate rather than just calling a method?

The answer, explained in the introduction, is simply that a delegate can be passed as a parameter to another method, so determining what method is called at run time. More widely a delegate can be used anywhere an object can, which means you can have references to a delegate and data structures of delegates such as arrays. In functional programming terms, a delegate converts a method or a function into a "first-class object" i.e. one that can be used like any other object.

There are two well-known patterns that demand the use of a delegate. The first is the "callback" or notification method which is supplied to an object for it to call with intermediate or final results of its working. Of course, in this instance the object is usually run on a separate thread and the method provides some asynchronous communication between the caller and the called thread. The second is event handling. A delegate can be set up within an object so that clients can provide a method to be called when an event occurs. If you think carefully you will see that there is little difference between the callback and the event pattern. In both cases a delegate is called when some condition occurs – a buffer is full, the user has clicked a button, an error condition has been detected etc. However, while events are based on delegates they add an additional structure, an add and remove accessor similar to a property. A third, slightly less common, pattern involves creating a new thread of execution.

Signatures and Methods

At this point it is worth making clear that the delegate's signature always determines how the method that the delegate wraps is called. That is, you always have to invoke the delegate with the parameter types specified and the delegate always returns the type specified. However, it is possible to create instances of the delegate that encapsulate methods that don't have exactly the specified signature.

To summarize:

A delegate type's signature specifies how the delegate is invoked – i.e. the parameters and return type are always given by the delegate's signature.

A delegate type's signature specifies what sort of methods an instance of the type can encapsulate.

Notice that the encapsulated method can be a static or an instance method. That is, the method can belong to an instance of the class or it can be a static "class method".

The delegate's `Target` property stores the instance and the `Method` property stores the method that that the delegate encapsulates. This is how a delegate "knows" what method to call. If the delegate encapsulates a static method then the `Target` is `null`, i.e. there is no instance. To encapsulate a method on a specific object you simply have to qualify the method name with the object's name, for example `this.hello` or `MyObject.hello`.

Covariance and Contravariance Revisited

In the simplest case a method's signature and return type have to match the signature of the delegate type that encapsulates it. However, there is more flexibility in how a method signature can match a delegate type signature. In the documentation this is called covariance and contravariance, just to make is sound more sophisticated. We have already met this idea twice before, in chapters 8 and 10, but it worth seeing how it works for delegates.

Put simply covariance allows the method to return a sub-class or derived type of the return type defined in the delegate. Assume for the moment that `MyClassA` is the base class and `MyClassB` is the derived class, that is:

```
public class MyClassA {};
public class MyClassB : MyClassA {};
```

If you now define the delegate type:

```
delegate MyClassA HelloType(MyClassB param);
```

then clearly a method returning `MyClassA` matches the signature. However, by covariance, so does any method returning a type that inherits from `MyClassA`, such as `MyClassB`. That is, you can use `HelloType` with a function like:

```
MyClassB myFunc1(MyClassB param);
HelloType myDelegate = new HelloType(myFunc1);
```

So the delegate type can encapsulate a method that returns a `MyClassB`. However, following the rule that the delegate signature determines its invocation, the return type is always treated as `MyClassA`. If the method does return a derived type, `MyClassB` say, you have to use a cast to work with the result as a `MyClassB` object, for example:

```
MyClassB myResult = (MyClassB) myDelegate(myB);
```

Contravariance allows the method to have parameters that are base types of the types specified in the delegate that encapsulates it. That is, if you define the delegate type as before:

```
delegate MyClassA HelloType(MyClassB param);
```

then a method that that has a parameter that is a base class for `MyClassB`, such as `MyClassA`, matches the signature. For example:

```
MyClassB myFunc2(MyClassA param);
HelloType myDelegate = new HelloType(myFunc2);
```

is perfectly acceptable.

Once again, you can only invoke the delegate by passing a `MyClassB` object:

```
MyClassA myResult= myDelegate(myB);
```

but this all works because the method that the delegate invokes can treat this as a more primitive type, i.e. as a `MyClassA` object, which is what it wants to work with.

Generic Delegates

To confuse matters even more, or should that be to confer further elegance and power, you can also create generic delegate types. Put simply, you can use a generic type anywhere within a delegate definition. For example:

```
delegate int HelloType<T>(T param);
```

creates a delegate type with a generic parameter.

To use the delegate you have to provide the type information. For example:

```
HelloType<int> HelloInst = new HelloType<int>(hello);
```

where `Hello` is a method which returns an `int` and has a single `int` parameter. You can also use the shorter:

```
HelloType<int> HelloInst = hello;
```

Before you start to invent clever ways of creating generic delegates for every purpose, I should warn you that, in the main, generic delegates should only be used within generic classes. In this context they provide a way to create delegate instances that "fit in" with the functioning of the entire delegate class. For example, you might create a delegate as a notification or event method which can be customized to work with the same data types as the rest of the generic class.

Postlude

Delegates are a central part of the .NET framework, but since .NET 2.0 it has been possible to save some typing and avoid unnecessary names by using anonymous, as opposed to named, methods. However as of .NET 3.5 anonymous methods have been overshadowed by lambda expressions. In both cases you can simply treat the new facilities as easier ways of defining a delegate. Anonymous methods are covered in depth in Chapter 14 together with lambda expressions. Also of interest is the way anonymous methods and lambda expressions enforce the adoption of closure, which is also discussed in that chapter.

Chapter 13

Multicast Delegates

Multicast delegates are useful in their own right, but they also form the basis on which the C# event system is built. In this chapter we take a close look at how they work and how to use them. For example, did you know you could add and subtract delegates?

A `Delegate` is a class that wraps a method so that it can be used in more sophisticated ways, such as being passed as a parameter to another method. But delegates are also ways of making lists of methods that can be called in sequence when the delegate is invoked. Now that you know how delegates work, it's time to look at the multicast delegate and their relationship to events.

Multicasting

If you look at the documentation you will find a `Delegate` class and a class derived from it, `MulticastDelegate`. In theory, the `Delegate` class can encapsulate a single method and the `MulticastDelegate` maintains a list of methods and so can encapsulate more than one method. In practice, this isn't true. Early on in the development of C# it was decided that `Delegate` and `MulticastDelegate` should do the same job and be merged. However, merging them would have created too many problems, so `Delegate` was left as the base class for `MulticastDelegate`, but the two are essentially identical.

At this point you might imagine that you would never use the `Delegate` class, but in fact it is still returned by some methods that expect to return a single method encapsulated by a `Delegate`. It also used to be the case that if you created a delegate which returned void then it was encapsulated by a `MulticastDelegate`, but if it returned a result then a `Delegate` was used. This distinction was made because of the difficult of determining which method's return value was actually returned in a multicast invocation. However, this was solved by simply encapsulating all methods using `MulticastDelegate` and, in a multicast situation, the last method called is the only one that returns a result.

All delegates are multicast delegates, but for efficiency reasons an invocation list is only created if there is more than one method encapsulated. That is, a delegate that encapsulates a single method stores this method in its `Method` and `Target` properties and has a null invocation list.

To summarize:

In C# the `delegate` keyword creates an instance not of the `Delegate` class but of the `MulticastDelegate` class.

That is, in C# an instance of a delegate type is always an instance of a `MulticastDelegate` which extends the basic `Delegate` class to include an invocation list which can store multiple methods.

Multicast In Action

The easiest way to follow this confusing situation is to try it all out. First we need two methods with the same signature that we can encapsulate in a suitable delegate:

```
public int hello(string param)
{
        MessageBox.Show("Hello "+param);
        return 1;
}

public int goodbye(string param)
{
        MessageBox.Show("Goodbye " + param);
        return 2;
}
```

A suitable delegate type is just:

```
delegate int greetType(string param);
```

Now we can create an instance of `MulticastDelegate` encapsulating two methods:

```
greetType DoGreet = hello;
DoGreet += goodbye;
```

The `+=` operator is overloaded to add a method to the invocation list and this should be familiar to you if you have hand-coded events.

Invoking the delegate is just the same if it has single or multiple methods:

```
int i= DoGreet("delegates");
```

If the invocation list contains multiple methods then these are called in the order that they were added. Any parameters are passed to each method in turn and the final method to be called returns a value. That is, in this case the `hello` method is called with its parameter set to "delegates" then `goodbye` is called with the same parameter. Only `goodbye` is allowed to return a result and hence `i` is set to 2.

You can use anonymous methods or lambda expressions, see the next chapter, to define delegates within multicast delegates, for example:

```
DoGreet += delegate(string param)
{
        MessageBox.Show("Goodbye " + param);
        return 2;
};
```

Or, more properly if you agree that lambda expressions should be used in preference to anonymous methods:

```
DoGreet +=    (string param)=>
              {
                      MessageBox.Show("Goodbye " + param);
                      return 2;
              };
```

Notice that any unhandled exceptions that are raised by the delegates in the invocation list bring the call sequence to an end.

An Arithmetic of Delegates

You are probably familiar with the += operator for adding to the invocation list but there is also an -= operator that can be used to remove methods. In this case -= b will remove the last occurrence (in execution order) of the delegate that is equal to b. Equality between delegates is defined so that equal delegates have to be of the same type and encapsulate the same Target and Method. Also notice that two MulticastDelegates are considered equal if their invocation lists are identical and in the same order.

Delegates don't provide direct access to their invocation list and you can't manipulate it directly. However, you can retrieve the invocation list as an array of Delegate elements. For example:

```
Delegate[] InvList = DoGreet.GetInvocationList();
```

returns a delegate array with two elements, a delegate wrapping hello and a delegate wrapping goodbye.

You can even invoke each delegate in the invocation list by enumerating the array:

```
foreach (Delegate D in InvList)
{
        D.DynamicInvoke("Loop");
}
```

You might be puzzled as to why we use DynamicInvoke rather than Invoke? When you use the classes directly in this way the invocation of the method cannot be checked at compile time, hence the need for a "DynamicInvoke".

Some of the simplicity of using a `MulticastDelegate` comes from the overloading of the += and -= operators, but there are other, perhaps surprising, ways that you can work with invocation lists. For example, you can create a delegate that has the combined invocation list of other delegates using the + operator:

```
greetType DelA = hello;
greetType DelB = goodbye;
greetType DelC;
DelC = DelA + DelB;
```

In this case `DelC` encapsulates the methods of `DelA` and `DelB`. Similarly, the - operator removes one delegate's invocation list from another. For example:

```
DelC = DelC - DelA;
```

removes all of the delegates in the invocation list of `DelA` from `DelC`.

It is also worth knowing that there are static methods defined on the `Delegate` class such as `Combine` and `Remove` which can be used to manipulate arrays of delegates as well as pairs of delegates.

Events

A common misconception is that .NET events are just multicast delegates. This is mostly true but an event has some additional added infrastructure. Notice that we are discussing .NET events not WPF's routed events which are much more sophisticated.

An event is a multicast delegate with the addition of two accessor functions, `add` and `remove`, that take over the adding and removal of delegates from the invocation list. Most of the time you can ignore the existence of the accessor functions as the system will provide default implementations for you and, as the += and -= operators are overloaded and call these default accessor functions, you can use an event as if it was a simple delegate.

The basic idea is that a class can provide an event that any clients can subscribe to simply by adding delegates to the invocation list of the event's multicast delegate. The event can only be "raised" by the class that owns the event and this results in each delegate in the invocation list being called.

Events are mostly generated automatically for us by Visual Studio, but to really understand what is going on you can't do better than implement a custom event manually. First we need a suitable delegate type:

```
public delegate int MyNewEventType(string param);
```

This we convert into an event:

```
public event MyNewEventType MyNewEvent;
```

MyNewEvent is now an event instance which wraps an anonymous instance of the delegate type. We can add a delegate to the event in the usual way:

```
MyNewEvent += new MyNewEventType(hello);
```

You can also use anonymous methods and lambda expressions to add delegates to an event:

```
MyNewEvent += (string param) =>
{
        MessageBox.Show("Goodbye " + param);
        return 2;
};
```

To raise the event, we simply call it as if it was a delegate:

```
MyNewEvent("New Event");
```

Invoking Events

This is slightly more subtle than it looks because, for a default event with no custom accessor functions, the compiler changes the reference to the event to a reference to the private internal instance of the delegate. This allows you to call the delegate using the name of the event, but if you have defined custom accessor functions they no longer work.

You can use Invoke if you want to, but notice that an event restricts the invocation of its delegate to the object in which it is declared. In other words, an object cannot raise another object's event.

The new event object has all of the methods of a delegate and can be used more or less as if it was a delegate. In particular, you can use BeginInvoke to fire an event asynchronously on a threadpool thread. If you are concerned about using up threadpool threads, you could even create a thread manually and run the delegate using it. By default an event delegate is called synchronously and this means that the code that raises the event is stalled until the event processing is complete.

Are asynchronous events a good idea? If you want to write a responsive program, then yes they are, but you need to understand the problems that can arise in a multithreaded approach. Even if you don't explicitly make use of a multithreaded approach, you have to allow for the possibility that your code will be used in this way. Objects running on different threads can, and do, add event handlers to your event - events are multithreaded.

For example, if you want to provide a custom add and remove accessor, then you need to code the event something like:

```
private MyNewEventType _MyNewEvent;
public event MyNewEventType MyNewEvent
{
        add
        {
                lock(this)
                {
                        _MyNewEvent += value;
                }
        }
        remove
        {
                lock(this)
                {
                        _MyNewEvent -= value;
                }
        }
}
```

Notice that you need to use a lock to stop other threads from updating the delegate while you are in the middle of doing so. Locking on the current object, i.e. this, isn't a good idea because other threads might well try to acquire a lock on some other resource using it, so producing unnecessary waiting for locks to be released. Notice also that you now have to provide a private member variable to store the delegate. You can't use MyNewEvent because using += on it would trigger the accessor functions in an infinite recursion.

As the compiler now has no idea what you have called this internal private variable, you can no longer raise the event using the event's name. The standard solution is to provide an "On" method something like:

```
private void OnMyNewEvent(string param)
{
        if (_MyNewEvent != null)
        {
                _MyNewEvent(param);
        }
}
```

Following this pattern means always calling the "On" method to raise the event.

This is the pattern used automatically for all built-in events within the .NET Framework. Notice, however, that it isn't threadsafe because you could check that the invocation list isn't null and start the call when another thread takes over and changes the invocation list. Again, a correct solution is to obtain a lock before processing the invocation list.

In short, events are inherently multithreaded and as such are dangerous.

Generic and Standard Events

Of course, most of us simply make use of predefined events, but there has been a change in the way that this works. Originally we needed a delegate type for each, even slightly different, event or we just passed object types to allow the event handler to work with a range of types. A better solution is to use generics and this is the approach now taken by the framework classes. For example, the original standard event handler was not generic:

```
public delegate void EventHandler(object sender, EventArgs e);
```

Using `object` as the first parameter allowed any class to raise the event and still notify the users of the event handlers that had raised the event.

The new generic version is:

```
public delegate void EventHandler<TEventArgs>(object sender,
        TEventArgs e) where TEventArgs : EventArgs;
```

which still leaves the sender untyped. A better version is:

```
public delegate void GenericEventHandler<S,A>(S sender,A args);
```

In this case the event would be set up using something like:

```
public event GenericEventHandler <MyClass,MyArgs> MyNewEvent;
```

Generics significantly simplify the implementation of events and by reducing the need to pass an object type increase overall type safety.

Postlude

Multicast delegates sound like they should be something rarely used – and they are unless you make use of or want to implement something like event handling. In this case they become essential and to fully understand events you need to understand multicast delegates.

Chapter 14

Anonymous Methods, Lambdas & Closures

Anonymous methods were introduced in .NET 2.0 and, while they sound like something designed to implement "dirty" shortcuts, were a welcome addition to C#. In modern C# they have been superseded by lambda expressions, but there is one thing that an anonymous method can do that a lambda can't so they are still worth knowing about. In addition, statement lambdas are just a slightly different syntax for anonymous methods so they are the foundations upon which lambdas are built.

The big problem with anonymous methods is figuring out what the problem is that they are designed to solve. So let's take a look at what they are for. On one level anonymous methods are just about making delegates easier to create. Let's briefly recap the stages of creating a delegate, which we've already covered in Chapter 12.

Too Many Names

So the steps to create and use a delegate are:

1. Create the delegate type which specifies the signature and return type.
2. Write the method that you want the delegate to "wrap".
3. Instantiate the delegate type created in step 1 and use it to wrap the method.

What all this means is that you have to invent multiple names for what in most cases are single ideas:

- the delegate type – `MyDelegateType`
- the method to be wrapped – `MyMethod`
- the instance doing the wrapping - `MyDelegate`

For example, if you want to wrap a "Hello World" function you first create a suitable delegate type:

```
delegate void MyHelloDelegateType();
```

then you have to create the function within some class or other:

```
void Hello(){
      MessageBox.Show("Hello From a Delegate");
}
```

and finally create an instance of the delegate type specifying the function that it is to wrap:

```
MyHelloDelegateType MyHelloDelegate1 =
                        new MyHelloDelegateType(Hello);
```

or equivalently:

```
MyHelloDelegateType MyHelloDelegate1 = Hello;
```

Calling the function via the delegate is just a matter of using its name:

```
MyHelloDelegate1();
```

You can see that we have had to invent three names:

- `MyHelloDelegateType` - the delegate type
- `Hello` - the method name
- `MyHelloDelegate1` - the wrapper instance

This is fine if you are going to create multiple instances of the type and wrap multiple functions, but in most cases the type, the delegate and the method are more or less a single entity. That is, you create a delegate because you want to use a method as if it was an object and often this is a one-off requirement.

Anonymous methods

The idea of an anonymous method allows you to fuse the identity of the delegate with the function it wraps. The syntax is easy, you simply use the `delegate` keyword to stand in for the name of the function you are trying to wrap and follow it by a definition of that function. Notice that this means that you don't have to create a separate method that has a life of its own that you then wrap in the delegate. It also saves having to give the method a name.

For example, we can create an instance of `MyHelloDelegateType`:

```
MyHelloDelegateType MyHelloDelegate1 = delegate(){
      MessageBox.Show("Hello From a Delegate");
};

MyHelloDelegate1();
```

One identifier fewer might not seem much of a victory, but now we can recast the code to express the fact that the delegate type is really about the signature and the delegate instance is about what actually happens by renaming the delegate "Hello", i.e. the name that we probably would have assigned the method:

```
MyHelloDelegateType1 Hello = delegate(){
    MessageBox.Show("Hello From a Delegate");
};

Hello();
```

You can specify parameters in the function definition by treating the keyword delegate as if it was the function's name, for example:

```
MyHelloDelegateType2 Hello2 = delegate(string Msg){
    MessageBox.Show(Msg);
};
```

However, for this to work we need to define another delegate type that matches the new signature:

```
delegate void MyHelloDelegateType2(string MyString);
```

Notice that the identifier used as the parameter in the type definition doesn't carry any meaning – it's just there for the syntax.

Perhaps the C-style signature specification:

```
delegate void MyHelloDelegateType2(string);
```

would be better, but this doesn't work in C#.

With the type defined we can now call the delegate in the usual way:

```
Hello2("Hello delegate 2");
```

The situation is a little more complicated than this simple example suggests.

In fact, the anonymous method doesn't have to match the signature of the delegate type exactly. As long as the delegate type has no out parameters then the anonymous method can be defined with no parameters. For example, the following is perfectly legal, even though the delegate type specifies a single string parameter:

```
MyHelloDelegateType2 Hello3 = delegate() {
    MessageBox.Show("Default message!");
};
```

However, you still have to call the delegate with the correct signature:

```
Hello3("dummy");
```

The parameter supplied is simply thrown away. You can see why this approach doesn't work with out parameters. If there is an out parameter defined, where would the return value come from?

Using Anonymous Methods

So what are anonymous methods good for? They certainly save one level of naming confusion, but in some cases they can remove the need for any new names at all. For example, consider the Find method of the Array object defined as:

```
public static T Find<T> (T[] array, Predicate<T> match)
```

The Predicate delegate is defined as:

```
public delegate bool Predicate<T> (T obj)
```

Without anonymous methods you would have to define a Predicate method, wrap in a delegate and pass it to the Find method.

With anonymous method it can be as simple as:

```
int result = Array.Find(A, delegate(int x) {return (x < 0);});
```

In short, anonymous methods are good for short functions that you want to use "at once", often as a parameter within a method call. However, in modern C# lambdas provide a simpler way of doing the same job and more. They work in the same way as anonymous methods and provide a neater way of writing the code.

Statement Lambdas

Lambdas sound esoteric; the name comes from lambda calculus which is important in computer science. You don't need to worry about theory because lambdas solve a very practical problem.

There are two slight variations on the basic idea of a lambda - statement and expression lambdas. A statement lambda can have a mix of expressions and statements whereas an expression lambda has only a single expression as its body and simply returns the result of the expression.

It makes sense to start by looking at statement lambdas because these are simply a more concise way of writing an anonymous method and return to expression lambdas later.

The basic syntax of a statement lambda is:

```
(comma separated parameters)=>{semicolon terminated statement list;}
```

The => symbol can be read as "becomes" to indicate that the parameters are transformed into the actions.

A lambda shares all its characteristics with anonymous methods. For example, to define the `Hello` anonymous method listed earlier using a statement lambda you would write something like:

```
delegate int HelloType(int param);
HelloType HelloInst = (int param1) =>
{
        MessageBox.Show("Hello delegate World" + param1.ToString());
        return ++param1;
};
```

The idea is that you are still creating an anonymous method, but the body of the method is now defined using a slightly different syntax. Once the lambda is encapsulated by the delegate instance everything works in the same way. Note there is nothing special about the name `param1` - you can call parameters whatever you want.

There are some tricks that you can use with statement lambdas to make the method definition even more concise and flexible. The first is that the compiler can deduce the type of the parameters from the delegate type. Essentially the lambda has to have the same number of parameters as the delegate and the return type, if any, has to be implicitly convertible to the return type of the delegate.

Thus the previous lambda can be written:

```
HelloType HelloInst = (param1) =>
{
        MessageBox.Show("Hello delegate World" + param1.ToString());
        return ++param1;
};
```

You can also leave out the brackets if the lambda has only one parameter:

```
HelloType HelloInst = param1 =>
{
        MessageBox.Show("Hello delegate World" + param1.ToString());
        return ++param1;
};
```

and you can use empty brackets () if there are no parameters at all.

```
HelloType HelloInst =  () =>
{
        MessageBox.Show("Hello delegate World");
        return 0;
};
```

You can use a lambda anywhere you would use an anonymous method and they are most often used as parameters as an easy way to pass a function to a method.

Expression Lambdas

A statement lambda can have a mix of expressions and statements. However, there is a particularly simple form of the lambda that is very common in other languages, the "expression lambda" which has only a single expression as its body and simply returns the result of the expression:

```
(parameters) => expression
```

For example:

```
x => x*x;
```

is an expression lambda that takes x and squares it. Notice that if there is only one parameter the parentheses are optional and you never need curly brackets. Expression lambdas are ideal for passing short chunks of code, Boolean conditionals for example, to other methods, which is what they were designed for.

The one problem with expression lambdas is that they can look more complicated than they are by the inclusion of comparison operators. For example, the confusing looking:

```
x => x <= 10;
```

defines a lambda expression that returns true if x is smaller than or equal to 10 and false otherwise, even though it looks like an expression for crushing an x between itself and 10.

Expression lambdas are used extensively in the framework classes where the standard delegate types often make this easier. For example, the Array type has a static Find method which accepts an array and a predicate and returns the first element that makes the predicate true. For example:

```
int i=Array.Find<int>(MyIntArray, x => x>0);
```

returns the first element in MyIntArray that is positive.

In short, expression lambdas are ideal for passing simple functions into methods.

Since C# 6.0 they can also be used to define a method, for example:

```
public int square(int x) => x * x;
```

You can use the same syntax to define a getter-only property:

```
public int total => t1 + t2;
```

When you use total the expression is evaluated to provide the value.

Slightly more esoteric is the use of a lambda in an indexer:

```
public MyClass this[int i] => myarray[i]
```

This will return an instance of MyClass stored in myarray[i] when you use an index on an instance of the class you are defining. For a short, but unrealistic, example we define the class:

```
class myArray
{
        private string[] myarray= { "test0", "test1" };
        public string this[int i]=>myarray[i];
}
```

Now we can create an instance and use the indexer:

```
myArray myArrayObject = new myArray();
MessageBox.Show(myArrayObject[0]);
```

Expression Trees

An expression lambda is also special because it can be converted to an expression tree. What is an expression tree? Put simply an expression tree is just an object which contains all of the information contained in the lambda. It is a representation of the function in data.

Why would you want to create an expression tree? An expression tree can be stored or transmitted to another system where it can be implemented at a later time or remotely. You can think of an expression tree as a data exchange format for a lambda, but they also allow you to create lambdas dynamically. You can create an expression tree without using a lambda and then use it to create the method that corresponds to the lambda. That is, the expression tree is one way of dynamically generating a method.

The main reason that expression trees were introduced was so that LINQ, which makes heavy use of expression lambdas, could turn a query into a data structure and send this "over the wire" to a remote server, but there are lots of alternative and innovative uses.

To see expression trees in action, let's take a simple expression lambda and convert it into an Expression object. When an expression lambda is assigned to an Expression variable it is automatically converted to an expression tree, for example:

```
Expression<Func<int, int>> ExTree = (x) => x * x;
```

Notice that you have to specify the delegate type that the Expression object is going to represent, in this case Func<int,int>. Following this instruction ExTree contains a data representation of the expression lambda.

You can explore the expression tree using its methods and properties. For example:

```
Console.WriteLine(ExTree.Body);
Console.WriteLine(ExTree.Parameters[0]);
Console.WriteLine(ExTree.ReturnType);
```

results in:

```
(x * x)
x
System.Int32
```

You can apply the method in an expression tree using the `Compile` method. For example:

```
Func<int, int> MyNewDelegate = ExTree.Compile();
int result=MyNewDelegate(3);
```

stores the expression lambda in `MyNewDelegate` and then uses it. You can also create and use the delegate on the fly:

```
int result= ExTree.Compile()(3)
```

An Expression Tree From Scratch

Now that we have taken an expression lambda and converted it to an expression tree and then taken the expression tree and converted it back to the lambda, all that is left is to build the expression tree from scratch. If you think about how complex a method can be, you can see that this is an equally complex topic. Most of the methods that you need to generate an expression tree from scratch are provided by the `Expression` static class and its methods.

As a simple example of how this all works, let's create the squaring lambda from scratch. First we need to define the parameter:

```
ParameterExpression param = Expression.Parameter(typeof(int), "x");
```

The parameter name "x" is only used in debugging and system messages. Next we need to define the body of the lambda and this is where things can get complicated:

```
Expression square = Expression.Multiply(param, param);
```

The `Multiply` method takes a left-hand side expression and a right-hand side expression and multiplies them together. In this case we simply multiply the parameter by itself. Now we can build the expression tree:

```
Expression<Func<int,int>> ExTree =
                Expression.Lambda<Func<int,int>>(square,param);
```

There are a number of different ways of creating an expression tree, but the Lambda method simply takes the body and parameter and puts them together using the specified delegate type to define the type of the lambda. Following this we can use the expression tree as if it had been derived from a lambda in the first place. For example:

```
Func<int, int> MyNewDelegate = ExTree.Compile();
Console.WriteLine(MyNewDelegate(3).ToString());
```

will display 9.

The most important point to understand is that you can build an expression tree that corresponds to a multiline method in this way. That is, you can only automatically convert a single line expression lambda to an expression tree, but you can build much more complex expression trees using the Expression static methods.

Closure?

You will often hear JavaScript and functional programmers talking about "closure" and now you can join in because C# also has "closure" in the form of the variable capture that anonymous methods and lambdas use. Consider the following code:

```
int i = 0;
MyHelloDelegateType1 Hello2 = ()=>
        {
                i++;
                MessageBox.Show(i.ToString());
        };
Hello2();
Hello2();
Hello2();
MessageBox.Show(i.ToString());
```

There is nothing really surprising here - the lambda has access to all of the variables that are in scope when it was defined. So each time you call Hello2, the local variable i is incremented. What is surprising is that this works even if the local variable has gone out of scope and been destroyed as far as the rest of the program is concerned. When you declare a lambda, or an anonymous method, a bond is created between it and all of the variables that are in scope when is was defined and this bond continues beyond the lifetime of the variables.

Usually the way that a function outlives the variables it was defined alongside is that it is referenced by a longer-lived variable or returned as the result of a method.

An easy to way to see that this happens is to make int i local to an inner code block:

```
MyHelloDelegateType1 Hello2;
{
        int i = 0;
        Hello2 = () =>
        {
                        i++;
                MessageBox.Show(i.ToString());
        };
}
Hello2();
Hello2();
Hello2();
MessageBox.Show(i.ToString());
```

If you try this you will find that you get a compiler error complaining that i doesn't exist when you try to display it using the Show method. This is reasonable as i is only in scope within the outer braces. However, a call to Hello2 still works and accesses the inaccessible variable.

This capturing of the variables is generally referred to as a closure.

Although the use of a variable with block scope is a very direct way to show that the captured variable persists, it is not the most common way that it occurs. In most cases the function could be referenced by a variable with a longer lifetime because it is declared outside of the method that creates the lambda or the lambda could be returned as a result by another method. For example, suppose we define a class member variable:

```
public partial class Form1 : Form
{
        delegate void mytest();
        mytest test;
```

and create a function referenced by the test variable in an initialization method:

```
public Form1()
{
        InitializeComponent();
        int c = 1;
        test = delegate ()
                {
                        button1.Text = c.ToString();
                };
        c = 0;
}
```

Notice that the delegate sets the button's text to the value of c. What value of c do you think is used, 1 or 0? To find out you have to call the function away from the initialization method:

```
private void button1_Click(object sender, EventArgs e)
{
        test();
}
```

Now you can see that the only reason that you can still call the function is that it is referenced by a class member that is in scope for the event handler. You can also see clearly why there is doubt about the value of c as the variable no longer exists. However, the test method captured the variable and its final value before it went out of scope and was destroyed. If you try the program you will find that c is 0. All of the variables captured are initially frozen at their final value before they go out of scope and are destroyed. The functions that capture the variables can change their values, but note that all anonymous functions defined within the same scope share the same set of captured variables. That is the captured variables for a single run environment exist for all of the functions defined at the same time.

To demonstrate how subtle the effects of closure can be, consider the following example:

```
MyHelloDelegateType1[] Count=new MyHelloDelegateType1[10];

for(int i=0;i<10;i++)
{
        Count[i] = ()=>
        {
                MessageBox.Show(i.ToString());
        };
}
```

Notice that we create an array of ten delegates and each one is the same anonymous method that simply displays the current value of i. What do you think is going to be the result of calling one of the delegates, Count[0] say? The simplest thing to do is call each of the delegates:

```
for (int j = 0; j < 10; j++)
{
        Count[j]();
}
```

This works perfectly and displays the value 10 for each delegate. What happens is that the variable i is captured when each of the delegates is created, but all of the delegates share the same variable with the local environment. When the outer function changes the variable, all the delegates see the change and, in this case, the captured copy of i slowly counts up to 10 as the for loop progresses.

When the loop ends the local version of the variable goes out of scope, but the captured copy of i lives on in the delegates and it has the value 10. That is we capture the very last value of i and all of the delegates share it.

Examples of closure can become more complicated than this simple for loop and if you find yourself using such constructions you probably should reconsider and find a more clear expression of what you are trying to do. However, the principle is simple enough; the compiler creates a hidden class wrapper for all of the variables in scope when the delegates are created. If a variable is recreated each time the delegate is created, then each delegate will capture a new copy. For example:

```
MyHelloDelegateType1[] Count = new MyHelloDelegateType1[10];

for(int i = 0;i<10;i++)
{
        int j = i;
        Count[i] = delegate()
        {
                MessageBox.Show(j.ToString());
        };
};
```

In this case the variable j is recreated each time through the loop and each delegate captures its own copy. If you now try calling each delegate in turn you will find that it now displays 0,1,2, and so on, reflecting the value of i at the time the delegate was created. Notice that j is out of scope when the loop ends so you can't discover what its current value is – only the captured copies survive the loop.

Using Closure 1 - More Parameters

Clearly closures are fun but what use are they? The answer is that they provide a context for a function which can furnish additional information without the need to use additional parameters. Why wouldn't you create some additional parameters? Most likely because the signature of the function you are trying to use isn't under your control. For example, consider the EnumWindows API call, which needs a callback function that is called for each window it enumerates.

The API call is:

```
[DllImport("user32.dll")]
[return: MarshalAs(UnmanagedType.Bool)]
        static extern bool EnumWindows(
                EnumWindowsProc lpEnumFunc,
                ref IntPtr lParam);
```

and the callback delegate is:

```
public delegate bool EnumWindowsProc(
        IntPtr hWnd,
        ref IntPtr lParam);
```

The problem with using the callback delegate is that it only has the two parameters, the handle of the current window and a pointer supplied in the call to the EnumWindows function. It is this pointer that is used to communicate between the callback function and the program needing the enumeration.

Closure, however, makes communication much easier. If you need a function to find a particular dialog box specified by its Owner and its Caption string then you could write a function something like:

```
public IntPtr getDialog(IntPtr Owner, String Caption)
{
```

Clearly, we need to pass the Owner and Caption to the callback delegate so that it can compare each of the enumerated windows to the target. The most natural way to do this is to provide these extra pieces of information to the callback via extra parameters, but to work as a callback it can only have the parameters defined by the API. The simplest solution is to define the callback delegate in the usual way, but use the fact that the Owner and Caption parameters are in scope and so are captured by an anonymous function:

```
EnumWindowsProc enumProc =
                    delegate(IntPtr handle, ref IntPtr pointer)
{
```

First we get the window text and compare it to Caption, which we can only access here thanks to closure:

```
int length = GetWindowTextLength(handle);
StringBuilder wTitle = new StringBuilder(length + 1);
GetWindowText(handle, wTitle, wTitle.Capacity);
if (wTitle.ToString() == Caption)
{
```

If they match we check that the class name is correct for a dialog box and then check that `Owner`, which is once again only accessible at this point because of closure, is the correct window:

```
int max = 100;
StringBuilder classname = new StringBuilder(max);
GetClassName(handle, classname, max);
if (classname.ToString() == "#32770")
{
    IntPtr Parent = GetParent(handle);
    if (Parent == Owner)
    {
            pointer = handle;
            return false;
    }
}
}
    return true;
};
```

This completes the anonymous callback delegate; now we can call `EnumWindows`:

```
IntPtr DlgHwnd = IntPtr.Zero;
EnumWindows(enumProc, ref DlgHwnd);
return DlgHwnd;
}
```

To follow what is going on here, you need to keep in mind that the callback is actually run by the API via the call:

```
enumProc(handle,pointer);
```

which passes in the handle to the window and a pointer to some additional data. The `Owner` and `Caption` variables are used within the callback courtesy of closure. Notice that the pointer in the callback delegate is used to return the handle of the dialog box that we have found, but this too could have been achieved using closure. Without any use of closure we would have had to pack the `Owner` and `Caption` into a data structure and passed this to the callback. Closure makes things much simpler in this case.

Using Closure 2 - Event Pattern

There is one very important situation where closure simplifies things, although not everyone agrees it's a good idea. In an event-oriented environment, the linear flow of actions is often made unclear by the need to pause processing until an event occurs. Situations like this occur all the time, but to make the explanation easier to follow, let's try to remain as general as possible. Suppose you are writing some code that works with some resources

and you get to the point where you need to load a new resource and this is a
time-consuming action, then there are two approaches, blocking synchronous
and non-blocking asynchronous. Blocking synchronous simply causes the
thread doing the work to pause until the resource is loaded:

```
work with resources
request new resource
wait(until resource loaded)
continue with processing
```

This has the advantage of simplicity and you can clearly see what is
happening, but if the processing thread is also processing events then all
event handling stops at the wait. This is a common problem that can be
partly alleviated by use of constructs such as DoEvents which sends the
thread off to process events while waiting:

```
work with resources
request new resource
Do Until (resource loaded)
      DoEvents
Loop
continue with processing
```

This approach has many problems - the biggest being reentrancy, i.e. what if
an event that occurs as the result of DoEvents restarts the entire method over
again. The second approach, non-blocking asynchronous, is to use an event
to trigger the resumption of the processing when the resource has loaded, for
example:

```
work with resources
setup "resource loaded" event handler
request new resource
end method
```

When the method ends, the thread can continue to process events and, when
the resource is loaded, the assigned event handler is invoked and processing
continues.

The problem with this is that the event handler has to be written elsewhere
and it's self-contained and doesn't share access to any of the resources of the
original processing method. That is, the logic of the program says:

```
do actions A
load  new resource
do actions B
end AB
```

A and B are linked in the sense that B might well need access to variables that were created as part of A, but the need not to block the thread waiting for the resource load means this has to be written as:

```
do actions A
set B to be onload event handler
load new resource
end A


onload
Do B
end B
```

Not only is the flow of control confused by this break, but B doesn't have access to the variables etc in the scope of A. At this point you should be thinking – closure. If the event handler is defined as an anonymous method in the scope of A then when it runs, whenever that might be, it has access to the original environment provided by A. That is:

```
do actions A
set B to be onload event handler
load new resource
onload anonymous method
Do B
end B
end A
```

It is clear that the flow of control is do A then do B, but B has access all of the variables defined in A and can continue the processing as if it hadn't had to wait for an event.

The use of closure to make non-blocking asynchronous coding look more like blocking synchronous coding is one of the big advantages of using a closure - but don't overuse it!

In modern C# a better way of handling events and asynchronous code is to use async and await, see Chapter 17.

Standard Delegates

Lambdas have made it much easier to use the standard types of function within the .NET framework and to make it even easier there are a range of standard pre-defined delegate types.

Action delegates provide a way to encapsulate a method that does something, i.e. is an "action", returning void and anything from zero to 16 parameters. For example:

```
Action<int> HelloInst = (param1) =>
{
        MessageBox.Show( Hello delegate World" + param1.ToString());
};
```

To use Action with additional parameters you simply keep specifying them up to the maximum. For example:

```
Action<int><int><string> MyAction=(p1,p2,p3) => ...
```

The Func delegate works in the same way as the Action delegate, but you can also specify a return type in addition to up to sixteen input parameters. The return type is specified as the final type, for example:

```
Func<int,int> HelloInst = (param1) =>
{
        MessageBox.Show("Hello delegate World"+ param1.ToString());
        return ++param1;
};
```

Using Action or Func you can create a delegate that can encapsulate almost any lambda, but notice that it might be better still to define your own delegate to convey the meaning of what the lambda is supposed to do.

The need to convey a meaning is the motivation behind there being a number of other standard predefined delegates as well as the Action and Func delegates. For example, a predicate in mathematical logic is a function which evaluates to true or false, i.e. a function returning a boolean. The Predicate<T> delegate can be used to wrap a lambda that accepts a single parameter and returns a boolean. That is, Predicate <T> is identical to Func<T><bool>.

Similarly, the Comparison<T> delegate takes two input parameters, x and y say, of the same type and returns an int that indicates the relative "size" of the two objects - negative means x<y, zero means x = y and positive means x>y, for example:

```
Comparison<int> Bigger(x,y)=>
{
        if(x<y) return -1;
        if(x=y) return 0;
        return 1;
}
```

There is also a Converter<Tin,Tout> delegate which represents a method that converts the input type to the output type:

```
Converter<int,string> MyConv (x,y)=>
{
        return x.ToString();
}
```

There are lots of other predefined delegates, but they rapidly become increasingly specialized like the EventHandler<TEventArgs> delegate.

Postlude

Anonymous methods and lambdas are a big improvement over the pure delegate approach to using functions as if they were objects. Closure might seem mystifying at first, but it is logical to allow a function to have access to its local context, even when that local context should no longer exist. Not only is it logical, it is also more useful than you might expect.

IV Async

Prelude

C# isn't a naturally asynchronous language in the sense that it isn't wedded to any particular UI framework, but it still needs to use asynchronous operations. As soon as you select a UI framework there are events to deal with and asynchronous code is an essential part of working with it. In a wider context you need asynchronous code to avoid having to wait for long running processes to come to an end. The first approach to the problem was to use threads, then the task parallel library came along and finally the oh-so-easy to use async and await.

Chapter 15

Threading, Tasks & Locking

A thread of execution is just that - a set of instructions that are carried out more or less independently of any other set of instructions.

The simplest and most common programming model is single threading. In .NET every GUI program has a single UI thread of execution which responds to all of the events generated by the user. The majority of programs really don't need anything more than this single thread of execution, but occasionally there is something to be gained in using more than one thread.

Generally speaking multi-threading can make a program more responsive to the user by splitting off worker threads that don't block the UI thread. Multi-threading can make a program actually run faster, although this is a much less common situation than you might think. The only gains in efficiency that are possible are if a single thread is repeatedly blocked waiting for something to happen and there is work that another thread could be getting on with. In this case, however, the single-threaded version of the program could also be made more efficient by simply getting it to do work while it would otherwise be idle.

Until quite recently most multi-threading was simulated by the operating system switching a single processor's attention between a set of active threads. In this case there is only one thread actually being obeyed at any one time, but the rate of switching between threads is sufficiently high to give the impression that all of the threads are being run. Simulating multi-threading is generally done by preemptive multi-tasking, but there are other ways of doing it.

With the rise of multi-core processors the possibility of real multi-threading, albeit limited to a small number of threads, has become possible and in this case the potential for speed increase is more real. All in all threading is becoming increasingly important. .NET makes the creation of multi-threaded programs very easy and while this can be considered a good thing it also has some negative consequences.

Using multiple threads properly is a very difficult and subtle task and not to be undertaken lightly. So while it is good that .NET facilitates their use, it should not be taken as an encouragement to proliferate threads without some careful thought. Here we explore how multi-threading works and, more importantly, how it can go very wrong. In particular, we take a look at some of the more obscure ways in which threading can become part of your program via Invoke and the background worker class, but first some standard threading.

Starting A Thread

There is more than one way that you can enter the world of multi-threaded programs. Some of them are so simple that you might not even notice the transition. For example, when you employ an asynchronous call using BeginInvoke you use a separate thread to run the method without having to do anything extra. However, no matter how you create a new thread, the same considerations apply.

There are two ways of explicitly using a thread in your program. The first is to use one of the existing threads in the thread pool. This has the advantage that you don't have the overhead of actually creating a new thread, but the number of threads available for use in the thread pool is limited. In general, you should only use a thread-pool thread for tasks that are short and release the thread back to the thread pool as soon as possible. The same concerns apply to using a thread-pool thread as one you create yourself.

As long as the task that you want the thread to do is sufficiently long-lived you are advised to create a thread for it. To do this you need to use the Thread class in System.Threading.

The Thread constructor accepts either a ThreadStart or a ParameterizedThreadStart delegate which wraps the method that will be executed by the new thread. For example, suppose we have a method like:

```
public void CountUp()
{
        for (int i = 0; i < 9999; i++)
                MessageBox.Show("Thread1 " + i.ToString());
}
```

then this can be run as a new thread using:

```
Thread  T1=new Thread(new ThreadStart(CountUp));
```

This creates the new thread object but doesn't actually start the thread running. To do this we have to use the Start method:

```
T1.Start();
```

You will now see the message box appear and as long as you keep clicking the OK button the thread will continue.

There are a number of thread methods that can be used to stop and pause threads and what these do and how they are used is fairly obvious. Here we will concentrate on more difficult aspects of threading.

Avoiding Race Conditions

We often use the term "thread safe" without really bothering to define what it actually means, as if using it often enough would make its meaning obvious. Basically a block of code, or an object, is thread safe if it works correctly and as desired if multiple threads make use of it at the same time. Most of the code you will encounter isn't thread safe and this includes most of the objects in the .NET class library and, of course, your own code. The important thing to realize is that in general code isn't thread safe unless you take steps to make it so.

What exactly is the problem? There is the obvious confusion caused by threads sharing the same data. For example, if a method has a counter then another thread starting the same method might well zero that counter and leave it in a state that is not as the first thread left it. For example, consider the following code:

```
public int count = 0;
public void A()
{
        for (int i = 0; i < 10000000; i++)
        {
                count++;
        }
}
public void B()
{
        for (int i = 0; i < 10000000; i++)
        {
                count++;
        }
}
private void button1_Click(object sender, EventArgs e)
{
        Thread T1 = new Thread(new ThreadStart(A));
        Thread T2 = new Thread(new ThreadStart(B));
        T1.Start();
        T2.Start();
        T1.Join();
        T2.Join();
        textBox1.Text = count.ToString();
}
```

Function A adds one to count in a loop and function B does the same. These are run as two independent threads and the main thread waits until they have completed before using the Join method. If you run this program then you will discover that the final value of count isn't predictable because it all depends on when the two threads get access to count. This is not thread-safe coding because the result changes each time you run it – it is subject to race conditions where both tasks attempt to update the variable at the same time and the result depends on which arrived at it first. In particular consider what happened if function A is updating the counter and reads 42 but is then interrupted by function B which also reads 42. They both add one to get 43 and store the result back in count which now holds 43 when it should hold 44 as there have been two updates.

In a deeper sense it isn't thread safe because access to the global resource, i.e. count, isn't controlled. In this case the increment is such a fast operation that the chance of being interrupted is low, but given enough updates the effect can be seen.

This is the sort of problem that thread-safe code is designed to avoid. Notice that, as this sort of threading error can have a low probability of occurring, it's possible for it to go unnoticed for many, many runs of the program and look to all intents and purposes like some sort of random hardware failure. This is what makes multi-threaded programs very difficult to debug.

Ensuring Thread Safety

There are three general approaches to making code thread safe, the first of which is to write reentrant code. If you only use local variables stored on the stack then restarting the function with another thread automatically saves the state of any original invocation. Restricting storage to the stack isn't always easy, so .NET also provides thread-local storage which ensures that each thread has its own private copy of any variables it used. Reentrant code is a good approach if you need a function that can be used by multiple threads to do a task, but it forbids any sharing of resources which would render the code non-reentrant.

A more general approach is to use access control which works by allowing only one thread to access a resource at a time. There are lots of facilities provided within .NET to allow you to implement mutual exclusion and more complicated access methods. The big problem with access control is knowing when a resource is in use by a thread and when it is free. Access control also brings with it problems connected with what happens when a thread wants to use a resource which is locked.

Finally we can resort to atomic operations - ones that cannot be interrupted by a change of thread. That is, once started an atomic operation will complete without yielding to another thread. In general, which operations are atomic is defined by the hardware, so this isn't a particularly stable multi-platform solution. However, it is one of the easiest of approaches to thread safety.

Atomic Operations and Volatility

Before moving onto more sophisticated ideas, let's consider some of the issues of low-level data access. The .NET CLR guarantees that all native integer operations are atomic in the sense that they cannot be interrupted by a task swap in mid operation. This avoids the problem of a variable being changed by another thread in the middle of an operation so resulting in invalid or inconsistent data.

The problem with this definition is that the native integer size varies according to machine type. So, is count++ an atomic operation? It all depends on the machine it is run on. If you want to be sure an operation is atomic then use the operations provided by the Interlocked class. For example:

```
Interlocked.Increment(ref count);
```

will add one to count without any risk that the process will be interrupted by another thread using a similar interlocked operation. Notice that it can potentially be interrupted by standard non-interlocked operations. For this approach to work, all of the threads have to use nothing but interlocked operations to access shared resources. The advantage of Interlocked is simplicity and its disadvantage is that it is limited to the methods provided. In most cases, it is much better to use a lock based on a Monitor, as described later.

If you do change the increment in function A and B to use:

```
Interlocked.Increment(ref count);
```

in the previous example you will find that the result is always 20000000 as no increments are ever interrupted.

There is another strange problem associated with the way a variable changes its state or not, referred to as volatility. During a non-atomic operation a variable might change its state due to another thread. However, it is possible that the compiler and/or machine architecture may make the assumption that a variable can't change if the current thread doesn't change it. This allows variables to be cached in fast memory, but the cached copy may not reflect the true value of the variable stored in main memory. In practice, this problem doesn't happen at all often but you can declare a variable as volatile if you need the compiler to check that it hasn't been changed by another thread. In practice it usually isn't necessary to use volatile as, once again, if you use a lock it performs a volatile read at the start and a volatile write at the end making sure everything is up-to-date.

Using Reentrant Code

Reentrant code can be executed concurrently because each time it is run essentially a new copy of everything it uses is automatically created. Reentrancy is the key idea in functional programming where it is the norm, but in most languages you have to put in some work to achieve it. In C# you can create a reentrant function in a number of ways, but essentially you have to avoid using global non-constant data.

To convert our two example functions to be reentrant all we have to do is remove the use of the global variable count. Once defined as local to each function, the variables are allocated on the stack and hence local to each thread as each thread has its own stack. Of course, this means that the two functions cannot interact with each other, but this is in the nature of re-entrant functions.

Consider now the possibility that a class wants to be reentrant, i.e. have nothing but reentrant methods. This is fine as long as it doesn't make use of global or static variables. A static variable is just a special case of a global variable, i.e. it's global to all instances of the class. If you still want your class to be reentrant then you have no choice but to use thread-local storage. The simplest way of doing this is to use the [ThreadStatic] attribute. For example, to make the public count variable in the previous example thread-local, we simply have to change its declaration to:

```
[ThreadStatic] static public int count;
```

Notice that now it's also a static variable shared by all instances of the class, but it isn't shared by different threads executing methods in the same or different instances of the class. Now if you run this program you will see 0 as each thread increments its own copy of count and the main UI thread has its own copy which remains at 0 as it doesn't increment it. Thread-local storage isn't shared, which is the whole point of using it.

The [ThreadStatic] attribute is the most efficient way of creating thread-local storage. You can also do it the hard way using named or unnamed data slots, but you need to keep in mind that these are less efficient and only slightly more useful. In this case you have to allocate the storage yourself and use special storage and retrieval functions. The details are straightforward and documented under Thread.AllocateDataSlot and associated methods. Now it's time to move on to a much bigger and more important topic, exclusion.

Exclusion Using Locking

In principle, exclusion is simple to implement. All you need is a flag that a thread can test to see if the resource is in use. If it is then the thread should wait, forming a queue if needs be, until the resource is free as indicated by the flag. In practice implementing the flag so that nothing goes wrong is difficult in the extreme. If you simply use a Boolean as a flag, for example, consider what happens when two threads test it at more or less the same time to discover that it is set to false and both proceed to set it to true and use the resource it guards. Not only do you now have two threads using the resource, when one of them has finished it will set the flag back to false and allow other threads to use the resource.

.NET provides a great many different locking facilities – so many that it's very confusing. Part of the reason for this excess is that the theory of locking has been developed by many different people who each invented their own favorite way of doing the job. Let's start with the simplest and most useful locking mechanism, the monitor, invented by Per Brinch Hansen in 1972.

Every object in .NET has a monitor associated with it. A thread can acquire or enter the monitor only if no other thread has already acquired it. If it can't acquire the monitor it simply waits, in a queue of other threads trying to acquire the same monitor, until the monitor is available. When the thread that has the monitor is finished it has to explicitly exit or release the monitor.

The monitor is implemented in such a way that the sort of problems described with simple locking on a flag cannot happen – acquiring a monitor is an atomic operation. However, there are other things that can go wrong and the first big problem that confronts any programmer wanting to use a monitor is which object to use for locking. Remember every object has a monitor and so can provide a unique lock restricting access to a resource. At this point you need to focus on the fact that in many ways it is the code which accesses the resource which is locked and not the resource. Suppose we have a block of code that manipulates a global variable, we clearly don't want this code to be active on more than one thread at a time so we acquire the lock at the start of the code and release it at the end of the block.

If there are multiple different blocks of code that access the same resource then each of these blocks has to be written to acquire the lock at the start of the code and release it at the end. You can now see that, whatever object you use to provide the lock, it has to be accessible to all of the blocks of code that need to use it. The object that you place a lock on also has to be a fairly obvious one for the job and it shouldn't be used, by accident, by another block of code to restrict access to another resource.

There is a great deal of custom and practice in which objects should be used. For example, it is often said that you should lock on `this` for instance methods and a type `object` for static methods. The logic is that each instance method will only access resources that belong to that instance and so thread locking only has to be specific to that instance. However, a static method is common to all instances and hence likely to need locking so that one thread can only access it at a time, irrespective of which instance it is called from.

These conventions have some sense, but an equally good, and some might argue better, approach is to create and use objects specifically to be used to lock a resource. Let's see how this works. First, we need an object to use as a lock:

```
static readonly object MyCountLock = new object();
```

As we want to access the object from everywhere it needs to be `static` and as we don't want anyone to change it set to `readonly`. To make use of it we have to modify the count method quoted earlier to read:

```
public void A()
{
        Monitor.Enter(MyCountLock);
        for (int i = 0; i < 10000000; i++)
        {
                count++;
        }
        Monitor.Exit(MyCountLock);
}

public void B()
{
        Monitor.Enter(MyCountLock);
        for (int i = 0; i < 10000000; i++)
        {
                count++;
        }
        Monitor.Exit(MyCountLock);
}
```

The calls to the static `Monitor` object acquire and release the lock using our `object`. If one of the threads tries to enter the monitor while the other thread hasn't exited then it will wait for the other to exit. To try this out we need the same `main` program as before.

If you place a breakpoint on the return you will see that the update is performed in an orderly fashion in the sense that neither thread interrupts the other during the update and no updates are lost. If you comment out either of the calls to the monitor then you will immediately see that the two threads do interfere with one another. Notice that the placement of the lock is important.

In the example above the resource is locked for the entire for loop – that is the first thread will complete before the second gets a chance to update the variable. Locks should be acquired as late as possible and given up as soon as possible:

```
public void A()
{
        for (int i = 0; i < 10000000; i++)
        {
                Monitor.Enter(MyCountLock);
                count++;
                Monitor.Exit(MyCountLock);
        }

}
public void B()
{
        for (int i = 0; i < 10000000; i++)
        {
                Monitor.Enter(MyCountLock);
                count++;
                Monitor.Exit(MyCountLock);
        }

}
```

This works and it only locks the variable while it is being updated. This allows both threads to work together, but at the expense of a lot more locking and unlocking operations. If you don't want to use a specially created object then you can use the more commonly encountered lock on this:

```
public void A()
{
        for (int i = 0; i < 10000000; i++)
        {
                Monitor.Enter(this);
                count++;
                Monitor.Exit(this);
        }
}
```

The other thread needs to be changed in the same way.

The lock using the current instance works equally well but imagine what would happen if the monitor was protecting a resource shared by multiple instances of the class. The result would be messy, to say the least, as each instance would obey the lock but threads from different instances would access it at the same time. Similarly a lock on this isn't very useful for controlling access from different objects. Another problem with locking on the current instance is that you might well forget that it is being used to protect a particular resource and accidentally use it to protect another, completely unconnected, resource. This would result in a thread accessing resource one, unnecessarily blocking all access to resource two.

In many ways it is better to create an object specifically to be used to lock a particular resource and include the name of the resource in the name of the lock. Don't make the common mistake of using a string or a value object to lock because there are pitfalls in using both. The string might well end up being shared due to optimization and the value object would be boxed and unboxed each time it was used, nullifying the effect of the lock.

Another potential problem with using `Monitor` in the way described is that if the code crashes while it has a lock then the lock never gets released. Similarly, you could accidentally forget to release the lock or attempt to release the lock on the wrong object. You can avoid the problem of a crash by wrapping the code in a try-catch statement, but it's much easier to use the equivalent `lock` statement. That is:

```
lock(object){list of instructions}
```

is equivalent to:

```
try{
            Monitor.Enter(object);
            list of instructions
}
finally{Monitor.Exit(object);
```

In other words, `lock` will try to obtain a lock using the specified object before executing the list of instructions within a try. No matter what happens, you can be sure that the lock will be released so that other threads can use the resource. For example, the previous code can be written in a more robust way as:

```
public void A()
{
      for (int i = 0; i < 10000000; i++)
      {
            lock (this)
            {
                  count++;
            }
      }
}
```

Notice that while this is rather more foolproof than using the basic `Monitor` methods, a thread that doesn't play by the rules and simply accesses the resource will spoil everything. The point is that you can't enforce locking, just hope that everyone remembers to use it.

There are other `Monitor` methods that are sometimes useful. For example, the `TryEnter` method will attempt to acquire a lock, after waiting for a specified time, but will allow the thread to continue if the lock cannot be acquired. Clearly in this case you need to test the return value, a Boolean, to see if the lock has been acquired and do something different if it hasn't.

The `wait` method will allow the thread that currently has the lock to free it and allow other threads to acquire it while it waits for a signal from another thread before attempting to acquire the lock again. Another thread, one that currently has the lock, can signal to the next waiting thread, (or to all waiting threads) to try to acquire the lock by using the `pulse` or `pulseall` method. To understand how this might be used, consider a thread that processes a buffer that is filled by another thread. The processing thread can call `wait` when it has finished processing the buffer and allow the filling thread to access it. As soon as the filling thread has finished its work, it can use `pulse` to tell the processing thread to try to acquire the lock and start work again. The clever part is that this mechanism generalizes to multiple work-creating and work-consuming threads and they can all queue in an orderly fashion to access the resource using wait and pulse.

Deadlock

There are other problems with locking and the most celebrated is perhaps the deadlock condition. Put simply, if thread A locks resource one and thread B locks resource two everything is fine unless thread A also wants a lock on resource two before it can complete and if thread B needs a lock on resource one before it can complete. The result is that both threads spend forever waiting for the other to finish and release the resource. This is deadlock and it can occur in much more complicated ways than this simple "A waits for B which waits for A" situation. It is possible to create a deadlock ring of dependency by having A wait for B, which waits for C, which waits for D which is waiting for A.

There isn't much you can do about deadlock except to be aware of it and design your access strategies with a great deal of care. You can try to avoid locking threads on more than one lock at a time but this can slow things down to unacceptable levels as threads have to wait while another thread acquires an oversized lock on resources, some of which it isn't actually using. A better strategy is to attempt to acquire all of the locks that a thread needs to complete at the start and release any that have been acquired if it isn't possible to acquire them all. Again this can result in a loss of performance.

Multi-threading with locks isn't easy and carries the seeds of disaster. Multi-threading without locks is easy but is always guaranteed to be a disaster.

You can do most of what you need just with the `Monitor`, but .NET does provide other locking facilities. For example, the mutex provides locking across process boundaries and the semaphore can be used to control the number of threads that can access a resource. All of these work in similar ways to the monitor and you should have no problems in understanding how they work – but if the `Monitor` does the job then use it.

Background Worker

There is an easy way to implement a thread intended to do some background computation, the `BackgroundWorker` control. It attempts to make threading seem easy by making it look like event handling. The idea is that the average programmer understands how to write an event handler, but isn't an expert on threading. The background worker does indeed make things easier, but it still brings with it all of the problems of threading.

The easiest way to create a background worker is to drag-and-drop it from the Windows Forms toolbox. This automatically generates the code needed for the event handler. If you don't want to use a control then you can create the background worker in code, it's only slightly more difficult.

```
BackgroundWorker BW1 = new BackgroundWorker();
```

You can also use this construction with WPF.

The key to understanding the way the `BackgroundWorker` object implements threading for you is to realize that its `DoWork` event handler is run using a separate thread obtained from the thread pool.

For example, define the event handler as:

```
BW1.DoWork +=delegate(object s,DoWorkEventArgs We)
{
        //do something else
};
```

The event handler has been defined using an anonymous method, but you can define it in the usual way via a named method wrapped in a `DoWorkEventHandler` delegate if you want to. Nothing happens until we use the command:

```
BW1.RunWorkerAsync();
```

This gets a thread from the thread pool and uses it to run the method associated with the `DoWork` event. You can monitor the new thread using

RunWorkerCompleted event and even get a result from the RunWorkerCompletedEventsArg object which is passed back.

There are a few potential well-documented pitfalls, but in the main BackgroundWorker is easy to use except that you can't access any of the UI components from the DoWork event handler and accessing shared resources is just as much a problem as if you had created the thread explicitly. The documentation simply says the equivalent of "don't do it".

There is an argument for keeping BackgroundWorker threads simple, but if you understand threading you can use Invoke in the same way as described to allow UI interaction in the next chapter. For example, you can use the addtext2 method, described in the next chapter using the self invoke approach:

```
addtext2("thread ending");
```

at the end of the DoWork event handler and it will display the message in the text box without any cross threading problems.

The BackgroundWorker control does make it possible to get some of the benefits of threading without having to worry about the problems. However, if you know about threading there is little to be gained by using it. It may stop you worrying about the problems, but they are still present.

Task – The .NET Way To Thread

Using threads as described so far is the low-level, yet surprisingly portable, way of implementing asynchronous code. Just about every language and every operating system has some form of threading, but .NET has a higher-level implementation of asynchronous code that is built on top of threads, the Task. A Task is a class that represents an operation that will run on a separate thread. The threads are taken from the collection of already constructed threads waiting to be used – the thread pool. This speeds things up as creating threads is a slow process.

There are two task-related classes, Task and Task<TResult> - the first doesn't return a result and the second returns a result of the specified type. Already we have something extra to the basic thread as threads need you to provide code to extract results from them.

There are a number of different Task and Task<Tresult> constructors but the simplest are Task(Action) and Task<Tresult>(Func<Tresult>) which create Task objects based on the Action or Func delegates.

The `Action` delegate is a set of delegates like:

```
Action()
Action<T1>()
Action<T1,T2>()
```

and so on and the `Func` delegate is a set of delegates like:

```
Func<TResult>
Func<T1, TResult>
Func<T1, T2, TResult>
```

and so on. They provide delegates suitable for functions with a different number of parameters and a return type. `Task` has constructors for `Action()`, `Func<TResult)`, `Action<object>` and `Func<object,Tresult>`. That is you can have one or no parameters and a result or no result.

Thus the previous example using threads for functions `A` and `B` can be written using `Tasks` as:

```
Action AA = new Action(A);
Task T1 = new Task(AA);
Action AB = new Action(B);
Task T2 = new Task(AB);
T1.Start();
T2.Start();
T1.Wait();
T2.Wait();
textBox1.Text = count.ToString();
```

Notice that use of `Wait` to halt the current thread until the `Task` is complete. This isn't the shortest way to write this code, but it does show the stages of creating the delegate, then the `Task` and starting it running.

The simplest version is probably:

```
Task T1 = Task.Run(A);
Task T2 = Task.Run(B);
Task.WaitAll(new Task[] { T1, T2 });
textBox1.Text = count.ToString();
```

The `Run` method takes a function of the correct type, creates a `Task` and runs it. The `WaitAll` method waits for all of the `Task` objects in the array to finish. The existence of `Wait`, `WaitAll` and `WaitAny` are good reasons for preferring tasks to threads. There is also `When`, `WhenAll`, `WhenAny` which run a `Task` when the specified tasks end. Notice that the `When` methods provide an easy way to chain `Task` objects so that one starts when one ends.

If you want to pass parameters to the `Task` you can use the alternative constructor and an `object`:

```
Task(Action,object)
Task<Tresult>(Func<Tresult>,object)
```

The object is passed to the Task and the only problem is how to pack the parameters into the object. One of the simplest but by no means the only scheme is to use a value tuple and casting.

For example, function A in the example can be rewritten to allow the start and stop values for the loop to be specified:

```
public void A(object pars)
{
        (int start,int stop) args = ((int start, int stop)) pars;
        for (int i = args.start; i < args.stop; i++)
        {
                Monitor.Enter(MyCountLock);
                count++;
                Monitor.Exit(MyCountLock);
        }
}
```

Notice that we cast the object to a named value tuple and then use its fields. With this definition we a can start a Task with parameters using:

```
Task T1 = new Task(A, (0, 10000000));
T1.Start();
```

You can use the same method to pass any number of parameters of any type.

Getting a result back is even easier. All you have to do is use:

```
Task<Tresult>(Func<Tresult>)
```

or:

```
Task<Tresult>(Func<Tresult>,object)
```

if you also want to pass in parameters.

For example, to make function A return a result we could use:

```
public int A(object pars)
{
        (int start,int stop) args = ((int start, int stop)) pars ;
        for (int i = args.start; i < args.stop; i++)
        {
                Monitor.Enter(MyCountLock);
                count++;
                Monitor.Exit(MyCountLock);
        }
        return count;
}
```

To make use of this we use:

```
Task<int> T1 = new Task<int>(A, (0, 10000000));
T1.Start();
textBox1.Text = T1.Result.ToString();
```

There are many advantages of using the Task class, but it is worth remembering that it is just a light wrapper for a thread. What this means is that you can use all of the locking and similar mechanisms already introduced.

There are lots of other methods and properties that are worth investigating and unless you have a good reason you should use Task in preference to a raw thread. In particular, a Task is cancelable and can therefore serve as the basis for other more abstract features such as async and await and the parallel for.

Postlude

Threads are the key to keeping an application's UI responsive and they are also the way to make servers able to deal with multiple clients at the same time. They are important but difficult to get right. You can use raw threads in C#, but task objects are so much easier and safer. Even so you have to be on the lookout for the unique problems that occur when you try to share resources between active threads. In all cases, simple is better.

Chapter 16

The Invoke Pattern

All of the well-known UI frameworks are single-threaded. The reason is that, when multi-threaded UIs have been attempted before, things didn't work out too well. A single-threaded UI means that only one control in the UI can be updated at any given time and that update is fully completed before another control can begin its update. Such single-threaded UIs are event-driven to make it look as if different parts of the UI were being updated at the same time. An event occurs and the appropriate event handler is called. This performs an update and runs to completion and then another event is handled. This all happens so fast that it looks as if changes are occurring to multiple elements and at the same time.

For Windows Forms and WPF things are a little more complicated as there isn't a single UI thread in the traditional sense. Instead, each control that is created can only be accessed by the thread that created it. In practice, this usually means that the main thread, which is generally used to create all of the controls, is the only thread that can work with the UI and so it becomes the de facto UI thread. Of course, you can think up more complex strategies with different components created by different threads, but even this restricts each component to its own personal UI thread.

When you first start to build apps there is a tendency to simply accept what the IDE creates as a project template and start coding. The problem here is that in many cases the template is for a single-threaded UI and any code you create is run on the UI thread. This isn't a good idea, but it generally works – at first. Later, when the program grows and starts to do significant amounts of work on the UI thread, the user notices that the UI is slowing down, becoming glitchy and generally not providing a good experience. The reason is that the UI thread is being used to do work which has nothing to do with maintaining the UI. Instead of sitting idle, waiting for the next event, the UI thread is actively engaged in accessing data, preparing graphics or calculating the 10000th digit of pi.

At some point the work of the program has to be split off into another thread and then the problem changes from keeping the UI thread free enough to be responsive to getting changes to the UI implemented at all. This problem is caused by the very simple fact that the UI code is single-threaded and not thread safe. What this means is that while it is fine for the UI thread to make any changes to the UI it isn't OK for other threads to interact directly with the UI controls. A non-UI thread can't simply print its results to a TextBox say. Accessing the UI from a non-UI thread is generally called cross-threading and the invoke pattern is a good solution to the problem.

The Workings of Async - The Dispatch Queue

A typical machine will have many threads of execution all managed by the operating system. This is how a machine can seem to be doing more than one thing at a time. If the machine actually has multiple cores then it can really be doing more than one thing at a time because each core can run a thread of execution at the same time. Making use of multiple threads in a reliable and bug-free way is difficult - so difficult that in many cases it is a good idea to confine programs to just one thread.

A C# program has just one default thread of execution – the User Interface, or UI, thread. The reason it is generally called the UI thread is that its sole purpose in life is to look after the User Interface. The UI thread simply responds to events generated by the UI. An event is generally something that happens as a result of what the user does. For example, when the user clicks a button, a click event is generated.

What happens is that the dispatcher maintains a queue of requests generated by UI events. Any event that occurs adds a record to the end of the queue with details of what code should be run as a response to the event. The UI thread takes a request from the front of the queue and runs the code associated with the event. When the event code completes the UI thread returns to the queue and deals with another request.

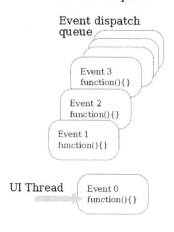

Notice that, once the UI thread starts to execute an event handler, it usually runs to completion before it moves on to deal with another event from the head of the queue. In this sense a simple event handler blocks the UI thread and renders the UI frozen until it releases the UI thread to move on to another event handler.

This continues until the queue is empty and all of the events have been dealt with. The UI thread then just waits for an event to occur.

Empty
Event dispatch
queue

UI Thread waits for event

You can see that this means that the user generates events and your program responds to them as quickly as possible and in the order in which they occur, but not necessarily at once.

If you have understood this simple dispatcher mechanism you should be able to understand a great deal of otherwise strange behavior. For example, if you write an event handler that takes a long time to complete then the user interface will appear to freeze because the UI thread cannot process any more events.

In fact for a responsive UI what you really need is for the UI thread to be idle most of the time just waiting for an event to occur. Whenever you are actually making use of the UI thread within an event handler then the user interface is frozen.

The ideal C# single-threaded program does nothing but wait for a UI event.
The big problem is that as the UI is single-threaded and the only thread you have to do any work is the UI thread, you have to find ways of using it that don't make the user interface freeze up.

As outlined in the previous chapter, C# in common with almost all modern languages has the ability to run more than just the UI thread, but it is worth pointing out that any thread can have its own event queue and can work in the same way as the UI thread. It is also tempting to think that the solution to the problem is to allow multiple threads to work with the UI so that it doesn't freeze if there is a lot of work to do. The problem is that writing reliable multi-threaded programs is difficult. This is the reason that most UIs are single-threaded.

Cross-Threading The UI

If any thread other than the one that created a UI control tries to access it then you will eventually see a cross-thread exception. This is a debug error message designed to help you find problems, but you can also get the exception at run time. Consider this example:

```
public void CountUp()
{
    for (int i = 0; i < 10; i++)
    {
        richTextBox1.Text += i.ToString() + Environment.NewLine;
    }

}

public void CountDown()
{
    for (int i = 10; i > 0; i--)
    {
        richTextBox1.Text += i.ToString() + Environment.NewLine;
    }
}
```

and:

```
Task T1 = Task.Run(CountUp);
Task T2 = Task.Run(CountDown);
```

We also need a richTextBox and probably a button to run the code that starts the Task objects on the form. If you don't want to use Task objects everything in this chapter works with raw threads just as well.

If you run the program you will see something like:

Microsoft Visual Studio

⚠ Exception thrown: 'System.InvalidOperationException' in System.Windows.Forms.dll ⌃

Cross-thread operation not valid: Control 'richTextBox1' accessed from a thread other than the thread it was created on.

If there is a handler for this exception, the program may be safely continued.

☑ Break when this exception type is thrown
Break and open Exception Settings

[Break] [Continue] [Ignore]

Exactly what you see depends on the version of Visual Studio, or more generally the IDE, you are using. You might not even see it at all if the debug environment is set up not to break on the exception.

You can turn off cross-thread checking with:

```
Control.CheckForIllegalCrossThreadCalls = false;
```

Now you can write to any control on the form without any cross-thread exceptions. If you try it out, however, you will discover that `richTextBox` isn't updated and shows blank after the `Task` objects complete. You could spend a long time trying to find out why the update doesn't work, but the `Text` property of a `richTextBox` is a complicated get/set function call and there are many things that could go wrong. Exactly what the problem is depends on the control you try to cross-thread but in most cases sooner or later something does go wrong - much better not to cross-thread at all.

Invoke

The mechanism embodied in `Invoke` is a fairly general way of transferring calls to methods from one thread to another. There are two versions, one for a delegate with no parameters, `Invoke(delegate)`, and another for parameters packaged into an object array, `Invoke(delegate,object[])` where `delegate` can return an `object` which packages a return value if the delegate has one or `null` otherwise. The delegate is placed on the UI thread's dispatcher's queue and is processed along with other events that might have occurred. The best way to think about this is to imagine that the delegate is an event handler that is invoked on the UI thread when its turn comes around. Also notice that `Invoke` is a thread-safe method that every control has just for this purpose.

Basically the idea is that the `T1` and `T2` threads in our example should ask the UI thread to run a method which achieves the desired result using `Invoke`. To do this we first need a new `delegate` type:

```
delegate void Delegate_addtext(string s);
```

There are a number of ways of creating the `delegate` instance and using anonymous methods is one way:

```
public void CountUp()
{
 Delegate_addtext addtext = delegate(string s)
 {
  textBox1.Text+= s+Environment.NewLine;
 };
 for (int i = 0; i < 99; i++)addtext(i.ToString());
}
```

```
public void CountDown()
{
 Delegate_addtext addtext = delegate(string s)
 {
  textBox1.Text+= s+Environment.NewLine;
 };
 for (int i = 99; i >0; i--) addtext(i.ToString());
}
```

Notice that the anonymous methods have to be defined within the form's methods to give them the correct context and access to the form's controls – don't worry, there is a much better way to do the job which is explained later.

Currently we are just using the delegates to do the same job as before and the text box is still being accessed by two threads. If you run the program you will see the same problems as before.

To run the delegate on the UI thread, we need to change the calls to addtext to:

```
Invoke(addtext, new object[] {i.ToString()});
```

We are using object initializers to create an object used to pass the string parameter to the delegate. You have to pack all of the parameters in the correct order within an object array to be passed to the delegate which is invoked on the UI thread.

Now if you run the program you will discover that its behavior is quite different. You get a rock solid complete list of all of the numbers produced by each of the threads. The pattern of thread access also settles down to thread 1, then thread 2, then thread 1, and so on because of the need for each thread to wait for the UI thread to be ready to process the Invoke. Notice that if the UI thread has some work to do after starting the tasks then the invoked delegates will wait until it has finished. It is also possible that events will be handled in between the invoked delegates.

Using Invoke makes the running of the delegate asynchronous, but from the point of view of the thread or task using it the Invoke method is synchronous and blocking. That is when thread 1, say, does:

```
Invoke(addtext,new object[] {i.ToString()});
```

it waits until the addtext delegate finishes running on the UI thread before proceeding.

There is an asynchronous non-blocking form of the Invoke method – BeginInvoke. When called it starts the delegate running on the UI thread and returns immediately to allow the calling thread to continue. The calling thread can get on with other jobs until it detects that the delegate has finished its job.

The simplest way of checking that the delegate has finished is to use
EndInvoke to test the IAsynchResult object returned by the BeginInvoke.
EndInvoke simply blocks until the delegate has finished. So, for example, you
could use something like:

```
IAsyncResult dotext = BeginInvoke(addtext,
                                new object[] { i.ToString() });
    ..get on with some other work
    ...
    ..when ready wait for addtext to end
this.EndInvoke(dotext);
```

Self Invoke

Although this demonstrates the basic invoke mechanism, there is a very
sophisticated way of doing the same job which is described in the
documentation as part of an overlong example. It is so good it's worth
repeating in case you miss it. The idea is that you make use of the
InvokeRequired method which compares the thread ID of the calling thread
to the ID of the creating thread. If they are different then an Invoke is required
but the clever part is the way the same method is used, but restarted on the
UI thread. The reduced version of the example starts:

```
public void addtext2(string s)
{
```

First we check to see if addtext2 is running on the UI thread:

```
if (this.textBox1.InvokeRequired)
{
```

If it isn't running on the UI thread, we wrap in in a delegate and use invoke to
call the addtext2 method again but this time on the UI thread:

```
 Delegate_addtext d =  new Delegate_addtext(addtext2);
 this.Invoke(d,new object[] { s });
}
```

If addtext2 was called on the UI thread, or has not been invoked on the UI
thread, a simple assignment completes the task:

```
else
{
 this.textBox1.Text += s +  Environment.NewLine;
 }
}
```

The complete function is:

```
public void addtext2(string s)
{
        if (this.textBox1.InvokeRequired)
        {
                Delegate_addtext d = new Delegate_addtext(addtext2);
                this.Invoke(d, new object[] { s });
        }
        else
        {
                this.textBox1.Text += s + Environment.NewLine;
        }
}
```

The for loop of each thread now just calls addtext2 without worrying about invoke or the UI thread:

```
addtext2(i.ToString());
```

That is, the new addtext2 method works out if it should have been invoked rather than called and, if it needs to be invoked, wraps itself as a delegate and uses Invoke to run itself on the UI thread.

If you want to give the UI thread time to process events then it's a good idea to add:

```
Application.DoEvents();
```

after updating the text box, but only if you are working with Windows Forms because WPF uses a very different dispatch system and doesn't support anything like a DoEvents method.

Asynchronous calls

The BeginInvoke/EndInvoke methods of running a delegate on the thread that created the control are also available to run any delegate on a thread from the thread pool.

All you have to do is wrap the method in a delegate and use the delegate class's implementation of BeginInvoke/EndInvoke.

For example, we can construct two delegates that do the same tasks as threads T1 and T2 defined earlier:

```
delegate void asyncTask();
asyncTask T1 = delegate()
{
        for (int i = 0; i < 999; i++)
                addtext2(i.ToString()); ;
};

asyncTask T2 = delegate()
{
        for (int i = 999; i > 0; i--)
                addtext2(i.ToString());
};
```

Where `addtext2` is defined as before and uses `Invoke` to run something on the UI thread.

We can use the `delegate Invoke` method to run them synchronously, that is on the same thread that created them, the UI thread.

```
T1.Invoke();
T2.Invoke();
```

In this case T1 completes before T2 begins. To run them on separate threads, i.e. asynchronously, we change `Invoke` to `BeginInvoke`:

```
IAsyncResult R1 =  T1.BeginInvoke(null, null);
IAsyncResult R2 =  T2.BeginInvoke(null, null);
T1.EndInvoke(R1);
T2.EndInvoke(R2);
```

The `EndInvoke` methods simply wait for the delegates to finish.

If you try this out you will discover it doesn't work. All that happens is that the entire program hangs at the first `EndInvoke` – see if you can work out why before reading on.

The reason is that when a thread calls `addText2` this switches execution to the UI thread, but the UI thread is blocked waiting for the tasks to end and so doesn't process the delegate!

This is a good example of deadlock – two threads, the UI and either of T1 or T2, waiting for each other to do something both blocked by the other. The solution is simple – don't block the UI thread. Unfortunately, the simplest way of not blocking the UI thread is to use a callback method to clean up when the thread has finished and this is not always simple.

For example, a suitable callback delegate that can clean up both of the threads is:

```
AsyncCallback C = delegate(IAsyncResult ar)
{
        asyncTask T = (asyncTask)ar.AsyncState;
        T.EndInvoke(ar);
};
```

To make this work we need to call the asynchronous delegates, passing both the callback and the delegate itself as the `ar` parameter:

```
IAsyncResult R1 = T1.BeginInvoke(C,T1);
IAsyncResult R2 = T2.BeginInvoke(C,T2);
```

With this change it all works as advertised.

The Invoke Pattern

You might be wondering why `Invoke` is used to run UI objects on the UI thread. Why not simply use locks to synchronize access to each control so that just one thread can be updating the control at a time? As long as each thread completes before the next one starts there is no danger of leaving the control in a strange, half-completed, state.

The reason for adopting the invoke approach is simply that the UI thread accesses controls as and when it needs to and it isn't going to play by the same rules as any threads that you create and this means that you can't limit access to controls to just one thread using locks, the UI thread will simply ignore them. For locks to work, all of the threads trying to access the resource have to honor the locking mechanism. Any thread that doesn't play by the rules simply makes a mess of the whole enterprise.

The `Invoke` pattern, however, can be implemented so as to force threads to behave nicely when they access an object. The object can test to see which thread is accessing it and throw an exception if it isn't the thread that created it - thus forcing the thread to access it via an Invoke.

This Invoke pattern is useful enough for us to want to know how to use it in our own classes. Put simply, how to you give a class an `Invoke` method that allows a thread to run a delegate on a thread of the class's choice?

The full answer is quite complicated and involves implementing the `ISynchronizeInvoke` interface which includes `Invoke`, `BeginInvoke`, `EndInvoke` and `Invokerequired`.

All controls define the `ISynchronizeInvoke` interface and these are the methods we have been using in this chapter. For simplicity let's restrict ourselves to just an implementation of `Invoke` and also assume that any delegates to be so invoked have no parameters. The extension to parameters and to the other "invoke" methods isn't easy, but it is a lot easier after you have seen the example. The class that implements the `Invoke` is a simple implementation of `Point` with two properties, x and y:

```
public class Point
{
 public int x;
 public int y;
```

We could store the details of the thread that created an instance of the `Point` class, but for this example it's easier to create a new thread to act as a "point worker thread":

```
Private Thread T;
```

that is, thread `T` is the one used to run any delegates that are invoked on the point instance.

If we wanted to use the thread that created the point instance to run the delegate we would have to add code to store the thread's identity and use it to run the delegate. In this case we can keep the thread ready to go because it is dedicated to doing nothing but servicing the instance of the `Point` class.

We need a member variable to hold the delegate to be invoked and an `AutoResetEvent` to use to start it when it has a delegate to invoke and to stop it when there is nothing to do:

```
Delegate _d;
static AutoResetEvent autoEvent;
```

We could have used the thread's `Suspend` and `Resume` methods to start and stop the thread, but these are marked as obsolete since .NET 3.5 and `AutoResetEvent` is now the correct way to control a thread. It can be used as a lock or a signal between threads. Threads can wait on an instance of `AutoResetEvent` using its `WaitOne` method. The instance can be initially set or unset and, when it is set, one thread that is waiting on it will be started and the instance is reset. The instance can be set again by calling its `Set` method.

You can see that `AutoResetEvent` allows a set of threads to wait for a signal, i.e. `Set` being called, and only one will start at a time.

215

The point constructor has to create a delegate, in this case called doInvoke, that it can run on its thread to get the method that is being invoked run on thread T:

```
public Point()
{
        ThreadStart doInvoke = delegate ()
        {
                do
                {
                        autoEvent.WaitOne();
                        _d.DynamicInvoke(null);
                } while (true);
        };
```

Notice that doInvoke is designed to be run on thread T and not the current thread. What happens in the doInvoke is that the thread is immediately suspended, waiting to woken up by another thread setting the AutoResetEvent object. That is, the thread that is going to be used to Invoke the method is suspended to wait for a method to run. When this happens we assume that there is a delegate stored in _d ready to be invoked. We have to use DynamicInvoke because we have no idea what the form of the delegate actually is and hence it has to be late bound. The DynamicInvoke method simply runs the delegate on the current thread, i.e. it is like a dynamic call to the method that the delegate wraps. The rest of the constructor creates the AutoResetEvent in an unset state and then creates and starts the thread T, giving it the doInvoke delegate to run:

```
        autoEvent = new AutoResetEvent(false);
        T = new Thread(doInvoke);
        T.Start();
}
```

You can now see how this is all going to work, but how it all fits together is intricate. We start a new thread running our doInvoke which then simply waits for the AutoResetEvent to be set before running the delegate in _d. The doInvoke delegate only ever runs on thread T and most of the time it is suspended and waiting to be woken up. When it is woken up it runs whatever delegate it finds in _d and then goes back to sleep again.

All that is missing is the invoke method that does the setting of the delegate and the waking up of the thread:

```
public void invoke(Delegate d)
{
     _d = d;
     autoEvent.Set();
     do
     {
           Application.DoEvents();
     }while (T.ThreadState == ThreadState.Running);
}
```

The invoke method simply stores the delegate to be invoked and signals, using autoEvent, that thread T should start running. As invoke is blocking, it then enters a loop to wait for the invoked delegate to complete and thread T to suspend itself again.

You can see that to implement BeginInvoke as a non-blocking invoke all you have to do is return immediately.

That's all there is to the invoke implementation in the Point class. All we need now is some code to try it out and this is very easy. First we create a point instance:

```
point p = new Point();
```

We also need a delegate to invoke:

```
asyncTask update = delegate()
{
 p.x = 10;
 p.y = 20;
};
```

Finally we invoke it:

```
p.invoke(update);
```

When the invoke returns, the x and y properties of the Point object are indeed set to 10 and 20 – and this has been done by thread T running the update delegate.

The extension of these ideas to delegates that pass parameters is easy enough – just pass an object array as in the case of the standard Invoke. The extension to non-blocking invokes is more complicated because you have to allow for the possibility that multiple delegates will be queued for execution. Yes, you need to use a queue to store all of the pending delegates. This complicates matters because you have to control access to the queue and arrange for thread T to empty the queue each time it is woken up. It is more complicated in the details, but the principles are the same.

Getting the invoke pattern and the asynchronous invoke pattern right can be difficult but if you are trying to supply objects which are going to be used by other people it can be very well worth it.

Postlude

The invoke pattern is a very easy way to manage the interaction of other threads with the UI. It reduces the need for other threads to manipulate the UI to events and hence treats them on the same level as all other interactions.

Chapter 17

Async Await

The async/await asynchronous programming facilities in .NET solve one of its longstanding problems - how to write an elegant application that uses the UI correctly. But to avoid problems you still need to understand both the problem and the solution.

As we have seen in the previous chapter, one of the biggest problems facing any Windows Forms, WPF or MAUI programmer is that you can't use the UI thread to do much work. If you do, the result is an unresponsive application. The proper solution is to use a new thread to do all of the heavy computation and leave the UI thread free to get on with what it is supposed to do, deal with user events. However, the computation thread usually has to provide evidence that it has done something and this means that it has to interact with the UI components.

As is well known, UI components aren't thread-safe - hence the rule that only the thread that created a component can access it. You can optionally turn this rule off and allow the worker thread to access the UI, but this isn't a good idea. The correct way, as described in the previous chapter, to allow the worker thread to access the UI is to use the `Invoke` method in the worker thread to ask the UI thread to run a delegate that does the update using data provided by the worker thread. This may be the correct way, but it results in very messy code and, given it is such a common requirement, we really could do with a simpler way of implementing two or more threads working with the UI and this is where `async` and `await` come into the picture.

The `Invoke` method allows a worker thread to run code on the UI thread. This has the advantage of allowing the worker thread to interact with the UI thread when it has something to say. The UI thread is not blocked waiting for the worker thread to complete or have an intermediate result. The async/await method turns this approach on its head and allows the UI thread to run code on another thread in an organized way that doesn't block the UI thread. The problem is that once the UI thread starts a worker thread it somehow has to deal with any result it returns.

Without async/await the only option is to either block the UI thread while the worker thread does its thing or supply a callback that the worker thread can wake up on the UI thread to process the result. The async/await mechanism does the same thing, but much more elegantly. It allows the UI thread to be freed to get on with processing events until the worker thread completes when the UI thread will seem to continue from where it left off. It's an "I'll comeback to you when you are ready" mechanism.

Hands-On Example

Start a new Windows Forms project and place two text boxes and one button - the button will start the process off and the text boxes will record its progress. The example given here will work perfectly with WPF with only changes to the controls and their names.

First let's look at the problem that we are trying to solve. The Button's click event handler calls a method that does a lot of work:

```
private void button1_Click(object sender, EventArgs e)
{
        textBox1.Text = "Click Started";
        DoWork();
        textBox2.Text = "Click Finished";
}
```

You can see that the first two text boxes are changed to show what is happening. For the purpose of this example, DoWork can be simulated by a routine that just loops and so keeps its thread occupied. You get the same overall result if DoWork simply waits for an I/O operation to complete - the important point is that as written it keeps the attention of the UI thread until it is complete. That is:

```
void DoWork()
{
        for (int i = 0; i < 10; i++)
        {
                Thread.Sleep(500);
        }
}
```

keeps the UI thread busy for 5 seconds and to use Thread.Sleep you also have to add:

```
using System.Threading;
```

What do you think you see if you run this program? If you aren't familiar with the way that single-threaded UIs work with a dispatcher, you might think that you see Click Started appear and then, after 5 seconds, Click Finished. What actually happens is that you see both messages appear after the 5 seconds are up, during which time the UI is frozen. The reason for this behavior is simply that the UI is frozen from the moment the DoWork method is called and this is usually before the "Click Started" text has been rendered to the display. This is exactly the reason you don't want any intensive computation on the UI thread - in fact you really don't want any computation on the UI thread at all! The ideal UI thread is idle for most of the time, ready to respond to the user's input.

Async and Await

Now we can look at how to implement this property using async and await. The first thing is to know is that any method that you put async in front of is an asynchronous method, which means it can be started and stopped rather than just run from first to last instruction. We could create a new method and mark it as asynchronous, but to keep the example as much like the synchronous case described above we can simply change the click event handler into an asynchronous method:

```
private async void button1_Click(object sender, EventArgs e)
{
        textBox1.Text = "Click Started";
        DoWork();
        textBox2.Text = "Click Finished";
}
```

If you do this the compiler will complain that you have an asynchronous method without any awaits and so it will run it as a synchronous method anyway. To take advantage of the asynchronous nature of the new event handler we have to await the completion of the DoWork method. However, if you write:

```
private async void button1_Click(object sender, EventArgs e)
{
        textBox1.Text = "Click Started";
        await DoWork();
        textBox2.Text = "Click Finished";
}
```

then the compiler will complain that you can't await a method that returns a void. Any method that you preface with await has to return a Task or a Task<T> object where T is the type it would normally return. In this case as nothing is returned we can use a simple Task object.

The next question is what Task object do we actually return? The answer is that we have to create a Task object that runs the worker code on a different thread. This how the UI thread can be released to do some other work and where the multi-threading comes into the picture. The awaited function generally creates a Task which does the work on another thread and this it

221

returns at once to the awaiting code. Notice that this means that the UI is blocked for all the time it takes to get to the return of the `Task` and clearly this needs to be minimized as much as possible. When the awaited function returns, the UI thread is released and free to get on with whatever events need to be processed. When the `Task` is finished the UI thread continues from the `await`. In this sense the code that comes after the `await` is much like a callback.

There are a number of possible ways of creating a `Task` to do the job, but the simplest is the `Task.Run` method that will take a `delegate` or a lambda expression and run it using a thread from the thread pool.

So the new `DoWork` method is:

```
Task DoWork()
{
        return Task.Run(() =>
            {
                for (int i = 0; i < 10; i++)
                {
                        Thread.Sleep(500);
                }
            });
}
```

You could use a delegate or an anonymous method to define the code to be run, but a lambda expression is so much easier. This completes the conversion of the synchronous implementation to asynchronous.

Now what do you expect to see if you run the program? The answer is you see what you would expect to see by a naive reading of the original program. That is, first you see `Click Started` appear, then there is a 5-second wait and `Click Finished` appears.

This just looks as if the `DoWork` method has been run in a blocking synchronous way, but no. The first program showed what happens if `DoWork` is run in a blocking synchronous way and this is different! If you look at the program more carefully you will also notice that the UI is responsive between the two messages appearing and we have solved the problem of the unresponsive UI.

Inner Workings

So what is happening? Let's take a detailed look. At this point I have to say that the purpose of constructs such as async and await is to hide the details of what is going on behind the scenes, but it still helps have a rough idea of what is happening.

What happens when the user clicks the Button is that the event is added to the dispatcher's queue and the UI thread eventually gets round to processing it. This takes the UI thread to the `button1_Click` event handler and the UI thread updates `textBox1`. This doesn't result in the change being rendered at this point, however.

Next the UI thread starts to execute the `DoWork` method but in this case as it's executed via an `await` within an `async` method it doesn't happen in the usual way. The UI thread creates the `Task` with the lambda expression that does all the work and returns to the event handler.

At this point what happens next might surprise you. When the UI thread returns from `DoWork` the event handler also executes a return and the UI thread goes back to the dispatcher to deal with any events that need dealing with. That is, the `await` frees up the UI thread and puts the event handler into an inactive, waiting, state. If you know the yield command in Ruby, JavaScript and so on you will recognize this as just such an operation.

Of course, all the while the UI thread is dealing with events and generally getting on with other stuff, the instructions in the `Task` that was returned by `DoWork` are being obeyed on the worker thread and so 5 seconds later the `Task` completes.

At this point the need for the UI thread to return to the event handler is added to the dispatcher's queue. Eventually the UI thread reaches this item in the dispatcher's queue and starts executing the event handler from where it left it - i.e. just after the `await`. You might recognize this as a "continuation", a construct found in other languages such as Ruby, Haskell and Scheme.

At this point the second "Click Finished" message is executed and after this the event handler finishes in the usual way and once again the UI thread can return to the dispatcher queue for more things to do.

The await causes the UI thread to return to the calling code, the dispatcher in this case, and then it causes the UI thread to pick up where it left off when the Task completes, i.e. a continuation.

This may sound complicated and it is even more complicated if you inquire a little deeper into how it is all achieved. In particular the state of the event handler has to be saved when the await is obeyed and restored when the event handler resumes. But from the programmer's point of view it looks as if the `await` has run the task in `DoWork` while letting the UI thread get on with other things and then has called the UI thread back to finish the event handler once the `Task` is complete.

Notice that all of the code in the event handler and `DoWork` is run on the UI thread - only the lambda expression in `DoWork` is run on a different thread. To make the point even more forcibly that await simplifies things compare the two versions and their flow of control:

```
private async void button1_Click(object sender, EventArgs e)
{
        textBox1.Text = "Click Started";
        DoWork();
        textBox2.Text = "Click Finished";
}
```

This looks as if it should display the first message, do something for 5 seconds and then display the second message, but of course it doesn't. Adding the `await` command makes it do exactly that:

```
private async void button1_Click(object sender, EventArgs e)
{
        textBox1.Text = "Click Started";
        await DoWork();
        textBox2.Text = "Click Finished";
}
```

In the second case the apparent flow of control through the event handler coincides with what it appear to be.

Pitfalls and Dangers

If you have used the DoEvents command in Visual Basic or some other event-handling construct in other languages, you might see that this is a very similar mechanism in that it allows the UI thread to process the Dispatch queue, but also notice that this is more sophisticated in that another thread is used to do the work.

Just as there were dangers in using DoEvents and similar constructs, there are even more dangers in using `async/await`. For example, as the UI stays responsive, the user can click the same button more than once and create multiple tasks. Usually this is not a good idea and so the event handler usually disables the button while the task is running:

```
private async void button1_Click(object sender, EventArgs e)
{
        button1.IsEnabled = false;
        await DoWork();
        button1.IsEnabled = true;
}
```

If you try writing this simple idea using threads and callbacks you will see just how neat the `async/await` pattern is.

This example just gets us started because it raises a few questions of its own. In particular, we still have the problem of allowing the worker code to update the UI. The key factor is that the event handler can update the UI each time it is restarted so we could use an approach where the work is broken into chunks which return to the event handler for an update, for example:

```
private async void button1_Click(object sender, EventArgs e)
{
        button1.IsEnabled = false;
        await DoWork();
        textBox1.Text = "First work done";
        await DoWork();
        textBox2.Text = "second work done";
        button1.IsEnabled = true;
}
```

In this case what happens is that DoWork runs for 5 seconds and then summons the UI thread back to continue the event handler from where it left off. This results in the text First work done being displayed. Then the second await lets the UI thread get on with processing the Dispatcher queue, only to be called back to continue from where it left off 5 seconds later. Hence we see the second work done update message.

You could break work down into chunks like this, and even put the chunks into a for loop, say, to automate the process:

```
private async void button1_Click(object sender, EventArgs e)
{
        button1.IsEnabled = false;
        for (int i = 0; i < 5; i++)
        {
                await DoWork();
                textBox1.Text = "Chunk "+i.ToString();
        };
        button1.IsEnabled = true;
}
```

However, if all you want to do is report the progress of a longer computation via the UI, then there is an alternative way of doing the job by passing in a method that can be called on the UI thread by the worker.

Getting Results

An even more important issue, however, is how the worker thread can return a result. For simplicity all of the examples so far have returned void, but in real life the worker usually returns some value, usually a complex object. Getting results back turns out to be remarkably easy.

To return a type T we simply change the Task to Task<T> and return a T at the end of the code run on the worker thread. For example, to return an int from DoWork you would write:

```
Task<int> DoWork()
{
    return TaskEx.Run(() =>
        {
            for (int i = 0; i < 10; i++)
                {
                    Thread.Sleep(500);
                };
            return 500;
        });
}
```

where the code run on the new thread returns 500 just to show that it works.

In the asynchronous method we simply call the new DoWork in the obvious way:

```
int result=await DoWork();
textBlock1.Text = result.ToString();
```

Notice that there are a few points of potential confusion.

The return type of DoWork is stated as Task<int> yet it actually seems to return an int to the calling routine. Also there now appear to be two returns in DoWork, the one that returns the Task<int> and the one that returns the int, but of course these are in separate functions run on different threads. If you have followed how all of this works then this should seem understandable, if potentially confusing.

The key idea is that the awaited function should return a Task as soon as possible and the Task runs on its own thread, while the UI thread gets on with running the UI, and eventually returns the final result.

Postlude

This is a brief introduction to the ideas of async and await. There are also lots of other facilities such as a cancellation mechanism, a progress reporting mechanism and so on that make the whole even more flexible. There is no single more important change to the way that asynchronous code is written than the introduction of async and await.

Chapter 18

The Parallel For

So far in our exploration of asynchronous code we have considered parallel execution without necessarily executing anything at the same time. Today's processors, however, have multiple cores and this means that it is possible to actually run threads in parallel and so hopefully speed things up. Asynchronous code is mostly about keeping the UI responsive by dividing the processor's attention between servicing the UI and doing useful work. True parallelism has the attraction of speeding up the useful work and thus is attractive even without considering the responsiveness of the UI.

The .NET parallel extensions are great. They are easy to use and provide a huge payback – but, and this is a big but, parallel programming isn't easy. If it was we would be using it all over the place and the parallel extensions would be nothing new.

Making parallel code easier to use is an important development, but making it easier also means you can use it without realizing what you are getting into. By being easy to use, `Parallel.For` encourages programmers who might never consider adding additional threads to their code simply because it promises to get the job done faster. Unless we can find a way of making parallel code both easy and safe you are still going to have to take care.

Parallel Race Condition

While we have looked at the problems of sharing resources in earlier chapters which applies to all asynchronous and true parallel methods, there is an addition problem with true parallel algorithms. Put simply trying to turn a sequential algorithm into a parallel one introduces the possibility that the algorithm will interact with itself in ways that aren't entirely obvious.

Parallelism is easy if you restrict your attention to completely unrelated tasks. If you have task A which has nothing to do with task B, then you can simply say to a processor "*get on with task A*" and to another processor "*get on with task B*". For example, if you have a shopping list then you can tear it in two and give one to shopper A and one to shopper B and tell them both to do the shopping at the same time. When they meet up at the checkout there is no problem and the shopping is done in half the time.

Things start to go wrong when the tasks are interrelated. For example, if the top half of the shopping list says *"buy bread"* and the bottom half says *"if you bought some bread buy some jam"*, there are problems. Now when you tear the list into two and hand the halves to shopper A and B what you get at the checkout varies – sometimes you get bread and no jam, sometimes bread and jam, and very rarely jam and no bread when shopper A picks up a loaf, but at the last minute notices it's stale and puts it back without getting another one.

If the list is processed by a single shopper buying things in the order the list specifies, there is no problem. As soon as you split the list then what you get depends on how the two tasks interact. Of course this is just another manifestation of the shared resource problem and the race conditions that can arise when it isn't clear what order things will happen in. What is new is that now we have the extra concern of how you split a sequential algorithm into portions that it is safe to execute in parallel. Until recently this is a problem that the average programmer could avoid by not trying to write parallel programs, but now C# has the `Parallel.For` construction it is very easy to convert a sequential algorithm into a parallel one without a moment's extra thought.

The Parallel For In Action

The `Parallel.For` loop makes it so easy that you can start parallel programming in a few minutes - no threads, no tasks, nothing at all that looks any different from normal programming. When you get a little deeper you discover that you have to do things like lock shared resources and so on, but problems can arise much earlier and at a much more basic level if you haven't thought about the consequences of implementing something in parallel.

To see parallel programming in action start a new C# project and add:

```
using System.Threading;
using System.Threading.Tasks;
```

`System.Threading` is the original threading library and `System.Threading.Tasks` is where the newer parallel features live.

Next place a button on a form and write a simple for loop in its click event handler:

```
int size = 1000000;
double[] data = new double[size];
Stopwatch sw = new Stopwatch();
sw.Start();
for (int i = 0; i < size; i++){
        data[i] = Math.Pow(new Random().NextDouble(), 0.6);
}
MessageBox.Show("done " + sw.Elapsed.TotalMilliseconds.ToString());
sw.Reset();
```

The loop simply does some arithmetic on a lot of random data. The Stopwatch class, which can record time accurately across multiple threads, is used to time how long the loop takes and to make use of this very useful class all you need to add is:

```
using System.Diagnostics;
```

We can turn this loop into a parallel loop very easily. The Parallel static class has a For method which accepts the start and end value for the loop and a delegate to execute. In general the command is:

```
Parallel.For(start,end,delegate);
```

The loop is run from *start* to *end-1* and must run in the forward direction, that is from smaller to bigger index values. There are variations on the Parallel.For command, including parameters to control the parallel iteration and a Parallel.ForEach, and the problem that we are about to encounter can happen with all of them.

The simplest way to provide the delegate is to use a lambda expression and so the following example will execute the code for values of i from 0 to size-1.

```
int size = 1000000;
double[] data = new double[size];
Stopwatch sw = new Stopwatch();
sw.Start();
Parallel.For(0, size, i => {
        data[i] = Math.Pow(new Random().NextDouble(), 0.6);
});
sw.Stop();
MessageBox.Show("done " + sw.Elapsed.TotalMilliseconds.ToString());
sw.Reset();
```

This all works and the results are impressive. On a dual-core machine the simple loop takes around 4000ms and the parallel loop takes 2500ms, which isn't quite half but still represents a very worthwhile speed up. If you use the Task Manager or the diagnostic tools to monitor CPU usage, you will see that the simple loop uses 100% of one of the cores while the parallel loop uses

229

100% of both cores. This in itself might not exactly be a good thing, as our parallel loop is a bit of a processor hog, but these are the sort of simple decisions that have to be made.

The bottom line is that the Parallel.For is very easy to use and produces a real gain in performance. It provides a lot for very little effort. However, it comes with its own set of dangers. We have just seen that it has apparently converted a loop that takes 6 seconds to one that takes 3 seconds, which is like doubling the machine's speed for free. However, unless you realize this isn't magic then there could be problems ahead.

You can't just convert any old for loop to a Parallel.For and expect everything to work – it only works if the for loop is essentially a set of independent operations. This sounds easy, but it can be difficult to spot because parallel implementation can render everything you have come to expect simply wrong.

Accessing Earlier Results

To show this in action let's implement the equivalent of the bread and jam shopping list. It is a truth drummed into every programmer by experience that if you have a for loop going in the positive direction then it is often perfectly safe to access the results of earlier iterations.

That is, if you have reached *index* in the loop it is OK to look at the result of *index*-1, or *index*-2 and so on, but this isn't the case in a Parallel.For.

Change the simple for loop to:

```
bool flag = true;
for (int i = 0; i < size; i++){
    data[i] = 1;
    if (data[new Random().Next(i)] == 0.0)
        flag = false;
}
MessageBox.Show(flag.ToString());
```

The second statement in the loop checks to see if an earlier element in the array is zero. The method Random().Next(i) generates a random integer in the range 0 to less than i. As the loop progresses from data[0] to data[size] then when you reach data[i] all array elements from data[0] up to data[i] have been set to a non-zero value i.e. 1. That is, if you run this loop you are guaranteed to see flag = true.

The same algorithm used with a `Parallel.For` is much trickier. Consider:

```
Parallel.For(0, size, i => {
      data[i] = 1;
      if (data[new Random().Next(i)] == 0.0)
            flag = false;
});
MessageBox.Show(flag.ToString());
```

In this case the order in which the elements are processed isn't guaranteed and in most cases there will be an earlier element that hasn't yet been processed and so the result is usually `flag = false`. However, notice that the actual situation is much worse than simply getting a different answer. It is possible that the order of evaluation will be such that all of the tested elements are non-zero and in this case the result will, very occasionally, be `flag = true` and so the outcome isn't even predictable – it's a race condition and this makes it non-deterministic. The result of the program can vary each time you run it as if its outcome was random.

No Fix!

The random nature of a program plagued by a race condition is often put down to an intermittent hardware fault, but notice that there is no easy remedy for this problem. It isn't a problem due to locking or the use of a shared resource or any other fixable problem. The algorithm that you are trying to implement needs to access the data in a particular order and a parallel implementation doesn't promise to evaluate in any particular order which means that the algorithm is inherently not parallel. You might be able to re-cast the algorithm in form that is suitable for parallel implementation but as its stands it just doesn't work.

This order of evaluation problem is, of course, the reason why you only get a forward implementation of `Parallel.For`, i.e. 1,2,3 4... and not a reverse form of a loop, i.e. ...4,3,2,1 As the order of evaluation isn't fixed, it would be a nonsense to let you specify it in reverse order. Any algorithm that requires a loop with a particular order isn't inherently parallel.

The only type of `Parallel.For` that is free of this problem is one that doesn't manipulate the index, i.e. all expressions are indexed by i and not, say, i+1 or i-3, etc.

Notice that this doesn't mean that the `Parallel.For` is useless or even very primitive. `Parallel.For` is doing a great deal of work on your behalf. It is choosing how to partition the loop, creating the threads necessary, running the partitions one per thread and making sure that everything waits until the final thread completes the task. If you were to try to implement it from scratch you would need to generate a lot of code. This is a great simplification over the DIY version and `Parallel.For` is well worth using. But at the end of the day you are still using separate threads to run different portions of the `for` loop and as such all of the usual problems arise and it is up to you to keep them under control.

A simple-minded approach is to restrict the use of `Parallel.For` to tasks that are truly isolated from one another and never do anything adventurous, but that would simply be missing an opportunity. There are algorithms that can be implemented using a `Parallel.For`, but they need some attention to resource sharing in the same way that a raw threads solution would. It is worth mentioning that the `Parallel.ForEach` loop suffers from the same problems and so does `Parallel.Invoke`, which runs an array of `Action` delegates possibly in parallel.

Postlude

Making concurrency easier is a good thing, but with it comes the usual set of new difficulties that we always encounter when multiple threads of execution are employed. The real danger is that, unless you know better, you can be led into believing that somehow the new features solve the old problems – they don't.

V Data - LINQ, XML & Regular Expressions

Prelude

All programming languages need to work with data and C# has some of the best data features around. LINQ is a general-purpose data query language built right into the core of C#. It provides a way to work with XML that is unique. The final jewel in C#'s data abilities are its regular expressions, which are more powerful than you might expect.

Chapter 19

The LINQ Principle

Language-Integrated Query (LINQ) isn't just for SQL, it's for languages. It is worth finding out how LINQ works at the most basic level and how it can be useful as a general language construct, even if you aren't using a database. LINQ may look like SQL, but this just a convenience so that LINQ can be used by people too lazy to learn new syntax.

You need to think of LINQ as an attempt to bring "querying" type operations into the mainstream of the .NET language of your choice. LINQ isn't really about database, this just happens to be a really good use of it. It's a general purpose and extensible approach to working with structured data. In a more general setting you can think of it as yet another aspect of the way functional programming is making its way into .NET.

A query is basically an operation where you specify a subset of the data that you actually want to work with. In many ways you can think of "querying" as the point where software creation becomes complicated and the real world enters the design problem. Put simply, data is messy, usually not organized in a way that suits and the task is always more difficult and fragile than you could possibly imagine. LINQ can't do anything about the inherent complexity of querying data, but it does deliver it in a uniform and integrated format.

The key idea is that LINQ is a set of classes and methods that will work with any class as a data source as long as it implements the `IEnumerable<T>` interface. As, in a sense, this is the foundation on which the rest of LINQ is built, it is a good place to start. In fact, it is probably a good idea to take one step further back and look at the whole idea of enumerators.

Implementing An Enumerator

The basic idea of an enumerator is to supply each item in a collection of data items one-by-one and usually in no specified order. In .NET an enumerator is a class that provides a number of methods in addition to the basic one-by-one enumeration of the items.

To be specific an enumerator has to supply:

- Reset – initializes the enumeration so that it starts over again
- Current – returns the current item
- MoveNext – updates the index to the next item

Of course, this all implies that there is a numeric index to the current item which starts off set to –1 to indicate that it "points" before the start of the collection. Calling Current repeatedly is allowed, but if the index is invalid then you are supposed to throw an exception. MoveNext returns true if the result is a valid index and false if the resulting index isn't pointing to a valid item. Put together these three methods make up the IEnumerator interface and any class that supports enumeration does so by implementing this interface.

You don't have to use a separate class to implement IEnumerator, you can do the job in the same class that implements the inner workings of the data collection if that's convenient. It is more usual to create the enumerator as a separate class and write a constructor that creates an instance of the enumerator ready to be use.

A Simple Enumerator

To see the simplest possible example of an enumerator, let's create everything in a single class. Our example is also going to be a little strange with regard to data collection in that no collection of data ever exists. Instead when the collection is instantiated the constructor is supplied with the size of the collection and from then on a random number generator is used each time a data item is required. This is clearly not very useful for anything other than testing, hence the name of the class:

```
class TestCollection:IEnumerator
```

Generating random data also has the advantage that the example doesn't use any of the existing collection data types which all supply enumerators and hence tend to confuse the issue. TestCollection doesn't make use of anything pre-built in the .NET framework to implement its enumerator.

To make it work you need to add:

```
using System.Collections;
```

To get us started we need some private variables, something to hold the instance of the random number generator, something to store the size of the collection and, of course, an index to the current position in the collection:

```
{
        private Random rnd;
        private int Size;
        private int loc = -1;
```

We need the constructor to set everything up ready for the collection to be enumerated:

```
public TestCollection(int s)
{
        rnd = new Random();
        Size = s;
}
```

Now we have to implement the methods of the IEnumerator interface. The reset method is simply:

```
void IEnumerator.Reset()
{
        this.loc = -1;
}
```

You don't really need the this, but it helps to emphasize the fact that the enumerator works with the instance.

The Current method takes the form of a read-only property:

```
object IEnumerator.Current
{
        get
        {
                if (this.loc > -1)
                        return this.rnd.Next(500);
                else
                        return -1;
        }
}
```

Notice that Current returns an object rather than an int. This is how it has to be as the interface defines the Current method in this way. Ideally we would like to return a result of a specified type, but without generics, which we have explicitly chosen to ignore, this is difficult. More about this problem later as to use LINQ we have no choice but to use a generic enumerator.

In principle, we should test to make sure loc is sensible, i.e. it actually indexes an element of the collection and throws an exception if it doesn't. In this case we simply return −1. In most cases, whatever is using the enumerator usually stops enumeration when the MoveNext method returns false to indicate that there is no next item:

```
bool IEnumerator.MoveNext()
{
        loc++;
        if (loc < this.Size)
                return true;
        else
                return false;
}
```

Now we have the complete enumerator and it's very easy to see how it works, but we can't as yet make use of it.

IEnumerable

The reason is that any class offering an enumerator has to also implement the IEnumerable interface. This has just a single method GetEnumerator which returns the instance of the class that provides the methods of the IEnumerator.

If you think about it for a moment it is obvious that IEnumerable has to be implemented by the data collection class that holds the items to be enumerated so we have to add it to the class definition:

```
class TestCollection:IEnumerator,IEnumerable
{
```

The single method that we have to implement is trivial as the instance of the TestCollection class concerned provides its own enumerators, i.e. it is the enumerator to be returned:

```
 IEnumerator IEnumerable.GetEnumerator()
 {
        return  this;
 }
}
```

The complete class is:

```
class TestCollection : IEnumerator, IEnumerable
{
        private Random rnd;
        private int Size;
        private int loc = -1;

        public TestCollection(int s)
        {
                rnd = new Random();
                Size = s;
        }

        void IEnumerator.Reset()
        {
                this.loc = -1;
        }

        object IEnumerator.Current
        {
                get
                {
                        if (this.loc > -1)
                                return this.rnd.Next(500);
                        else
                                return -1;
                }
        }

        bool IEnumerator.MoveNext()
        {
                loc++;
                if (loc < this.Size)
                        return true;
                else
                        return false;
        }

        IEnumerator IEnumerable.GetEnumerator()
        {
                return this;
        }
}
```

Now we can write some code that makes use of our data collection with enumeration. The simplest thing to try out is a `foreach` loop:

```
TestCollection col = new TestCollection(5);
foreach (object o in col)
{
    MessageBox.Show(o.ToString());
}
```

Notice that the iterator `o` has to be defined as an `object`. We can use an `int` in the `foreach` loop as it supports implicit casting. For example:

```
foreach (int o in col)
{
    MessageBox.Show(o.ToString());
}
```

works perfectly unless you happen to return something that can't be cast to an `int` at run time with the result that an exception is raised. If you want to do better then you need to change the enumeration interfaces to their generic forms, which is what we have to do anyway to use LINQ.

Separating The Enumerator

Before moving on it is worth commenting on why we usually implement the enumerator as a separate class. Consider what happens if we try to use the current enumerator in a nested `foreach` loop? The same enumerator would be returned by `GetEnumerator` and hence the nested loops would interfere with each other. If you want to write nested loops or allow multiple enumerations to happen concurrently you need to implement the enumerator as a separate class and you need to create an instance of that class each time an enumerator is called for by `GetEnumerator`.

As nesting of queries is very common we need to do the job properly before moving on to consider LINQ. All we need to do is separate out the enumeration methods into a new class. This class has to keep track of where it is in the enumeration and it needs to keep track of which instance of the collection it is enumerating:

```
class TestCollectionEnumerator:IEnumerator
{
    private TestCollection m_Instance;
    private int loc = -1;
```

If you create the enumeration class as an inner class of the data collection, i.e. `TestCollection`, it will have access to all of the data collection's variables and methods and this makes it easier for the two classes to work together.

The only new method we need is a constructor that initializes the enumerator with the current instance of the data collection:

```
public TestCollectionEnumerator(TestCollection Instance)
{
        m_Instance = Instance;
}
```

The other enumeration methods now have to use m_Instance instead of this to make sure they work with the correct instance of the data:

```
void IEnumerator.Reset()
{
        loc = -1;
}
object IEnumerator.Current
{
        get
        {
                if (loc > -1)
                        return m_Instance.rnd.Next(500);
                else
                        return -1;
        }
}
bool IEnumerator.MoveNext()
{
        loc++;
        if (loc < m_Instance.Size)
                return true;
        else
                return false;
}
```

We also need to change the data collection class so that its GetEnumerator actually creates a new instance of the enumerator:

```
class TestCollection:IEnumerable
{
        private Random rnd;
        private int Size;
        IEnumerator IEnumerable.GetEnumerator()
        {
                return new TestCollectionEnumerator(this);
        }
```

Notice how the use of this makes the final connection between the instance and any number of enumerators that are generated.

Now our example code is slightly more complicated, but you can use it within nested foreach loops and, as we shall see, nested LINQ queries.

The complete class is:

```
class TestCollection : IEnumerable
{
        protected Random rnd;
        private int Size;
        public TestCollection(int s)
        {
                rnd = new Random();
                Size = s;
        }
        IEnumerator IEnumerable.GetEnumerator()
        {
                return new TestCollectionEnumerator(this);
        }
        class TestCollectionEnumerator : IEnumerator
        {
                private TestCollection m_Instance;
                private int loc = -1;
                public TestCollectionEnumerator(
                                        TestCollection Instance)

                        m_Instance = Instance;
                }
                void IEnumerator.Reset()
                {
                        loc = -1;
                }
                object IEnumerator.Current
                {
                        get
                        {
                                if (loc > -1)
                                        return m_Instance.rnd.Next(500);
                                else
                                        return -1;
                        }
                }
                bool IEnumerator.MoveNext()
                {
                        loc++;
                        if (loc < m_Instance.Size)
                                return true;
                        else
                                return false;
                }
        }

}
```

Generic Enumeration

It is generally better to use a generic form of the interfaces so add to the start of the program:

```
using System.Collections.Generic;
```

The generic form of the IEnumerator interface inherits from the non-generic IEnumerator interface.

Note that when an interface inherits from another interface, for example IA:IB then when you add IA to a class it's exactly the same as writing :IA,IB and you have to implement the methods of IA and IB. This sounds bad as it now looks as if we are going to have to implement both the non-generic and generic forms of the interface. Fortunately, the generic interface only extends the non-generic interface by one method.

The generic form of the IEnumerator interface defines a single generic version of Current, after all this is the only method that needs to use the data type. To complicate things a little, it also inherits the Dispose method from IDisposable, but we can ignore this at the moment by adding a null implementation.

The generic form of the IEnumerable interface simply adds a generic form of GetEnumerator. So to make our class use the generic interface all we have to do is change its definition to:

```
class TestCollection : IEnumerable,IEnumerable<int>
```

and add to it a second generic GetEnumerator method:

```
IEnumerator<int> IEnumerable<int>.GetEnumerator()
{
        return new TestCollectionEnumerator(this);
}
```

The enumerator class also has to implement the generic interface:

```
class TestCollectionEnumerator:IEnumerator<int>
{
        rest of class definition
```

and has to have two new methods added to it. The first is:

```
int IEnumerator<int>.Current{
 get
 {
        if (loc > -1)
                return m_Instance.rnd.Next(500);
        else
                return -1;
 }
}
```

The second:

```
void IDisposable.Dispose()
{
}
```

Notice that you have to keep the existing non-generic implementations and that the new generic method is almost identical to its non-generic version apart from the use of the int data type. Now you can write:

```
foreach (int o in col)
{
        MessageBox.Show(o.ToString());
}
```

The complete class is:

```
class TestCollection : IEnumerable,IEnumerable<int>
{
        protected Random rnd;
        private int Size;

        public TestCollection(int s)
        {
                rnd = new Random();
                Size = s;
        }
        IEnumerator IEnumerable.GetEnumerator()
        {
                return new TestCollectionEnumerator(this);
        }
        IEnumerator<int> IEnumerable<int>.GetEnumerator()
        {
                return new TestCollectionEnumerator(this);
        }

        class TestCollectionEnumerator : IEnumerator<int>
        {
                private TestCollection m_Instance;
                private int loc = -1;

                public TestCollectionEnumerator(
                                        TestCollection Instance)
                {
                        m_Instance = Instance;
                }
                void IEnumerator.Reset()
                {
                        loc = -1;
                }
```

```
    object IEnumerator.Current
    {
        get
        {
            if (loc > -1)
                    return m_Instance.rnd.Next(500);
            else
                    return -1;
        }
    }


    int IEnumerator<int>.Current
    {
        get
        {
            if (loc > -1)
                    return m_Instance.rnd.Next(500);
            else
            return -1;
        }
    }
    void IDisposable.Dispose()
    {
    }
    bool IEnumerator.MoveNext()
    {
        loc++;
        if (loc < m_Instance.Size)
                return true;
        else
                return false;
    }
    }
    }
}
```

LINQ and Extension Methods

Now we have a simple generic IEnumerable class we can start to use LINQ
with it – and it really is this simple. What the LINQ system does it to add
extension methods, something we have already encountered in Chapter 7, to
the IEnumerable generic interface. For the moment just accept the fact that
there are a large number of additional methods available to any class that
implemented the IEnumerable generic interface and most of these return an

IEnumerable object - which is a more important observation than you might think. To make use of the extension methods you need to add:

```
using System.Linq;
```

To get started, let's look at the Where extension method. If you look at its definition you will discover that it is:

```
public static IEnumerable<T> Where<T>(this, IEnumerable<T> source,
                                      Func<T, bool> predicate
)
```

Ignore the this for the moment because it's part of every extension method.

The parameter, source, is an IEnumerable that will be "scanned" for all of the entities that predicate returns true for. The predicate is just a generic delegate that "wraps" a function that accepts a single input parameter of the first specified type and returns a result of the second specified type. In this case predicate can be seen to accept a single parameter of type T and return a Boolean result. If we are going to use Where the first thing we need is a suitable predicate. This can be created in many ways, but to keep the explanation simple let's do it the old-fashioned, but rather long-winded, way of first defining a suitable function and then wrapping it in a delegate.

First define the function:

```
bool MyTest(int i)
{
        return i > 250;
}
```

This simply tests to see if the value is greater than 250 and returns true if so and false otherwise. To make use of this we have to first wrap it in a delegate:

```
Func<int, bool> MyDelegate = new Func<int, bool>(MyTest);
```

Next we create the data collection as before:

```
TestCollection col = new TestCollection(5);
```

And finally use the Where method with the delegate we have defined:

```
IEnumerable<int> q = col.Where<int>(MyDelegate);
```

If you try this out nothing happens. This is because LINQ queries are nearly always lazy-evaluated, that is the operation of enumerating and extracting the entities smaller than 250 is only performed when it is required.

In practice evaluation is triggered by calling the generic GetEnumerator method, usually within a foreach loop.

For example:

```
foreach (int o in q)
{
        MessageBox.Show(o.ToString());
}
```

To emphasize, the results of the query are only stored in q when we start the foreach loop.

The complete main program is:

```
bool MyTest(int i)
{
        return i > 250;
}
Func<int, bool> MyDelegate = new Func<int, bool>(MyTest);

TestCollection col = new TestCollection(5);
IEnumerable<int> q = col.Where<int>(MyDelegate);
foreach (int o in q)
{
        MessageBox.Show(o.ToString());
}
```

And remember you need to add:

```
using System.Linq;
```

You should find this pleasing and exciting. The LINQ extension functions have been added to a class that you have created that simply implements IEnumerable. You have not just a collection of data, but a collection that you can query and manipulate in quite complex ways. Of course, there are many facilities in C# that can make using the Where query much simpler, but this is LINQ in the raw and it illustrates exactly how it all works. It also makes it clear how clever the idea is and demonstrates that LINQ isn't just SQL added to C#.

There are lots of other extension methods and, as they all extend IEnumerator and as they all return an object of type IEnumerator, you can simply chain them together. For example, to apply a second Where condition to the same query you would write something like:

```
IEnumerable<int> q = col.
            Where<int>(MyDelegate1).
                Where<int>(MyDelegate2);
```

If you look up the range of extension methods provided you will see that it's very easy to build up complicated queries and as it's also easy to add your own extension methods to make LINQ capable of whatever query you want it to.

Syntactic Sugar

So far the LINQ query example given above doesn't look a great deal like any other LINQ example you will find in the documentation and the reason is that it doesn't use any of the syntactic sugar introduced to make LINQ look more like SQL and to make it generally easier to use. Now the time has come to add such finishing touches and package it all up.

The first simplification is that we can use a lambda expression to create the predicate method. This makes it possible to do away with the separate function and write something that looks like a condition as a parameter to most of the extension methods. If you recall from Chapter 14, a lambda expression is a function without a name that returns a single value and can be assigned directly to a delegate. For example:

```
Func<int, bool> MyDelegate2 = i => i > 250;
```

creates a delegate that can be used in the call to `Where` just as in the previous example. However, as the `Where` method has a parameter of type `Func(int,bool)`, we can do the job directly without the need to create an explicit delegate:

```
IEnumerable<int> q = col.Where<int>(i => i > 250);
```

With this simple change the query is beginning to look a lot more like SQL. We can also go one better. It is up to each .NET language to choose to provide a linguistic wrapper for the LINQ system and they can do it however they like. In practice, there is a lot of sense in using something close to a dialect of SQL. C# and VB both wrap LINQ with SQL-like instructions. For example, our simple query can be written:

```
IEnumerable<int> q = from i in col where i > 250 select i;
```

This is compiled to the same set of method calls given earlier and is completely equivalent.

You can even make is slightly simpler by allowing the compiler to work out the type of `q` from the return result of the method calls, i.e. use an anonymous type:

```
var q = from i in col where i > 250 select i;
```

Now you can see why these features were introduced to C#.

In general, a LINQ query expression always starts with:

```
from variable in IEnumerable object
```

This specifies the object to be used in the query and the parameter to be passed to all of the methods, the "range" variable. Then there's a wide choice of possible clauses which correspond to each of the extension methods and, when used, cause them to be called with the parameters and predicates specified. Finally, every LINQ query expression has to end with a select. The select is easy to use, but often not so easy to understand how it is implemented. The idea is that select performs a projection or transformation on the basic data item used in the query. That is, it takes a data type and projects it to a "smaller" subtype. This idea deserves a deeper explanation.

Custom Select

The nature of the select depends on the nature of the data item. For example, if the item takes the form of a row of a table then a select can pick out individual columns. If the data item is an array then it can select individual elements.

You can see that selecting part of the data item could be a complex operation. It helps greatly to know how LINQ works in terms of extension methods in understanding what it does and how to make use of it. For example the definition of one overlay of the Select extension method is:

```
public static IEnumerable<TResult>  Select<TSource, TResult>(
     this IEnumerable<TSource> source,
        Func<TSource, TResult> selector)
```

You can clearly see that you have to specify a source type and a result type and a function that does the conversion between the two types.

When you write a C# query expression using Select all you do is specify the transformation function and let the compiler work out the types of the source and result data. For example:

```
var q = from i in col
      where i > 250
              select i*2;
```

The final select now creates a function:

```
Func<int, int> MySelect=i->i*2;
```

and passes the call to the Select method, as a lambda expression:

```
var q = col.Where<int>(i => i > 250).Select<int,int>(i=>i*2);
```

A little thought reveals that this mechanism is more sophisticated than it looks. For example, you can call methods defined in the source data type to perform more complicated data transformations such as:

```
var q2 = col.Where<int>(i => i > 250).
                    Select<int,string>(i=>i.ToString());
foreach (string o in q2)
{
      MessageBox.Show(o);
}
```

Of course, you can add custom methods to the class that do much more by way of conversion and manipulation.

More Selection

Understanding how the query expression is converted into calls to the query extension methods greatly clarifies how LINQ works and what you can do with it. If you want to stay with a clear design you should always use Select as a "projection operator". That is, it should reduce the data item to something that is a subset of itself. For example, if the data item is a struct then the select should specify which fields are to be extracted and returned in a "smaller" struct. This is a common and interesting task so let's look at another simple example. First we need a class or struct to hold the data:

```
public struct Contact
{
        public string name { get; set; }
        public string address1 { get; set; }
        public int phone { get; set; }
}
```

The default property implementations are just enough code to allow us to initialize a List of such structs directly:

```
List<Contact> AddressBook= new List<Contact>(){
        new Contact(){
                name="mike",
                address1="Anywhere1",
                phone=123},
        new Contact(){
                name="Ian",
                address1="Anywhere2",
                phone=124},
        new Contact(){
                name="john",
                address1="Anywhere3",
                phone=125}
        };
```

As List supports IEnumerator we can now move immediately to using LINQ to query it. To extract a single field, say name, you would use a query something like:

```
var q = from N in AddressBook select N.name;
foreach(var n in q)
{
        MessageBox.Show(n);
}
```

Notice the use of var to avoid having to state the data type. If you don't want to use an anonymous type then you can replace var with string.

It is easy to see how this translates to the call to the select extension method which has to return just the single field as a string, but how do you return multiple fields? The problem is that you don't have a data type, i.e. a struct, that holds a subset of fields. You could define a suitable struct, but the standard solution is to create a new anonymous type on the fly:

```
var q = from N in AddressBook select new { N.name, N.phone };
foreach ( var n in q)
{
      MessageBox.Show(n.name.ToString + n.phone.ToString());
}
```

You can see that these "dynamic" facilities are required to make LINQ look simple.

Postlude

Basically we have been looking at LINQ to objects, but the same principles apply to all the other implementations - LINQ to SQL, XML and ADO, for example. You should now be in a position to see how these work, even if you still need to dig out the details. What is even more impressive is that if you have a data source that LINQ doesn't support, you should be able to add it by implementing IEnumerable.

LINQ is such a powerful and compact way of working with data that many suggest it should be used in place of alternative methods of processing. In other words, use a LINQ expression in favor of a foreach loop whenever possible.

251

C# has some really easy-to-use facilities for creating and editing XML, eXtensible Markup Language. Many of these facilities were introduced to make LINQ to XML work better, but you can make use of them in more general situations. There always was good XML support in .NET, but LINQ adds a set of classes that makes it easier to work with XML, particularly if you're not an XML specialist.

There are a number of standard protocols and ways of working with XML, Xpath, SAX, DOM and so on. All of them are good but they all focus on some specific particular aspect of XML and a particular way of getting the job done. LINQ's version of XML goes "back to basics".

Even if you aren't interested in working with XML, looking at how LINQ handles a more complicated data structure, a tree in this case, is instructive and has a lot to teach you about the way LINQ is designed, how it works and how you might extend it to other data structures. In this chapter we look at how to construct the tree structure that XML is all about and in the next we look at how to use such structures with LINQ.

Tag Rules and Tree Structure

The core of XML is the tag as in an opening tag, e.g. <Record> and a closing tag, e.g. </Record>. The rules for XML are simple – tags occur, almost always, in matched pairs and you can nest tags as if they were brackets. The only exception to the matched pairs rule is a tag that is its own closing tag, as in <Record/> which opens and closes the tag in one go. This is, of course very similar to HTML.

It's not difficult to see that you can use tags to build a general tree structure and all you need to represent it in a program is a class that has a collection of itself as a property. This is exactly how the xNode class, and the more useful xElement descended from it via xContainer, operate. The important point is that xElement has a Nodes collection which can be used to store an element's child elements.

A simple example will make this clear.

First we need a root node:

```
XElement root = new XElement("Record");
```

The string Record is automatically converted to an XName object and this is used to set the Name property of the new XElement. An XName is used instead of a simple string because XML names have some additional behavior because of namespaces, which we return to later.

Now we have a root for our tree let's create a leaf node:

```
XElement child1 = new XElement("Name");
```

and hang it off the tree:

```
root.Add(child1);
```

If you place a text box on a form you can see the XML that the tree represents using:

```
textBox1.Text = root.ToString();
```

What you will see is:

```
<Record>
<Name />
</Record>
```

You can carry on in the same way to build up a tree of any complexity you like. For example:

```
XElement root=new XElement("Record");
XElement child1=new XElement("Name");
root.Add(child1);
XElement child2=new XElement("First");
XElement child3=new XElement("Second");
child1.Add(child2);
child1.Add(child3);
XElement child4=new XElement("Address");
root.Add(child4);
```

creates the following XML:

```
<Record>
 <Name>
  <First />
  <Second />
 </Name>
 <Address />
</Record>
```

The idea of nesting XElement within another is fairly obvious, but there are neater ways of achieving the same result.

For example, you can combine the two Add methods into a single call:

```
child1.Add(child2,child3);
```

The reason this works is due to an overload of Add not mentioned in the documentation:

```
public void Add(params object[] content);
```

You can, of course, construct a list of child objects to insert into multiple instances of XElement if you want to.

Another style of XML tree construction is based on the use of the XElement constructor. One overloaded version allows you to specify the contents of an XElement. So to create an XElement with two children you would use:

```
XElement root = new XElement("Record",
              new XElement("Name"),
               new XElement("Address"));
```

You can continue this nested construction to any level you require. For example, the following creates the same XML tree we had earlier:

```
XElement root = new XElement("Record",
              new XElement("Name",
                new XElement("First"),
                new XElement("Second")),
              new XElement("Address"));
```

This is generally referred to as "functional construction" and if you format it correctly then it looks like the tree it is constructing and it has the advantage that you can pass it directly to any method that cares to make use of it. Of course, in this style of construction you don't get variables to keep track of each node, but in most cases you don't need them.

Converting XML To XElement Trees

There are two additional very easy ways of converting XML into an XElement tree, the static Load and Parse methods. Load will take a file specification as a URI or as a TextReader or XmlReader and parse the text stream into an XElement tree. The Parse method does the same, but by accepting a string of XML tags. For example, to construct the same XML tree given earlier:

```
string XML = @"
 <Name>
  <First />
  <Second />
 </Name>
 <Address />
</Record>";
XElement root= XElement.Parse(XML);
```

If the XML you try to load or parse is syntactically incorrect then you will have to handle the resulting exception.

If you want to go the other way to using Parse then there is a Save method and you can specify options on the Save and the ToString methods that control some aspects of formatting.

Content

Now you can see how to build an XElement tree, but what about content? A tree of XML tags isn't usually the whole story. The main data payload in XML is supposed to be anything you put between opening and closing tags. In the XElement tree any text between tags is stored as an XText node in the node collection, i.e. it is just another type of child node. As such you can add XText nodes using all of the methods described earlier – if you try to add a string object as a child then the methods simply convert it to an XText object and add it to the collection of nodes. For example:

```
XElement root = new
XElement("Record","Address Record",
       new XElement("Name",
              new XElement("First","Mike"),
              new XElement("Second")),
              new XElement("Address"));
```

This adds Address Record and Mike as text between the specified tags. It is also worth knowing that if an XElement object has only a single XText child then this is also its string Value property.

Attributes

Text between the tags isn't the only sort of data carried by XML. You can also specify any number of name value pairs within the tags themselves as attributes. Attributes are supposed to be used as "metadata", i.e. they describe the nature of the data between the tags - formatting, time zone, context, etc - and within the XElement tree they are stored as XAttribute objects within the Attributes collection. The reason for this is that if you enumerate the tree you will list each of the tags and text between tags but not the attributes. Once you have found a tag, i.e. an XElement object, you can enumerate its attributes. Viewed in this way it should be clear that the main distinction between attributes and other nodes is that attributes are not part of the tree structure, but are simply stored at each node of the tree.

The rule that you have to keep in mind is that if you add an XAttribute object to an XElement object then it will automatically be added to the Attributes collection.

For example:

```
XAttribute Att1 = new XAttribute("Epoch",1900);
root.Add(Att1);
```

adds an attribute `Epoch` "1900" to the `Attributes` collection. The XML generated reads:

```
<Record Epoch = "1900"> ...<Record>
```

You can achieve the same result using the function method of constructing an XML tree:

```
XElement root = new XElement("Record",
      new XAttribute("Epoch", 1900),
      new XElement("Name",
       new XElement("First","Mike"),
       new XElement("Second")),
      new XElement("Address"));
```

The Constructor Rules

What the constructor or the Add method does with an object you supply to it depends on the object's type. The rules are:

- If it's null, nothing happens
- If it's descended from `XNode` then it is added to the Nodes collection
- If it's an `XAttribute` then it is added to the Attributes collection
- If it's a string then it is converted to `XText` and added to Nodes

Less obvious behavior is that if you supply an object that implements `IEnumerable` then it is enumerated and the resulting objects are treated according to the above rules, and if an object is anything that can't be handled by the rules it's converted to a `String` and then to an `XText` object and added to `Nodes`. This `IEnumerable` behavior is very handy because it means you can add a collection of objects in one step.

Manipulating The Tree

Constructing a tree is usually just the beginning of the problem. You usually want to process, i.e. examine and change, the tree as a result. As an `XElement` tree is dynamic this is fairly easy. You can of course use `Add` to add additional elements of any kind and there are also two remove methods – `RemoveNode` and `RemoveAttribute`. These simply remove the object that they belong to from the parent's collection. For example:

```
root.Add(child4);
child4.Remove();
```

This first adds child4 to the node collection of `root` and then removes it.

A particularly useful method is `SetElementValue`, which modifies an element's value and creates a new object if it doesn't already exist. For example, the instruction:

`root.SetElementValue("Tel","123");`

will set an existing `XElement` child of `root` with `XName` "Tel" to a value of "123" or if such a `XElement` doesn't exist it will first create a new instance.

There is some apparently odd behavior here in that the value "123" is applied between a new pair of tags <Tel>123</Tel> but it is also appended to root's `Value` property as if it was new text located between the <root></root>. The reason for this is that the `Value` property is the concatenation of all the `XText` objects contained within its opening and closing tags. This often makes the Value property less than helpful. Notice that if you add some additional text in the form of a string then it is simply added to any existing `XText` object as a concatenation. If you first explicitly create `XText` objects and add these then you get new child objects, which seems reasonable behavior.

The `SetAttributeValue` method works in much the same way but on the `Attribute` collection. For example:

`root.SetAttributeValue("Epoch", "2000");`

updates or adds an `Epoch` attribute. As an attribute generally has only one value, its `Value` property is much more useful.

Two other useful methods are `AddBeforeSelf` and `AddAfterSelf` which, as their names suggest, allow the adding of elements above and below the current element in the tree.

There are lots of other methods that modify the tree structure, but they are all fairly obvious and contain no surprises, check the documentation for details.

Values

XML is about a standard format for data and just occasionally we need to actually access the data. As already mentioned, if an `XElement` has a single `XText` child node then you can access this data as a string using the `Value` property. However, if it has multiple `XText` child objects, perhaps contained within other `XElement` child objects, then the `Value` property contains a concatenation of these strings. This makes processing data contained within tags a matter of navigating down to the `XElement` object which corresponds to the last pair of tags that enclose the text in question. Again, as already mentioned, `XAttributes` are easier to deal with in this sense because they always correspond to a single name/value pair. In this case the `Value` property always contains the data we are interested in. For simplicity the following examples will deal with `XAttributes`, but the same methods work with

XElement objects. You could just assign a new value to the Value property, but it is usually easier to use the SetValue method because this performs automatic type conversions. For example:

```
XAttribute Att1 =new XAttribute("Epoch",2000);
Att1.Value = "2000";
```

works and sets the attribute to a string "2000".

However:

```
Att1.Value = 2000;
```

generates a run-time error because you need an explicit conversion, such as:

```
Att1.Value = 2000.ToString();
```

The good news is that:

```
Att1.SetValue(2000);
```

works without the need for an explicit conversion, as does:

```
Att1.SetValue(DateTime.Now);
```

Going the other way is almost as easy, but you do have to use an explicit cast and don't need to use Value. For example:

```
DateTime T = Att1.Value;
```

doesn't work, neither does:

```
DateTime T = (DateTime) Att1.Value;
```

but, perhaps surprisingly:

```
DateTime T = (DateTime) Att1;
```

does.

You can cast an XAttribute to any numeric, bool, DateTime, TimeSpan and Guid. You can also cast to nullable versions of each of these data types, which can make handing missing data easier.

Converting To Real XML

There is more to XML than a node tree. You can add many of the XML "decorations" by wrapping the root XElement node in an XDocument object. This can have only one XElement object as the root, but also a single XDeclaration, a single XDocumentType and any number of XProcessingInstruction and XComment objects. As you can easily work out, each of these objects adds a corresponding "meta" tag to the XML that the XDocument represents. There are various, very reasonable, rules about when declarations are emitted, default declarations, and other bookkeeping concerns, which are all very obvious.

Namespaces are also fairly simple and deserve a simple example. All `XNames` are created by default with an empty namespace. There are lots of different ways of adding a namespace specifier, but the most useful is via the `XNamespace` class. For example, to add a namespace to a name you could use:

```
XNamespace ns = "http://www.i-programmer.info";
XName fullname = ns + "root";
```

Notice that an `XName` has `LocalName`, `NameSpace`, and `NameSpaceName` properties to allow you to work more creatively with XML names. Also, remember that all strings that you use in `XElement`, `XAttribute` etc names are automatically converted to `XName` objects. If you use a namespace then you have to explicitly include it when creating each element of the tree and you have to use it when searching for elements with specific names.

Postlude

XML is still a good choice for encoding data and C# makes it very easy to use. If you are tempted by formats such as JSON, just remember how much more sophisticated XML is.

XML, which is all about tree-structured data, and LINQ, which is all about querying collections, might not seem to be related, but they work together perfectly. As discussed in Chapter 19, LINQ isn't just about SQL and it isn't even just about database. It is a mechanism for querying collections with a wide range of structures and working with XML is probably its second most common application. The basics of working with the XML facilities are covered in the previous chapter.

LINQ Queries

LINQ queries are provided by extension methods applied to objects that implement the generic IEnumerable interface. In the case of XML the main objects don't implement IEnumerable but some of their methods return objects that do. This is a slight expansion of the basic LINQ idea, but a fairly obvious one. For example, the Elements method returns an IEnumerable supporting a   collection of all   the child elements of the object. This means you can write a foreach loop to step through each of the child elements:

```
foreach( XElement ele in root.Elements()){
      textBox1.Text += ele.ToString();
}
```

You can also make use of the usual LINQ extension methods, although this isn't the most common way of explaining how LINQ to XML works.

For example, assuming we have an XML tree something like:

```
<Record>
 <Name>
  <First />
  <Second />
 </Name>
 <Address />
</Record>
```

you can use the `Where` method to filter the collection of child nodes:

```
var q = root.Elements().Where<XElement>(E=>E.Name=="Address");
foreach( XElement ele in q){
      textBox1.Text += ele.ToString();
}
```

which, of course, selects only those child elements that are "`Address`" tags.

You can chain together a set of LINQ extension methods to produce something more complicated and you can use the syntactic shortcuts introduced into C# to make it even easier. For example the previous query can be written as:

```
var q = from E in root.Elements()
      where  E.Name == "Address"
             select E;
```

and the compiler translates it back into the method calls.

If you understand the general workings of LINQ then the only new element is using a method, i.e. `Elements`, that returns an `IEnumerable` collection rather than an object that implements `IEnumerable`. This may appear to be a small difference, but it does alter the "flavor" of using LINQ ever so slightly.

The point is that the XML tree is quite a complicated data structure and there are lots of different ways that its nodes or attributes could be enumerated. This is the reason why it doesn't just implement the `IEnumerable` interface in its own right and why it is preferable to delegate the enumeration to other methods called XML "axis methods" in the LINQ to XML jargon.

This small difference gives us a lot of power, but it can also be confusing because it often provides more than one way of doing things. For example, most LINQ to XML instructors would not demonstrate finding an `XElement` with a specific name using the `Where` method. The reason is simply that the `Elements` method comes with the ability to construct a collection of child nodes that are restricted to a single name. This means that you can return a collection of elements named "`Address`" in one simple step:

```
var q=root.Elements("Address");
```

No need for LINQ proper here as the axis method does the job of picking out the specific objects and returns them as a collection. Notice, however, that this isn't returned as a standard collection type. The axis method adheres to the "deferred" execution model of LINQ by returning an `Xcontainer.GetElements` type, which is only enumerated when the enumeration is really needed.

Another slightly confusing issue that is solved by axis methods is determining which type of object needs to be returned. For example:

```
var q = root.Attributes();
```

is a query that returns all of the attributes set on the root object. Once you have constructed the query, you can step through it in the usual way using a foreach loop.

Most of the axis methods allow the user to specify some simple filtering conditions that often mean that you don't need to use a full LINQ query at all. Some axis methods are so specific that they return a single element. For example, FirstNode and LastNode return the first and last node respectively. Similarly Element(*"name"*) returns the first matching element which should be contrasted with Elements(*"name"*) which returns all child elements that match.

As well as working with sequences of elements that go "down" the tree you can work back up to the top most level using the Ancestors method. For example:

```
var q = root.LastNode.Ancestors();
```

returns a collection of all of the elements in the tree by, perversely, starting at the last node and extracting all of its ancestors.

Subtrees

What about querying subtrees? This is very easy and almost doesn't need any thought. All you have to do is find the node that is the root of the subtree and use its Descendants method. For example:

```
var q=root.Element("Name").Descendants();
```

returns all of the child nodes below the Name XElement in the tree, i.e. First and Second in our earlier example. Notice that Descendants is "recursive" in the sense that it returns all of the child nodes of the first node specified, then the child nodes of each of those and so on. The order in which the child nodes are returned is described as "document order", i.e. the order in which the tags appear when the XML is listed down a page.

If you use a LINQ query to return an element you automatically get its "deep" value – i.e. all of the child nodes it contains. Because of this, the query:

```
var q2 = from E in root.Elements()
      where E.Name == "Name"
            select E;
```

returns a subtree starting at the XElement "Name". It is slightly different from the previous example because it includes the "Name" node and not just the subtree below it.

You can also chain axis methods, just as you can chain standard LINQ methods. For example:

```
var q=root.Element("Name").Attributes();
```

finds the first element that matches "Name" and then returns a sequence of its attributes, if any.

Some things are much easier to do with axis methods, which are designed to work with a tree structure, and some are easier using standard LINQ queries, which are designed to work with flat collections. Sometimes a combination of the two works even better. For example:

```
var q = from E in root.Elements()
        where (E.Element("First")!=null)
            select E;
```

selects all of the elements that have at least one "First" child element. Again, as a deep value is returned, you actually get the subtree below any node that has a "First" child node.

Once you start to follow the relentless logic of IEnumerable and its LINQ methods it becomes almost fun to try and work out the most "interesting" way of obtaining a result. Not necessarily good programming practice, but a good way to master the techniques.

Select and The Projection

The select part of a LINQ expression normally works as a projection operator that "reduces" the size of the data structure returned by a query. For example, it can be used to select which "columns" are returned from a SQL query which otherwise would return a complete record. So, the query:

```
var q = from E in root.Elements()
        where E.Name == "Name"
            select E;
```

returns a deep copy in the sense that the XElement corresponding to Name brings with it an entire subtree.

Suppose you want a "shallow" copy, i.e. just the node and its text value. In this case we can project the XElement to a string that contains all of the XText in the subtree:

```
var q = from E in root.Elements()
        where E.Name == "Name"
            select E.Value;
```

However, projection can also be used to create a larger or completely different type using the data returned by the query. For example, you could perform a LINQ to SQL query to return some values and then package them up into an XML tree.

To understand how this works all you really have to do is focus on the role of the "range" variable. It is set to each of the objects that match the selection criterion and eventually this can be used to construct any other data type. For example, suppose you wanted to reconfigure the XML tree that stored the First and Second names in our example into a different XML tree. You could do the job using a slightly more advanced select projection:

```
var q = from E in root.Elements()
        where E.Name == "Name"
            select new XElement("NameRecord",
              new XElement("Name1", XElement("First").Value),
               new XElement("Name2", E.Element("Second").Value)
);
```

In this case we take each of the selected elements and build a new XML tree using their values and it is a collection of these new XML trees that are returned. While this isn't a particularly useful transformation, it gives you the basic idea, i.e. use the result of the query to build new types, and you can generalize it to other situations. In more complex transformations it can even be useful to work out intermediate results to be used later within the select clause.

To create a variable within a LINQ expression you simply use the let keyword. For example, the previous query can be re-written:

```
var q = from E in root.Elements()
        where E.Name == "Name"
            let z1=E.Element("First")
            let z2=E.Element("Second")
        select
            new XElement("NameRecord",
            new XElement("Name1",z1.Value),
            new XElement("Name2",z2.Value));
```

In this case the let keywords create two new variables z1 and z2 which are used to hold the child elements that match the two sub-queries. Notice that the result is exactly the same if you don't use the temporary variables.

Notice that you can even use the select to modify the existing XML tree using SetValue and so on. But a tree is a complicated structure and you need to be sure that what you are trying to do can be done in every case.

In most cases it is much better to use the functional approach to build a new tree as part of the select clause. Notice that this is made even more powerful by the simple fact that the constructors can accept IEnumeration sequences and will automatically iterate through all of the objects thus adding them to the new tree.

For example:

```
var q = from E in root.Elements()
        where E.Name == "Name"
            select
              new Xelement("NameRecord", root.Attributes(),
                new Xelement("Name1",E.Element("First").Value),
                new Xelement("Name2",E.Element("Second").Value));
```

Notice that the use of root.Attributes adds all of the attributes in the collection to the new XElement corresponding to the tag <NameRecord>.

Postlude

LINQ, and LINQ to XML in particular, provides so many ways of doing things that it can leave you feeling slightly queasy about the whole thing and it is certain that you can write code that is deep and impenetrable – don't.

Chapter 22

Regular Expressions

If you think regular expressions are trivial and boring, you've not seen the whole picture. Here we reveal that in .NET they are amazingly powerful and not to be missed.

Regular expressions are addictive. Playing with these compressed and cryptic patterns is better than solving a Sudoku. If you are wondering what this is all about because, obviously, regular expressions are just the use of "*" and "?" then read on. The truth is a lot more subtle and the result is a lot more powerful than you might suspect. If you already know the basics of regular expressions then jump to a section where you will find some deeper explanations of less common features.

Regular Fundamentals

The idea of a regular expression starts with the idea of specifying a grammar for a particular set of strings. All you have to do is find a pattern that matches all of the strings you are interested in and use the pattern. The simplest sort of pattern is the string literal that matches itself. So, for example, if you want to process ISBN numbers you might well want to match the string "ISBN:" which is its own regular expression in the sense that the pattern "ISBN:" will match exactly one string that is exactly "ISBN:". To actually use this you have to first create a `Regex` object with the regular expression built into it:

```
Regex ex1 = new Regex(@"ISBN:");
```

The use of the @ at the start of the string is optional, but it does make it easier as we can often avoid the use of / the escape character. Recall that strings starting with @ are represented "as is" without any additional processing or conversion by C#.

To evaluate the regular expression we need one of the methods offered by the Regex object. The most obvious to start with is the Match method which applies the expression to a specified string and returns a Match object which in turn contains a range of useful properties and methods that let you track the operation of applying the regular expression to the string. For example, if there was a match the Success property would be set to true with:

```
MessageBox.Show(
        ex1.Match(@"ISBN:978-1871962406").Success.ToString());
```

The Index property gives the position of the match in the search string:

```
MessageBox.Show(
        ex1.Match(@"ISBN: 978-1871962406").Index.ToString());
```

which in this case returns 0 to indicate that the match is at the start of the string.

To return the actual match in the target string you can use the ToString method. Of course, here the result is going to be identical to the regular expression, but in general this isn't the case. Notice that the Match method returns the first match to the regular expression and you can use the NextMatch method which returns another Match object.

Pattern Matching

If this is all there was do regular expressions they wouldn't be very interesting. The reason they are so useful is that you can specify patterns that spell out the regularities in a type of data. For example, following "ISBN:" we expect to find a digit – any digit. This can be expressed as "ISBN:\d" where \d is character class indicator which means "a digit".

If you try this out you will discover that you don't get a match with the example string because there is a space following the colon. However

"ISBN:\s\d"

does match as \s means "any white-space character" and:

```
Regex ex1 = new Regex(@"ISBN:\s\d");
MessageBox.Show(ex1.Match(@"ISBN: 978-1871962406").ToString();
```

displays "ISBN: 9".

You can look up the available character set indicators in the documentation. The most useful are:

- .   (i.e. a single dot) matches any character.
- \d   digit
- \s   white-space
- \w   any "word" character including digits

There is also the convention that capital letters match the inverse set of characters:

- `\D`   any non-digit
- `\S`   any non-white space
- `\W`   any non-word character

The inverse sets can behave unexpectedly unless you are very clear about what they mean. For example. `\D` also matches white space and hence `@"ISBN:\D\d"` matches `ISBN: 9`.

You can also make up your own character group by listing the set of characters between square brackets. So, for example, `[0-9]` is the same as `\d`. Negating a character set is also possible and `[^0-9]` matches anything but the digits and is the same as `\D`.

There are also character sets that refer to Unicode but these are obvious enough in use not to need additional explanation.

Anchors

As well as characters and character sets you can also use location matches or anchors. For example, the `^` (caret) only matches the start of the string. For example, `@"^ISBN:"` will match only if the string starts with `ISBN:` and doesn't match if the same substring occurs anywhere else. The most useful anchors are:

- `^`   start of string
- `$`   end of string
- `\b`   word boundary, i.e. between a `\w` and `\W`
- `\B`   anywhere but a word boundary

So for, example, `@"^\d+$"` specifies a string consisting of nothing but digits. Compare this to `@"^\d*$"` which would also accept a null string.

One subtle point only emerges when you consider strings with line breaks. In this case, by default, the `^` and the `$` match only the very start and end of the string. If you want them to match line beginnings and endings you have to specify the m option either by setting the `RegexOptions.Multiline` parameter in the method call or by including `?m` in the regular expression. It's also worth knowing about the `\G` anchor which matches only at the point where the previous match ended. It is only useful when used with the `NextMatch` method, but then it makes all matches contiguous.

Greedy and Lazy Quantifiers

We now have the problem that it isn't unreasonable for an ISBN to be written as `ISBN:9` or `ISBN: 9` with perhaps even more than one space after the colon. We clearly need a way to specify the number of repeats that are allowed in a matching string. To do this we make use of "quantifiers" following the specification to be repeated. The most commonly used quantifiers are:

- `*`   zero or more
- `+`   one or more
- `?`   zero or one
- `{n}`   exactly n times
- `{n,}`   n or more times
- `{n,m}`   at least n at most m times

In many ways this is the point at which regular expression use starts to become interesting and inevitably more complicated. You could even say that the use of * and + is what makes a regular expression into a regular grammar in the wider technical sense. Simple examples not hard to find. For example:

`@"ISBN:\s*\d"`

matches `ISBN:` followed by any number of white-space characters including none at all followed by a digit. Similarly,

`@"ISBN:?\s*\d"`

matches `ISBN` followed by an optional colon, any number of white-space characters including none, followed by a digit.

Quantifiers are easy, but there is a subtlety that often goes unnoticed. By default, quantifiers are "greedy", that is they match as many entities as they can, even when the regular expression provides a better match a little further on. To illustrate this by the simplest example, suppose you need a regular expression to parse some HTML tags:

`<div>hello</div>`

If you want to match just a pair of opening and closing tags you might well try the following regular expression:

`Regex ex2 = new Regex(@"<div>.*</div>");`

which seems to say *"the string starts with <div> then any number including zero of other characters followed by </div>"*. If you try this out on the example given above you will find that it matches:

`MessageBox.Show(ex2.Match(@"<div>hello</div>").ToString());`

However, if you now try it out against the string:

```
<div>hello</div><div>world</div>
```

as in:

```
MessageBox.Show(ex2.Match(@"<div>hello</div>
                            <div>world</div>").ToString());
```

you will discover that the match is to the entire string.

That is, the final `</div>` in the regular expression is matched to the final `</div>` in the string, even though there is an earlier occurrence of the same substring. This is because the quantifiers are greedy and attempt to find the longest possible match. In this case the * matches everything including the first `</div>`. So why doesn't it also match the final `</div>`? The reason is that if it did the entire regular expression would fail to match anything because there would be no closing `</div>`. What happens is that the quantifiers continue to match until the regular expression fails, then the regular expression engine backtracks in an effort to find a match. Notice that all of the standard quantifiers are greedy and will match more than you might expect based on what follows in the regular expression.

If you don't want greedy quantifiers the solution is to use "lazy" quantifiers which are formed by following the standard quantifiers by a question mark. To see this in action, change the previous regular expression to read:

```
Regex ex2 = new Regex(@"<div>.*?</div>");
```

With this change in place the result of matching to:

```
@"<div>hello</div>world</div>"
```

is just the first pair of `<div>` brackets, that is `<div>hello</div>`. Notice that all of the quantifiers, including ?, have a lazy version and you can write ?? to mean a lazy "zero or one" occurrence.

The distinction between greedy and lazy quantifiers is perhaps the biggest reason for a reasonably well-tested regular expression to go wrong when used against a wider range of example strings. Always remember that a standard greedy quantifier will match as many times as possible while still allowing the regular expression to match, and its lazy version will match as few as possible times to make the regular expression match.

Grouping and Alternation

Regular strings often have alternative forms. For example, the ISBN prefix could be simply ISBN: or it could be ISBN-13: or any of many other reasonable variations. You can specify an either/or situation using the vertical bar |, the alternation operator, as in x|y which will match an x or a y. For example, @"ISBN:|ISBN-13:" matches either ISBN: or ISBN-13:.

This is easy enough but what about:

@"ISBN:|ISBN-13:\s*\d"

At first glance this seems to match either ISBN: or ISBN-13: followed by any number of white space characters and a single digit, – but it doesn't. The | operator has the lowest priority and the alternative matches are everything the left and everything to the right, i.e. either ISBN: or ISBN-13:\s*\d. To match the white space and digit in both forms of the ISBN prefix we would have to write:

@"ISBN:\s*\d|ISBN-13:\s*\d"

Clearly having to repeat everything that is in common on either side of the alternation operator is going to make things difficult and this is where grouping comes in. Anything grouped between parentheses is treated as a single unit, a subexpression, and grouping has a higher priority than the alternation operator. So, for example:

@"(ISBN:|ISBN-13:)\s*\d"

matches either form of the ISBN prefix followed by any number of white space characters and a single digit because the brackets limit the range of the alternation operator to the substrings to the left and right within the bracket.

The greedy/lazy situation also applies to the alternation operator. For example, suppose you try to match the previous ungrouped expression, but without the colon, @"ISBN|ISBN-13". In this case the first pattern, ISBN, will match even if the string is ISBN-13. It doesn't matter that the second expression is a "better" match. No amount of grouping will help with this problem because the shorter match will be tried and succeed first. The solution is to swap to the order of the subexpressions so that the longer comes first or to include something that always marks the end of the target string. In this case for example, if we add the colon then the ISBN: subexpression cannot possibly match the ISBN-13: string.

Capture Groups

Now that we have explored grouping it is time to introduce the most sophisticated and useful aspect of regular expressions, the idea of "capture". You may think that brackets are just about grouping together items that should be matched as a group, but there is more. A subexpression, i.e. something between brackets, is said to be "captured" if it matches, and captured expressions are remembered by the engine during the match. Notice that a capture can occur before the entire expression has finished matching – indeed a capture can occur even if the entire expression eventually fails to match at all.

The .NET regular expression classes make captures available via the `capture` property and the `CaptureCollection`. Each capture group, i.e. each subexpression surrounded by brackets, can be associated with one or more captured string. To be clear, the expression:

```
@"(<div>)(</div>)"
```

has two capture groups which by default are numbered from left to right with capture group 1 being the `(<div>)` and capture group 2 being the `(</div>)`. The entire expression can be regarded as capture group 0 as its results are returned first by the .NET framework. If we try out this expression on a suitable string and get the `GroupCollection` result of the match using the `Groups` property:

```
GroupCollection Grps = ex2.Match(
                @"<div></div><div></div><div></div>").Groups;
```

then, in this case, we have three capture groups – the entire expression returned as `Grps[0]`, the first bracket, i.e. capture group 1, returned as `Grps[1]`, and the final bracket, i.e. capture group 2, as `Grps[2]`. The first group, i.e. the entire expression, is reported as matching only once at the start of the test string – after all we only asked for the first match.

Getting the first capture group and displaying its one and only capture demonstrates this:

```
CaptureCollection Caps = Groups[0].Captures;
MessageBox.Show(Caps[0].Index.ToString()+
                " "+Caps[0].Length.ToString()+
                    " "+Caps[0].ToString());
```

It displays 0 11 <div></div> corresponding to the first match of the complete expression.

The second capture group was similarly only captured once at the first `<div>` and:

```
CaptureCollection Caps = Groups[1].Captures;
MessageBox.Show(Caps[0].Index.ToString()+
               " "+Caps[0].Length.ToString()+
                  " "+Caps[0].ToString());
```

displays 0 5 `<div>` to indicate that it was captured by the first `<div>` in the string.

The final capture group was also only captured once by the final `</div>` and:

```
CaptureCollection Caps = Groups[2].Captures;
MessageBox.Show(Caps[0].Index.ToString()+
               " "+Caps[0].Length.ToString()+
                  " "+Caps[0].ToString());
```

displays 5 6 `</div>`.

Now consider the same argument over again, but this time with the expression:

```
Regex ex2=new Regex(@"((<div>)(</div>))*");
```

In this case there are four capture groups including the entire expression.

Capture group 0 is the expression `((<div>)(</div>))*` and this is captured once starting at 0 and matches the entire string of three repeats, i.e. length 33.

The next capture group is the first, i.e. outer, bracket `((<div>)(</div>))` and it is captured three times, corresponding to the three repeats. If you try:

```
CaptureCollection Caps=Groups[1].Captures;
for (int i = 0; i <= Caps.Count - 1; i++){
  MessageBox.Show(Caps[i].Index.ToString() +
                 " " + Caps[i].Length.ToString() +
                    " " + Caps[i].ToString());
}
```

you will find the captures are at 0, 11 and 22.

The two remaining captures correspond to the `<div>` at 0, 11 and 22 and the `</div>` at 5, 16 and 27. Notice that a capture is stored each time the bracket contents match.

Advanced Capture

There are other capture group constructs, but these are far less useful and, because they are even more subtle, have a reputation for introducing bugs. The balancing group is, however, worth knowing about as it gives you the power to balance brackets and other constructs, but first we need to know about a few of the other less common groupings, the assertions. There are four of these and the final three are fairly obvious variations on the first. They all serve to impose a condition on the match without affecting what is captured, they have zero-width in the jargon:

- (?=*regex*) - zero-width positive lookahead assertion
  continues the match only if the regex matches on the immediate right of the current position but doesn't capture the regex or backtrack if it fails. For example, \w+(?=\d) only matches a word ending in a digit, but the digit is not included in the match. That is, it matches Paris9 but returns Paris as capture 0. In other words, you can use it to assert a pattern that must follow a matched subexpression.

- (?!*regex*) - zero-width negative lookahead assertion

  works like the positive lookahead assertion, but the regex has to fail to match on the immediate right. For example, \w+(?!\d) only matches a word that doesn't have a trailing digit.

- (?<=*regex*) Zero-width positive lookbehind assertion

  again works like the positive lookahead assertion, but the regex has to match on the immediate left. For example, (?<=\d)\w+ only matches a word that has a leading digit.

- (?<!*regex*) Zero-width negative lookbehind assertion.

  the negation of the Zero-width positive lookbehind assertion. For example, (?<!\d)\w+ only matches a word that doesn't have a leading digit.

Now that we have seen the assertions we can move on to consider the balancing group:

(?<*name1*-*name2*>*regex*)

which works by deleting the current capture from the capture collection for *name2* and storing everything since the last capture in the capture collection for *name1*. If there is no current capture for *name2* then backtracking occurs and, if this doesn't succeed, the expression fails.

Back References

What can you use captures for? The answer is two-fold – more sophisticated regular expressions and replacements. Let's start with their use in building more sophisticated regular expressions. Using the default numbering system described above you can refer to a previous capture in the regular expression. That is, if you write \n where n is the number of a capture group the expression will specify that value of the capture group. It's easy once you have seen it in action.

Consider the task of checking that html tags occur in the correct opening and closing pairs. That is, if you find a <div> tag the next closing tag to the right should be a <\div>. You can already write a regular expression to detect this condition but captures and back references make it much easier. If you start the regular expression with a subexpression that captures the string within the brackets then you can check that the same word occurs within the closing bracket using a back reference to the capture group:

```
Regex ex2= new Regex(@"<(div)></\1");
```

Notice the \1 in the final part of the expression tells the regular expression engine to retrieve the last match of the first capture group. If you try this out you will find that it matches <div><\div> but not <div><\pr>, say.

You could have done the same thing without using a back reference but it's easy to extend the expression to cope with additional tags. For example:

```
Regex ex2= new Regex(@"<(div|pr|span|script)></\1>");
```

matches correctly closed div, pr, span and script tags. If you are still not convinced of the power of capture and back reference try writing a regular expression that detects repeated words without using them.

The solution using a back reference is almost trivial:

```
Regex ex2= new Regex(@"\b(\w+)\s+\1\b");
```

The first part of the expression simply matches a word by the following process – start at word boundary, capture as many word characters as you can, then allow one or more white space characters. Finally check to see if the next word is the same as the capture. The only tricky bit is remembering to put the word boundary at the end. Without it you will match substrings that repeat as in "the theory".

As well as anonymous captures, you can also create named captures using (?<name>*regex*) or (?'name'*regex*). You can then refer to the capture by name using the syntax \<name> or \'name'. Using a named capture our previous duplicate word regular expression can be written as:

```
@"\b(?<word>\w+)\s+\<word>\b"
```

If you need to process named captures outside of a regular expression, i.e. using the Capture classes, then you still have to use capture numbers and you need to know that named captures are numbered left to right and outer to inner after all the unnamed captures have been numbered.

If you need to group items together but don't want to make use of a capture you can use (?:regex). This works exactly as it would without the ?:, but the bracket is left out of the list of capture groups. This can improve the efficiency of a regular expression, but isn't usually an issue.

Reduction

In many cases all you are doing is trying to reduce the capture count for name2 and in this case you can leave out any reference to name1. This sounds complicated but in practice it isn't too difficult. For example, let's write an expression that matches any number of As followed by the same number of Bs:

```
Regex ex3 = new Regex(@"^(?<COUNT>A)+(?<-COUNT>B)+");
```

This works, up to a point, in that it matches an equal number of A and Bs starting from the beginning of the string, but it doesn't reject a string like AABBB, which it simply matches to AABB.

Each time the first capture group hits an A it adds a capture to the capture set, so in this case there are two captures when the second capture group hits the first B. This reduces A's capture set to 1 and then to zero when the second B is encountered which causes the match to backtrack to the second B when the third B is encountered and the match succeeds.

To make the entire match fail we also have to include the condition that should now be at the end of the string:

```
Regex ex3 = new Regex(@"^(?<COUNT>A)+(?<-COUNT>B)+$");
```

This now fails on AABBB, but it matches AAABB because in the case the second capture group doesn't fail before we reach the end of the string.

We really need a test that amounts to *"at the end of the string/match the count capture group should be null"*. To do this we need some sort of conditional test on the capture and .NET provides just this:

```
(?(name)regex1|regex2)
```

will use *regex1* if the capture is non-empty and *regex2* if it is empty. In fact this conditional is more even general in that name can be a general regular expression. You can leave *regex2* out if you want an "if...then" rather than an "if...then...else".

With this our new expression is:

```
Regex ex3 = new Regex(@"^(?<COUNT>A)+(?<-COUNT>B)+(?(COUNT)^.)$");
```

The ^. doesn't match any character and so it forces the match to fail if the capture group isn't empty.

A more symmetrical if…then…else form of the same expression is:

```
Regex ex3 = new Regex(@"^(?<COUNT>A)+(?<-COUNT>B)+
                                  (?(COUNT)^.|(?=$))");
```

In this case the else part of the conditional asserts that we are at the end of the string.

Replacements

So far we have created regular expressions with the idea that we can use them to test that a string meets a specification or to extract a substring. These are the two conventional uses of regular expressions. However, you can also use them to perform some very complicated string editing and rearrangements. The key to this idea is the notion that you can use the captures as part of the specified replacement string. The only problem is that the substitution strings use a slightly different syntax to a regular expression. The Replace method:

```
ex1.Replace(input,substitution)
```

simply takes every match of the associated regular expression and performs the substitution specified. Notice that it performs the substitution on every match and the result returned is the entire string with the substitutions made.

There are other versions of the Replace method but they all work in more or less the same way. For example, if we define the regular expression:

```
Regex ex1 = new Regex(@"(ISBN|ISBN-13)");
```

and apply the following replacement:

```
MessageBox.Show(ex1.Replace(@"ISBN: 978-871962406","ISBN-13"));
```

then the ISBN prefix will be replaced by ISBN-13. Notice that an ISBN-13 prefix will also be replaced by ISBN-13 so making all ISBN strings consistent. Also notice that if there are multiple ISBNs within the string they will all be matched and replaced. There are versions of the method that allow you to restrict the number of matches that are replaced.

This is easy enough to follow and works well as long as you have defined your regular expression precisely enough. More sophisticated is the use of capture groups within the substitution string. You can use @"$n" to refer to capture group n or @"${name}" to refer to a capture group by *name*. There are a range of other substitution strings but these are fairly obvious in use.

As an example of how this all works consider the problem of converting a US format date, mm/dd/yyyy, to a UK/European format date, dd/mm/yyyy. First we need a regular expression to match the US format:

```
Regex ex1 = new Regex(@"(?\d{1,2})/(?<day>\d{1,2})/(?<year>\d{4})");
```

This isn't a particularly sophisticated regular expression, but we have allowed one or two digits for the month and day numbers but insisted on four for the year number. You can write a more interesting and flexible regular expression for use with real data. Notice that we have three named capture groups corresponding to month, day and year. To create a European-style date all we have to do assemble the capture groups in the correct order in a substitution string:

```
MessageBox.Show(ex1.Replace(@" 10/2/2008",
                            "${day}/${month}/${year}$"));
```

This substitutes the day, month and year capture groups in place of the entire matched string, i.e. the original date.

Postlude

Regular expressions are addictive in a way that can ultimately be unproductive. It isn't worth spending days crafting a single regular expression that matches all variations on a string when building one or two simpler alternatives and using a wider range of string operations would do the same job as well, if not as neatly. Resist the temptation to write regular expressions that you only just understand and always make sure you test them with strings that go well outside of the range of inputs that you consider correct – greedy matching and backtracking often result in the acceptance of a wider range of strings than was originally intended. If you take care, regular expressions are a very powerful way of processing and transforming text without the need to move to a complete syntax analysis package.

VI Unsafe & Interop

Prelude

Type safety and managed code is a big advantage, but there usually comes a time when you have to talk to legacy unmanaged code, often the operating system. To make this possible, C# provides the interop subsystem which, in the form of PInvoke (Platform Invocation Services), can be used to call operating system functions in DLLs or Linux libraries. If you are working under Windows then you can also interface to COM objects, which are still very important. Finally there is unsafe code, which allows you use pointers and manage memory directly.

All .NET code is managed code. What this means is that objects are garbage collected and code can't accidentally overrun limits and read and write areas it isn't supposed to, although see Pointers later on. In an ideal world all code would be managed code, although not everyone would agree with this statement. There are lots of examples of important unmanaged code – all major operating systems for example are unmanaged. If you want to call an operating system function from C# then you need to use interop, specifically PInvoke, Platform Invoke, to allow managed code to call an unmanaged function.

PInvoke has a long history of use under Windows but it also works, with some restrictions under Linux. Under Windows we also have many facilities implemented as COM objects and to use COM objects from managed code we need a slightly different flavor of interop and this is described in the next chapter. In both cases the big problem is converting the data from its representation in C# to the external representation used by the unmanaged code, usually C/C++. This is called "marshaling" and it is handled by applying attributes to the declaration of the external functions.

Marshaling works in both directions so when you are writing managed code you can use unmanaged functions and vice versa. In this account we focus on using unmanaged functions from managed code because this is the common requirement. However, the same ideas apply if you are trying to write a function in C# that can be called by other languages.

Basic PInvoke

The whole of interop is governed by the use of attributes which modify how the definition of an external function is interpreted by the system. This use of attributes is a good demonstration of how useful they can be and they are the subject of Chapter 25. The most important attribute is Dllimport which, despite its name, will import functions from a range of different library types including .DLLs and Linux .SO.

For example, for Windows [DllImport("mylib")]will look for mylib.exe or mylib.dll. For Linux it looks for mylib.so, libmylib.so, mylib and libmylib. For Mac OS the extension is .dylib. Notice that you can specify the library in more detail including path and extension to make sure you get the library you want.

There are also ways of loading a library at runtime dynamically. For example, under Windows you can use the GetSystemMetrics OS function which is stored in user32.dll using:

```
using System.Runtime.InteropServices;

[DllImport("user32.dll")]
static extern int GetSystemMetrics(int smIndex);

private void button1_Click(object sender, EventArgs e)
{
        textBox1.Text = GetSystemMetrics(0).ToString();
}
```

Notice that as the function is marked extern you cannot follow the declaration by a function body. In addition the function has to be declared static.

Once you have the declaration you can use the function as if it was a managed function within your program. However, you need to keep in mind that when you call it the interop system converts the parameters to an unmanaged data representation and converts the result back to a managed representation. For int this is so simple that you can rely on the system to do the job by default. A very simple Linux example is:

```
[DllImport("libc.so.6")]
private static extern int getpid();

int pid = getpid();
```

The main problem is finding the function and the library file it is stored in and then working out what the parameters are. For more sophisticated functions you also have to customize the marshaling from managed to unmanaged data.

Custom Marshaling

One of the big problems in using interop is controlling the way parameters are marshaled. Often you can simply ignore the problem and allow default marshaling to do the conversion without you having to think about it. For anything more complicated you need to use custom marshaling.

The key to

this is the MarshalAs attribute which can be applied to any parameter and the return type of a function. You can place:

`[param:MarshalAs(UnmanagedType.type)]`

in front of any parameter and:

`[return:MarshalAs(UnmanagedType.type)]`

in front of the entire function definition to indicate the return type. The param and return just indicate if the conversion is to be performed as an input, i.e. convert from the unmanaged type to the managed, or an output, i.e. convert the managed type to the unmanaged type. Of course, you also need to know what type to use from the UnmanagedType collection. As I4 is a four-byte integer, we can write the previous example in a much longer and explicit form as:

```
[DllImport("user32.dll")]
    [return:MarshalAs(UnmanagedType.I4)]
        static extern int GetSystemMetrics(
            [param:MarshalAs(UnmanagedType.I4)]  int smIndex);
```

This works in exactly the same way as the previous version. Notice that you don't need the param qualifier as the system can work out that you mean the MarshalAs an input:

```
[DllImport("user32.dll")]
   [return:MarshalAs(UnmanagedType.I4)]
 static extern int GetSystemMetrics(
 [MarshalAs(UnmanagedType.I4)]  int smIndex);
```

According to the documentation, the types that you can use are:

AnsiBStr	An ANSI character string – length-prefixed character array.
AsAny	A dynamic type that determines the type of an object at run time and marshals the object as that type.
Bool	A 4-byte Boolean value (true != 0, false = 0). This is the Win32 BOOL type.
BStr	A Unicode character string that is a length-prefixed double byte array. It is the default string in COM and String data.
ByValArray	When the Value property is set to ByValArray, the SizeConst field must be set to indicate the number of elements in the array. The ArraySubType field can optionally contain the UnmanagedType of the array elements when it is necessary to differentiate among string types. You can use this UnmanagedType only on an array that whose elements appear as fields in a structure.

ByValTStr	Used for in-line, fixed-length character arrays that appear within a structure. `ByValTStr` types behave like C-style, fixed-size strings inside a structure (for example, `char s[5]`). The character type used with `ByValTStr` is determined by the `CharSet` argument of the `StructLayoutAttribute` attribute applied to the containing structure. Always use the `SizeConst` field to indicate the size of the array.
Currency	A currency type. Used on a `Decimal` to marshal the decimal value as a COM currency type instead of as a `Decimal`.
CustomMarshaler	Specifies the custom marshaler class when used with the `MarshalType` or `MarshalTypeRef` field. The `MarshalCookie` field can be used to pass additional information to the custom marshaler. You can use this member on any reference type. This member is valid for parameters and return values only. It cannot be used on fields.
Error	A native type that is associated with an `I4` or an `U4` and that causes the parameter to be exported as an `HRESULT`.
FunctionPtr	An integer that can be used as a C-style function pointer.
HString	A Windows Runtime string for use with the `String` data type.
I1	A 1-byte signed integer.
I2	A 2-byte signed integer.
I4	A 4-byte signed integer.
I8	An 8-byte signed integer.
IDispatch	A COM `IDispatch` pointer (`Object` in Microsoft Visual Basic 6.0).
IInspectable	A Windows Runtime interface pointer. You can use this member on the `Object` data type.
Interface	A COM interface pointer. The `Guid` of the interface is obtained from the class metadata. Use this member to specify the exact interface type or the default interface type if you apply it to a class. This member produces the same behavior as `IUnknown` when you apply it to the `Object` data type.
IUnknown	A COM `IUnknown` pointer. You can use this member on the `Object` data type.
LPArray	A pointer to the first element of a C-style array. When marshaling from managed to unmanaged code, the length of the array is determined by the length of the managed array. When marshaling from unmanaged to managed code, the length of the array is determined from the `SizeConst` and `SizeParamIndex` fields, optionally followed by the unmanaged type of the elements within the array when it is necessary to differentiate among string types.

LPStr	A single byte, null-terminated ANSI character string. You can use this member on the String and StringBuilder data types.
LPStruct	A pointer to a C-style structure that you use to marshal managed formatted classes. This value is supported only for platform invoke and not for COM Interop.
LPTStr	A Unicode character string. This value is supported only for platform invoke and not for COM Interop.
LPUTF8Str	A pointer to a UTF-8 encoded string.
LPWStr	A 2-byte, null-terminated Unicode character string. You cannot use the LPWStr value with an unmanaged string unless the string was created by using the unmanaged CoTaskMemAlloc function.
R4	A 4-byte floating-point number.
R8	An 8-byte floating-point number.
SafeArray	A SafeArray, which is a self-describing array that carries the type, rank, and bounds of the associated array data. You can use this member with the SafeArraySubType field to override the default element type.
Struct	A VARIANT, which is used to marshal managed formatted classes and value types.
SysInt	A platform-dependent, signed integer: 4 bytes on 32-bit Windows, 8 bytes on 64-bit Windows.
SysUInt	A platform-dependent, unsigned integer: 4 bytes on 32-bit Windows, 8 bytes on 64-bit Windows.
TBStr	A length-prefixed, Unicode char string. You rarely use this BSTR-like member.
U1	A 1-byte unsigned integer.
U2	A 2-byte unsigned integer.
U4	A 4-byte unsigned integer.
U8	An 8-byte unsigned integer.
VariantBool	A 2-byte, OLE-defined VARIANT_BOOL type (true = -1, false = 0).
VBByRefStr	A value that enables Visual Basic to change a string in unmanaged code and have the results reflected in managed code. This value is supported only for platform invoke and not for COM Interop.

Even a quick look at this table indicates that things can be complicated. You also need to be aware that you cannot apply any unmanaged type to any managed type. For example, you cannot convert a string to an I4 or anything similar. The marshaling logic is restricted to what it reasonable. In many cases this means that you don't have to select a marshaling type because there is only one choice. For example, you cannot marshal a standard 32-bit int to anything other than I4. Of course, there is nothing stopping you casting or converting the int into something else before it is marshaled.

String Marshaling

Strings are a particular problem because there are so many encodings and representations. Most system functions either use UnmanagedType.LPStr or UnmanagedType.LPWStr, both of which are passed as pointers to a null terminated "C-style" string, the former using ANSI and the latter using Unicode characters. For functions implemented in "higher-level" situations such as COM, a UnmanagedType.BStr type is appropriate which has its length as the first character. For example, the MessageBox system function either uses byte or two-byte characters and so LPStr or LPWStr is appropriate depending on whether or not you are using Unicode, which can be determined by the CharSet option:

```
[DllImport("User32.dll", CharSet = CharSet.Unicode)]
public static extern IntPtr MessageBox(
        int hWnd,
        [MarshalAs(UnmanagedType.LPWStr)] String text,
        [MarshalAs(UnmanagedType.LPWStr)] String caption,
        uint type);
```

and you can call it using something like:

```
MessageBox(0, "Hello PInvoke World", "PInvoke", 0);
```

Notice that the marshaling is more active than you might expect. The managed string is copied to an area of memory, a null is added to the end and a pointer is set to reference the first character. The pointer is passed to the unmanaged function.

Strings are immutable so any changes made by the unmanaged function have no effect on the managed string.

StringBuilder is mutable and changes are allowed, but you can only use LPStr, LPTStr, and LPWStr. What this means is that it can be used to accept character data from unmanaged functions as a parameter. For example, the GetWindowsText function uses a C-style string parameter to return the Window text:

```
int GetWindowText( HWND hWnd,  LPTStr lpString,  int nMaxCount);
```

The lpString buffer has to be a fixed size as given by nMaxCount.

To do this we need an initialized `StringBuilder` of the correct size. We also need a system call to get the handle of the active window:

```
[DllImport("User32.dll", CharSet = CharSet.Unicode)]
static extern void GetWindowText(IntPtr hWnd,
                         StringBuilder lpString, int nMaxCount);

[DllImport("User32.dll", CharSet = CharSet.Unicode)]
static extern IntPtr GetForegroundWindow();

private void button1_Click(object sender, EventArgs e)
{
        IntPtr hwnd = GetForegroundWindow();
        StringBuilder Buff = new StringBuilder(200);
        GetWindowText(hwnd, Buff, 100);
        textBox1.Text= Buff.ToString();

}
```

Notice that `StringBuilder` uses UTF16 so each character takes two bytes and it can be larger than the string it currently holds. For this reason it is safe to use 200 as the number of bytes in the buffer.

Exactly what type of string you need and what character encoding is a big problem and one that has no easy solution.

Array Buffers

You can use `StringBuilder` as a mutable buffer, but often this confuses the issue with concerns about encodings. A simple solution is to use an array. You can marshal a standard C# array into a C-style array pointer using `LPArray`. For example, in the previous example an alternative declaration is:

```
[DllImport("User32.dll", CharSet = CharSet.Unicode)]
static extern void GetWindowText(IntPtr hWnd,
            [MarshalAs(UnmanagedType.LPArray)] byte[] array,
            int nMaxCount);
```

To use this new version of `GetWindowText` we need an array of the correct type:

```
IntPtr hwnd = GetForegroundWindow();
byte[] Buff = new byte[100];
GetWindowText(hwnd, Buff, 100);
textBox1.Text= Encoding.Unicode.GetString(Buff);
```

Notice also that to display the result we now have to convert the raw bytes to a string using the appropriate encoding. This is the extra work entailed if the buffer really is text and not just bytes. Also notice that you can often modify how you define an imported function so that it works with the type of managed data you want it to work with.

Blitable Types, In, Out and Pinning

The term "blitable" means that the representation of the managed and unmanaged types are the same. You can "blit", i.e. copy, the bit pattern of a blitable data type as a block and simply start using it at its new location. If this is possible then marshaling is very easy because all that is involved is a block copy and perhaps creating a pointer to use to pass to the unmanaged function. All of the basic .NET data types, `int`, `float` and so on, are blitable as all of the machine types that .NET supports use the same representation for numeric values and pointers. Also all arrays are blitable.

At this point you might be hard pressed to imagine a non-blitable type. A good example is almost any date and time representation. These tend to differ in their layout in memory and marshaling involves rearranging data. If you think for a moment it should be clear that all of these non-blitable types are essentially formatted data or structs, see Chapter 27.

If a blitable parameter is passed by value then it is copied to the unmanaged stack without modification. A reference type is also passed by value, but as a pointer - to what? If the managed code references a blitable then we have the option of not making a copy or making a copy and adjusting the pointer to the new copy. If no copy is made then the original data is pinned in place and cannot be moved by the system so that the unmanaged code doesn't lose track of its data. Pinning is usually automatic, but there are occasions when you need to use it explicitly to make sure that a block of data isn't moved while you are working with it. When data is not-pinned, i.e. it is copied, then you have the option of asking the system to make a copy of the data when the unmanaged code has finished for the managed code to work with. Usually the system works out if a second copy process is needed, but you can control what happens using the `In` and `Out` attributes. Any parameter marked as `Out` is only copied to the managed code from the unmanaged. Any parameter marked as In is only copied from the unmanaged code. Using both `In` and `Out` allows two way copying. Notice that the system uses `In` for any reference type and `Out` for a parameter marked as out. `StringBuilder` is an exception to this rule and is passed as `[In,Out]`. So, for example, the previous `StringBuilder` buffer example could be declared as:

```
static extern void GetWindowText(IntPtr hWnd,
                         [In,Out]StringBuilder lpString,
                         int nMaxCount);
```

This works exactly as the default. If you change the attribute to [In] it also works, but without a copy to the unmanaged code. However, if you change it to [Out] you don't see any result.

If you try the same thing with the array buffer example you will find that In and Out are ignored as the array isn't copied. It is pinned and in this case any changes the unmanaged program makes are seen by the managed program, no matter how you set In and Out.

Terms Used In Unmanaged Code

To make good and confident use of interop you need to understand what is going on in the managed and the unmanaged code and this is a problem. If you don't write C or C++ then you are unlikely to know what many unmanaged data types are. Add to this the fact that Windows programmers have added other types to the list and the problem is even worse.

The following table from the documentation covers the most common types:

Unmanaged type in Windows APIs	Unmanaged C language type	Managed type	Description
VOID	void	System.Void	Applied to a void function.
HANDLE	void *	System.IntPtr or System.UIntPtr	32 bits on 32-bit Windows, 64 bits on 64-bit Windows.
BYTE	unsigned char	System.Byte	8 bits
SHORT	short	System.Int16	16 bits
WORD	unsigned short	System.UInt16	16 bits
INT	int	System.Int32	32 bits
UINT	unsigned int	System.UInt32	32 bits
LONG	long	System.Int32	32 bits
BOOL	long	System.Boolean or System.Int32	32 bits

DWORD	unsigned long	System.UInt32	32 bits
ULONG	unsigned long	System.UInt32	32 bits
CHAR	char	System.Char	Decorate with ANSI.
WCHAR	wchar_t	System.Char	Decorate with Unicode.
LPSTR	char *	System.String or System.Text.StringBuilder	Decorate with ANSI.
LPCSTR	const char *	System.String or System.Text.StringBuilder	Decorate with ANSI.
LPWSTR	wchar_t *	System.String or System.Text.StringBuilder	Decorate with Unicode.
LPCWSTR	const wchar_t *	System.String or System.Text.StringBuilder	Decorate with Unicode.
FLOAT	float	System.Single	32 bits
DOUBLE	double	System.Double	64 bits

Using PInvoke

Getting a PInvoke function declaration right can often be difficult due to subtleties in the way that managed and unmanaged types can be used. However, once you have a declaration that works using it is often very easy and very obvious. Clearly there is scope for sharing interop declarations and this is what the PInvoke.NET wiki sets out to do. If you visit https://www.pinvoke.net you will find an extensive collection of declarations relating to a wide range of APIs. At this point you might think *"why bother learning about interop - why not just use the declarations?"*. The answer is that many of the declarations often need slight tweaks to make them work in your particular situation and this requires understanding. In addition, there are some functions that haven't been converted yet and you might need to modify one of the existing declarations. There is also the small matter that you can create declarations which allows your custom .NET code to be called by unmanaged programs and these won't be in any predefined catalogs.

Postlude

Using PInvoke is a matter of discovering where the native function you want to use is stored, i.e. which library file it is in. Then you have to work out what its parameter types are and ensure that the managed types that you are using are correctly marshaled to and from the call. This sounds easy, but in practice it is a very fiddly process that generally involves trial and error.

Using COM objects from .NET can be a difficult subject and it is where interop becomes most confusing. The reason is not just that it is poorly documented, but the range of implementation styles of COM objects is so great that it's confusing. You might think at this stage "*if it's so difficult why bother?*" The answer is that, despite the fact that .NET makes it obsolete, COM is deeply embedded in the existing Windows technology. First generation Windows API technology was based on the DLL as a function library – these functions you can use via PInvoke as described in the previous chapter. Second generation Windows used the same basic idea, but collected the functions together into COM interfaces. Microsoft has provided .NET classes that wrap much of the API, but there is still a great deal that is simply untouched. Then of course there are the legacy COM objects that we created in an effort to take advantage of object-oriented code reuse. It looks as if COM and the humble DLL is going to be with us for a while yet.

IJW (It Just Works) is perhaps the aspect of COM Interop that Microsoft likes to emphasize. The idea is that you add a reference to a COM object and the system imports it for you by automatically creating a class wrapper for it. It has to be said that this is the ideal and you should always try importing a COM object by adding a reference to the file it is stored in before resorting to the techniques described in this article. The big problem with IJW is that if It Doesn't Just Work (i.e. IDJW) then you really are dumped into a great unknown territory and, as the key COM interface is named IUnknown, perhaps that should be "great IUnknown territory".

The supplied documentation on manually creating wrappers is poor. What has been provided is spread out under a range of different topic headings and seems to have a strange reluctance to simply tell you what it is all about. If you study the few supplied examples and try to match them to the documentation, it is still very difficult to discover exactly what is going on. To really understand you need to know a little about how COM works and some of the variations on the basic theme that you encounter in real life.

Just Enough COM

The idea of a COM object is very simple. It's essentially a C++ class with some public virtual methods that you can call. In theory, it doesn't have to be implemented in C++, but that's the language that the technology was based on. A virtual method is simply a function that you can access via a pointer, like a virtual method in C# it is late-bound and a COM object organizes these pointers to functions into an array called a vtable. At a slightly higher-level we can view this vtable as an interface, i.e. a collection of functions of defined type and signature. It's important to notice that the type/signature aspects of an interface aren't part of its run-time implementation – it really is just an array of function pointers and you could use it to call one of the functions with any parameters you care to supply. Of course, if you don't supply the parameters it expects, nothing works and the whole thing crashes.

COM formalizes the interface idea to allow you to write code that "discovers" what interfaces an object supports at run time. The idea is that all COM objects offer a basic interface called IUnknown which has just three methods, QueryInterface, AddRef and Release. AddRef and Release just increment and decrement a use counter so that the COM object knows when it still has users and you can mostly ignore them.

The QueryInterface method is much more useful in that it will return a pointer to any other interfaces the object supports. Rather than using a name to specify the interface you want to find, you specify its IID (Interface ID), that is the Guid (Globally Unique Identifier) that was allocated to the COM object stored in the registry when it was installed. Indeed, the COM object itself is identified by another GUID in the registry known as its clsid (CLaSs ID).

Thus far the story is simple. To use a COM object you first create an instance of it using the standard API function CoCreateInstance. You pass it the clsid of the COM object and it passes back to you a pointer to the object's IUnknown interface. You then pass the IUnknown QueryInterface the IID of the interface you want to use and it passes back a pointer to it. You also need to know that every interface "inherits" from IUnknown and so every vtable starts off with a pointer to QueryInterface, AddRef and Release. Interfaces can also "inherit" from other interfaces, but this really only means that the vtable starts off with the entire vtable for the base interface before the pointers to any new functions.

Interfaces based on IUnknown are very simple. In fact, they are so simple that COM needed more infrastructure to cope with the real world. A wide range of additional technologies have been added to the basic IUnknown mechanism to make using COM more "automatic", in particular IDispatch interfaces and IDL.

IDispatch

An `IDispatch` interface is a special type of `IUnknown` interface that includes methods that allow other methods to be called by name at run time. To call a method in a simple `IUnknown` interface all you need is to know is where in the `vtable` the function pointer is. So, for example, to call `MyMethod` you would need to know that it is the sixth method defined in `MyInterface` and so its pointer is in `vtable[5]`, given that the first function pointer is in `vtable[0]` and points at `QueryInterface`.

Using `IDispatch` you can call the function by name. You simply use the `GetIDsOfNames` method and then the `Invoke` method of the `IDispatch` interface. You can think of this as equivalent to the .NET reflection mechanism that allows late binding. In the case of COM, the `IDispatch` interface was mostly used by other software tools to allow the programmer to access interfaces without the bother of learning COM. `IDispatch` is what allows you to use an `ActiveX` object or automation facility from a script without worrying about COM. The important point here is that this is still what .NET uses when it constructs a wrapper for a COM object. Indeed most of the COM Interop IJW facilities only "Just Work" when the COM object has an `IDispatch` interface and there are great many that only support the pure `IUnknown` interface.

IDL

We also need to know a little about IDL, Interface Definition Language, which is used to describe the type of an Interface. It allows the COM designer to specify GUIDS for classes and interfaces, interface names, method names, method signatures, how parameters are passed and even general data types to be used in conjunction with the COM object. You can think of IDL as a general purpose data type description language.

Most COM objects have an IDL file associated with them, but they don't have to. You can find the IDL files corresponding to the COM objects that implement parts of the Windows API in the Platform SDK which you can download from the Microsoft website. IDL files aren't actually used directly by a programming language but are converted into either C/C++ header files or into "type libraries" by the IDL compiler, MIDL.

A type library is what you need if you are going to try to use a COM object in IJW mode. This is what the .NET system uses to create class wrappers for the COM object but, as already explained, it only works if the object supports `IDispatch`. In practice, even an `IDispatch` interface isn't a guarantee that automatic wrapping will be possible – it has to be OLE Automation compatible and use nothing out of the ordinary for it to be 100% successful.

As you can see the basic COM mechanism is simple, but it has been elaborated to a point where it can seem very complicated. When you add to this the fact that COM programmers often found "inventive" ways of creating COM objects and interfaces then things become even more difficult. There is also the fact that COM programmers use different styles to write their IDL files and to implement their COM interfaces. Reading through some IDL files quickly raises the question *"how many ways does a COM programmer need to define a 32-bit word?"* DWORD, HRESULT, ULONG, HWND, Reserved, Flag and so on, all just mean Int32.

There are also generations of Windows to take into account. You will find FARPOINTER being used as a data type in the days when pointers were mostly 16-bit and a 32-bit pointer was the exception. You also have the problem of ANSI 8-bit versus UNICODE 16-bit character data and the large number of different ways there are ofr representing sophisticated data types such as strings, arrays and structures. It all adds up to a very threatening mess for any programmer about to tackle an IUnknown and it's a good example of how an initially good idea was allowed to run wild. What you need to keep in mind is that the IUnknown interface is essentially simple and if you proceed step-by-step you can get it all working.

Creating COM Objects

It's time to put theory into practice and we might as well start at the beginning and look at how we can create a COM object. As an example let's use the Windows TaskScheduler which has a fairly complicated COM-based API. You can find a header file MsTask.h and an IDL file MsTask.idl for it in the Platform SDK (in the Include directory). Reading either file will supply all the information you need about the GUIDs, data types and interfaces that the COM object is associated with.

If the COM object is playing by the rules, then there are three basic ways to bring an instance into existence using .NET. The first is to use the COM API function CoCreateInstance as if you were a C++ programmer. You can do this in C# using the standard PInvoke mechanisms. For example, to create an instance of the TaskScheduler we first need to define CoCreateInstance:

```
[DllImport("ole32.Dll")]
static public extern uint CoCreateInstance(
  ref Guid clsid,
  [MarshalAs(UnmanagedType.IUnknown)] object inner,
  uint context,
  ref Guid uuid,
  [MarshalAs(UnmanagedType.IUnknown)] out object rReturnedComObject);
```

This is simply a matter of looking up its definition in the documentation and translating it to a PInvoke-style declaration. The only unusual part is the use of the `UnmanagedType.IUnknown` type which marshals the returned pointer to `IUnknown` into an object wrapper of type `System._ComObject`. To use this to create an instance of the `TaskScheduler` we first need to read its `CLSID` from the IDL file and include the `IID` of the `IUnknown` interface, which is standard:

```
Guid CLSID_Ctask=new Guid("{148BD52A-A2AB-11CE-B11F-00AA00530503}");
Guid IID_IUnknown = new Guid("00000000-0000-0000-C000-000000000046");
```

With the addition of a constant and an object to store the returned interface pointer, we can now call `CoCreateInstance`:

```
object OSched;
const uint CLSCTX_INPROC_SERVER = 1;
CoCreateInstance(
                ref CLSID_Ctask,
                null,
                CLSCTX_INPROC_SERVER,
                ref IID_IUnknown,
                out OSched);
```

The `OSched` object is now a reference to the COM class and its `IUnknown` interface. How this is used is described later.

The second way of creating a COM object is to use the .NET reflection facilities to create a `Type` from a `Guid` and then an object from a type:

```
Type TSched = Type.GetTypeFromCLSID(CLSID_CTask);
OSched = Activator.CreateInstance(TSched);
```

As before, `OSched` is now an object that wraps the COM class and its `IUnknown` interface.

The final method is to make direct use of the .NET COM Interop facilities to define a class that wraps the COM object:

```
[ComImport, Guid("148BD52A-A2AB-11CE-B11F-00AA00530503")]
        class CTaskScheduler
        {
        };
```

Now we have a .NET class that wraps the COM object and `IUnknown` and we can create an instance in the usual way:

```
CTaskScheduler OSched = new CTaskScheduler();
```

In this case the .NET Framework does all of the initialization and calls to `CoCreateInstance` etc and looks after the lifetime of the object.

Which of the three methods is best? The answer is that using the `ComImport` attribute has to be the easiest, but it sometimes doesn't work or sometimes doesn't provide you with the control you need over how or when the class is created. In such cases try one of the others.

Raw IUnknown

At this point we have the COM object and, implicitly, its `IUnknown` interface. However, .NET doesn't expect you to want to use the object's `IUnknown` interface and therefore doesn't provide an easy way to do it. For other interfaces the COM Interop makes it very easy – in fact all you have to do is cast the object to a suitable interface type and COM Interop looks after calling `QueryInterface` and wrapping the returned interface pointer. This is certainly the way that you should use COM in .NET, but as a demonstration of how you can use a COM interface directly let's explore `IUnknown`.

The first thing to say is that .NET does provide methods that you can use to work with `IUnknown`, but they aren't entirely satisfactory. Again, it's important to note that this isn't the way that you would use a typical COM interface. The `Marshal` static object has a great many methods that can be used in the conversion of managed and unmanaged types. In this case there are four methods of direct relevance: `GetIUnknownForObject`, which returns a pointer to a pointer of the object's `IUnknown` interface; `QueryInterface`, which returns a pointer to a pointer for a specified interface; `AddRef`, which increments the use count; and `Release` which decrements the use count. All of them use the `IntPtr` type to specify and return pointers to interface pointers.

All will become clear with a simple example. First get a pointer to the `IUnknown` interface pointer for the scheduler:

```
IntPtr pIUnk = Marshal.GetIUnknownForObject(OSched);
```

Now we can use `AddRef` and `Release` as a demonstration that it works:

```
Int32 usecount1 = Marshal.AddRef(pIUnk);
Int32 usecount2 = Marshal.Release(pIUnk);
```

Finally, to show how a pointer to another interface would be retrieved, we use `QueryInterface` to get a pointer to the `ITaskScheduler` interface with its IID obtained from the IDL file:

```
IntPtr pISched;
Guid IidSched = new Guid("148BD527-A2AB-11CE-B11F-00AA00530503");
Int32 result = Marshal.QueryInterface(pIUnk, ref IidSched,
                                             out pISched);
```

When this method returns we have a pointer to the `ITaskScheduler` interface pointer.

This is all very well but how do we call the methods in an interface given that all we have is a pointer to the interface pointer? There might well be a way to cast such a pointer into an interface wrapper type, but I can't find one! One possible solution is to access the `vtable` directly as a pointer array and then cast each pointer to a function to a suitable delegate. Despite my best efforts I've only had limited success with this approach in C# - it's probably something to do with the calling convention used as it tends to fail when there are parameters.

Casting Interfaces

The examples given above of using the IUnknown interface are perhaps a little too low-level for most applications. Once you have created the COM object and its IUnknown interface, you don't really need to access it because the .NET Framework knows how to use it on your behalf. If you want to call methods defined in MyInterface all you have to do is define a C# interface with the correct number of functions, in the same order as in the vtable, and with the correct parameters. You then simply cast the COM object to this interface type and the Framework automatically calls the QueryInterface method and wraps the returned pointer to an interface pointer in a new class. You can then use all of the methods of the new class as if nothing unusual was afoot. Of course, there are a few fine details to consider and the main problem, as with all interop tasks, is sorting out how parameters should be handled.

In principle, this is no different from parameter handling when calling a DLL function but there are a few new features. Let's look at a real example and implement the definition of the ITaskScheduler interface. The IDL file defines this as:

```
interface ITaskScheduler : IUnknown
{
// Methods:
        HRESULT SetTargetComputer([in] LPCWSTR pwszComputer);
        HRESULT GetTargetComputer([out] LPWSTR * ppwszComputer);
        HRESULT Enum( [out] IEnumWorkItems ** ppEnumWorkItems);
        HRESULT Activate([in] LPCWSTR pwszName,[in] REFIID riid,
                                            [out] IUnknown ** ppUnk);
        HRESULT Delete([in] LPCWSTR pwszName);
        HRESULT NewWorkItem([in]   LPCWSTR pwszTaskName,
                            [in]   REFCLSID    rclsid,
                            [in]   REFIID      riid,
                            [out] IUnknown ** ppUnk);
        HRESULT AddWorkItem([in] LPCWSTR pwszTaskName,
                            [in] IScheduledWorkItem * pWorkItem);
        HRESULT IsOfType(   [in] LPCWSTR pwszName,
                            [in] REFIID  riid);
}
```

You can copy and paste the IDL or the header file specification of the interface into your C# program and then edit it to create a working definition. It is helpful to realize that only the order of the functions matters in relating them to the vtable.

So, for example, an absolutely minimum specification for this interface would be:

```
[Guid("148BD527-A2AB-11CE-B11F-00AA00530503"),
      InterfaceType(
      ComInterfaceType.InterfaceIsIUnknown)]
          private interface ITaskScheduler
{
      void SetTargetComputer();
      void GetTargetComputer();
      void Enum();
      void Activate();
      void Delete();
      void NewWorkItem();
      void AddWorkItem();
      void IsOfType();
}
```

This defines where each function is in the vtable, but without parameter information. Of course, if any function really doesn't have any parameters you could use this definition to call it without further refining the definition of the interface. This allows us to work incrementally when developing an interface definition. A simple way to work is to paste the IDL or header file definition into the C# program and initially comment out all of the parameters.

The Guid quoted at the start is the IDD of the interface obtained from the IDL file and this is used by the Framework when it calls QueryInterface. Notice that the ComInterfaceType doesn't mean that this is an IUnknown interface, but that it should be treated by the Framework as if it was derived from IUnknown. Also notice that the Framework saves you the trouble of having to define the QueryInterface, AddRef and Release functions as they are part of every IUnknown interface. You start the definition from the first new function added to the basic IUnknown.

To try out an interface definition it's usually a good idea to pick the simplest function defined and attempt to define its parameters. If this works then you know that you have the interface you want and it is functioning correctly. Defining the rest of the interface is then just a matter of crafting the parameter definitions. Let's start with GetTargetComputer:

```
HRESULT GetTargetComputer( [out] LPWSTR * ppwszComputer);
```

This translates to:

```
void GetTargetComputer([Out, MarshalAs(UnmanagedType.LPWStr)]
                        out StringBuilder ppwszComputer);
```

There are a number of traps waiting for the eager programmer in this definition. The first is that you do need to use `LPWStr` because this COM Interface uses Unicode. You also need the `out` modifier because this is a pointer to a `LPWStr` – most strings are passed as pointers to strings not, as here, pointers to pointers to strings. There is also the small puzzle as why the return type is void and not `Int32` or similar? The answer is that the COM Interop system converts all `HRESULT` error codes into exceptions which you should handle. As a result we don't get an `HRESULT` and so the function should be defined as void.

With this change to the interface definition we can test it. To get the new interface we simply cast the original object:

```
ITaskScheduler ITaskSchd = OSched as ITaskScheduler;
```

Now we can use it, but be careful to only use those methods that you have actually defined, i.e. `GetTargetComputer` in this case:

```
StringBuilder name = new StringBuilder(50);
ITaskSchd.GetTargetComputer(out name);
MessageBox.Show(name.ToString());
```

Now that we have this much working we can move on to more interesting methods. As methods within an interface tend to use the same range of parameters, interface definition tends to become easier as you progress through the list. So for example, only a small modification is required to define `SetTargetComputer`:

```
void SetTargetComputer(
        [In, MarshalAs(UnmanagedType.LPWStr)] String pwszComputer);
```

Notice that in this case a `String` is easier to use and this parameter is a pointer to a string.

Interfaces As Parameters

In the simple COM model the only way interfaces are returned is via `QueryInterface` and a suitable IID. However, COM programmers didn't keep to this simple model as they found it more or less essential to write other interface functions that returned interface pointers, sometimes with the help of an IID but mostly without one. Consider for a moment `NewWorkItem`:

```
HRESULT NewWorkItem(
        [in]   LPCWSTR      pwszTaskName,
        [in]   REFCLSID     rclsid,
        [in]   REFIID       riid,
        [out]  IUnknown **  ppUnk);
```

This takes a `clsid` and an Iid and returns a pointer to an `IUnknown` Interface pointer to the Interface specified. This appears to be horribly complicated, particularly the use of a pointer to a pointer and probably not worth trying to translate, but in fact the .NET Framework can handle it with ease. The translation is:

```
void NewWorkItem(
        [In, MarshalAs(UnmanagedType.LPWStr)] String pwszTaskName,
        [In] ref Guid rclsid,
        [In] ref Guid rIid,
        [Out, MarshalAs(UnmanagedType.IUnknown)] out object ppUnk);
```

The string is marshaled as in earlier functions and the Framework knows how to deal with converting the Guid to the string of bytes which the function needs. What is more surprising is that the Framework also implements the marshaling of the returned interface into an object wrapper. To use this function we simply need the Clsid of the Task object:

```
Guid CTask = new Guid(0x148BD520, 0xA2AB, 0x11CE, 0xB1, 0x1F, 0x00,
                                  0xAA, 0x00, 0x53, 0x05, 0x03);
```

and the IiID of the ITask interface:

```
Guid ITask = new Guid(0x148BD524, 0xA2AB, 0x11CE, 0xB1, 0x1F, 0x00,
                                  0xAA, 0x00, 0x53, 0x05, 0x03);
```

Next we use these to create a new Task object and its associated interface:

```
object itask;
ItaskSchd.NewWorkItem("Test", ref CTask, ref ITask, out itask);
```

To make use of the ITask interface we have to cast it to a .NET ITask interface type and this means that we have to define another interface. This isn't difficult, but in this case we can also cast it to one of the standard interfaces that many COM objects support.

It's also worth noting that CTask is a COM class in its own right and can be created complete with its IUnknown Interface using any of the three methods described earlier, for example:

```
[ComImport, Guid("148BD520-A2AB-11CE-B11F-00AA00530503")]
        class CTask{}
```

After this you can create CTask objects using new and cast them to ITask interfaces.

Standard COM Interfaces

As COM developed there was a need to define standard interfaces that would do common tasks in a uniform way. For example, many COM objects need to save their state and rather than expect the user to create a custom save routine the IPersist interface and its derived interfaces were introduced so that the user could simply call IPersistFile.Save and the COM object would save its state to disk. Not all COM objects implement IPersistFile, or any other standard interface, but when they do it's worth making use of them. In this case the TaskScheduler object implements both IUnknown and IPersistFile and we can use this to save the new task that we have just created.

Most of the standard COM Interfaces are defined in:

System.Runtime.InteropServices.ComTypes;

You can find older definitions in the UCOM namespace.

Adding a:

using System.Runtime.InteropServices.ComTypes;

allows us to write:

```
IPersistFile PFile = itask as IPersistFile;
PFile.Save(null, true);
```

That is, we cast to the predefined interface type IPersistFile and then use its Save method to create an unscheduled task in the default machine's scheduler.

Inheritance and Interfaces

You can continue with this approach to expanding the facilities that you have access to in .NET. Mostly it's just a matter of pasting and editing the IDL definitions. However, you have to be sure to take account of interface inheritance. For example, if you plan to implement the ITask interface, its IDL definition starts:

```
interface ITask;
[
        local,
        object,
        uuid(148BD524-A2AB-11CE-B11F-00AA00530503),
        pointer_default(unique)
]
interface ITask : IScheduledWorkItem
{
// Properties that correspond to parameters of CreateProcess:
        HRESULT SetApplicationName([in] LPCWSTR pwszApplicationName);
```

The inclusion of interface ITask : IScheduledWorkItem means that ITask inherits from IScheduledWorkItem. For interfaces, inheritance is particularly simple. All that happens is that the vtable starts off with all of the items in IScheduledWorkItem and then the new functions in ITask.

Thus the first function in our .NET Interface definition isn't
SetApplicationName, but CreateTrigger, the first function in
IScheduledWorkItem:

```
interface IScheduledWorkItem;
[
        local,
        object,
        uuid(a6b952f0-a4b1-11d0-997d-00aa006887ec),
        pointer_default(unique)
]
interface IScheduledWorkItem : IUnknown
{
// Methods concerning scheduling:
        HRESULT CreateTrigger(
                [out] WORD *              piNewTrigger,
                [out] ITaskTrigger ** ppTrigger);
```

That is, COM interfaces really do implement inheritance as concatenations of
vtables. For some reason the fact that one interface inherits from another is
often overlooked in the documentation and a careful look at the IDL file is
usually a good idea.

Signature Problems

The fact that COM Interop is clever enough to intercept the HRESULT return
value, decode it and then trigger an exception if it is an error code is usually a
good thing. However, sometimes methods return status information in
HRESULT, even though they shouldn't. For example, in the old Outlook
Express COM API – defined in msoeapi.idl and msoeapi.h which are both in
the Platform SDK Includes folder – the GetFirstFolder and GetNextFolder
functions in the IStoreNamespace interface return an HRESULT of 0 if they have
retrieved a sub-folder and 1 if there are no more sub-folders. To process this
result we have to add the [PreserveSig] attribute, which forces the COM
Interop mechanism not to interfere with HRESULT:

```
[PreserveSig]
Int32 GetFirstSubFolder(
[In, MarshalAs(UnmanagedType.U4)] Int32 dwFolderId,
[Out, MarshalAs(UnmanagedType.Struct)]  out _FOLDERPROPS pProps,
[Out, MarshalAs(UnmanagedType.U4)] out Int32 phEnum);


[PreserveSig]
Int32 GetNextSubFolder(
[In, MarshalAs(UnmanagedType.U4)] Int32 hEnum,
[Out, MarshalAs(UnmanagedType.Struct)] out _FOLDERPROPS pProps);
```

Now you can test the HRESULT return value to see if there is a folder to process, but notice that you now also need to test it for more general error conditions and throw your own exceptions to signal the problem. An interesting trap waiting for the innocent programmer is that if you leave off the [PreserveSig] then everything works, but the return value is always set to zero by COM Interop.

Postlude

Using COM from C# is easy as long as it just works. Troubleshooting requires a lot of deep knowledge about COM and about the way it is actually implemented and used. In most cases you can make it work as long as the implementation doesn't deviate too far from the basics.

Chapter 25

Custom Attributes

Attributes don't really seem to be necessary as part of a programming language. After all why "decorate" code with attributes when you can achieve the same results by more direct routes? In nearly all cases an attribute is an excuse for not implementing a property that does the same job. However, attributes provide a useful extension to the standard language syntax and a way of adding features after the event and without having to extensively rework the classes that that attributes are applied to as exemplified by the interop facilities that we've looked at in earlier chapters. In this context attributes are a natural way to apply modifiers to default behavior. In other words, the classes that you apply attributes to don't necessarily need to know anything about the attributes you apply. In this sense attributes have been likened to "code patching" brought up-to-date.

You can use an attribute to add a behavior without modifying the core code and you can take this behavior away just as easily.

C# has supported and usefully employed attributes for some time, but there is still a great deal of confusion about when custom attributes might or might not be useful.

Runtime Metadata

In .NET an attribute is an item of data associated with a programming construct that is stored in the assembly and which can be accessed by the use of reflection. Some confusion is caused by the fact that some built-in attributes also additionally affect the way that the compiler seems to work. In the main this is not something that most attributes, and certainly not custom attributes, do. Essentially a custom attribute is a "code comment" that gets compiled into your code, as metadata, and which other code, including your own, can retrieve and possibly act on.

This is the standard explanation of an attribute, but the attribute mechanism has more to offer. When you retrieve an attribute an instance of a class that represents the attribute is created. Understanding how this mechanism works means that you can think about exactly how attributes might be useful and how things can go wrong.

There is a sense in which an attribute can always be replaced by a property. For example, you might mark a class as using ASCII encoding for its text and hence implement an [ASCII] attribute. Any other class that makes use of a class so marked would have to inspect it to discover that it was ASCII and then arrange to treat it correctly.

It should be fairly obvious that an alternative is to use an ASCII property set to `true` or `false` to indicate the same information. Notice that the two approaches have some similarities and some differences:

- ◆ Any client that uses the class has to implement retrieving and testing the attribute or the property and act accordingly, that is, nothing is enforced in either approach.

- ◆ A property can be set at compile time and can be changed at run time. An attribute on the other hand is set at compile time and generally isn't changed at run time.

- ◆ A property is associated with instances of a class but an attribute can be associated with many different entities, including classes, methods, parameters and so on.

Attributes don't change and can be associated with a range of entities

This seems to sum up the situation, but notice that with such a flexible implementation you can always change the way things work. This is the standard and most appropriate way of working with attributes.

Implementing a Custom Attribute

Implementing a custom attribute such as [ASCII], mentioned in the previous section, is fairly easy as long as you don't read into it more than there is. All you have to do is create a class that inherits from `Attribute`:

```
public class ASCIIattribute : Attribute
{
}
```

It is usual to use a name of the form *X*attribute and if you do the system will treat the names *X* and *X*attribute as the same. Unfortunately if you do declare the class following this convention, e.g. `ASCIIattribute`, then IntelliSense prompts with the full name.

Personally I'd rather keep attribute names short and meaningful so I prefer:

```
public class ASCII : Attribute
{
}
```

Now you can apply the attribute to any class as in:

```
[ASCII]
public class MyClass
{
}
```

Of course, nothing happens if you do this as there is no default attribute behavior worth worrying about, but it is legal syntax – now to give it some semantics.

Attribute Semantics

The key to understanding what is going on here is to realize that the attribute class you have defined is instantiated when anything queries the custom attributes of `MyClass`. To query custom attributes we use the `GetCustomAttributes` static method of the `Attribute` class:

```
Attribute.GetCustomAttributes(t)
```

This returns an array consisting of an instance of each attribute class corresponding to the attributes that have been applied to the specified type t. Notice that this returns an array containing one instance of every attribute applied to t. For example, the instruction:

```
Attribute[] attrs = Attribute.GetCustomAttributes(typeof(MyClass));
```

returns an array with, in this case, a single element `attrs[0]` which contains an instance of `ASCII`. A cast to `ASCII` is all you need to make use of the instance.

This way of retrieving attributes is the one you most often encounter in examples of attribute use. However, in many situations there is an alternative which is arguably better. In most cases you don't really want to retrieve all the attributes applied to an entity because you are writing code which is going to handle just one attribute type, i.e. the custom attribute you are currently implementing.

There is a fairly easy way to retrieve specific attributes from the type to which they are applied using the `GetCustomAttributes` method of the `Type` object to return attributes of a specified type.

For example, to retrieve any ASCII attributes applied to MyClass you would use:

```
object[] attrs = typeof(MyClass).
                    GetCustomAttributes(typeof(ASCII), false);
```

This returns an array of objects that can be cast to the attribute type you are looking for. The final Boolean parameter determines if the instance's inheritance chain is searched for attributes - false restricts us to only directly applied attributes.

If you want to make things easier you can perform the cast on the returned array:

```
ASCII[] attrs = (ASCII[]) typeof(MyClass).
                    GetCustomAttributes(typeof(ASCII), false);
```

This always works because only attributes of ASCII type will be returned or a null reference which can also be cast to ASCII.

The Attribute Constructor

Currently the instance of the attribute's class isn't doing us a lot of good as the class has no methods and, more importantly, no properties. There are two ways of providing it with properties. The first is to provide a constructor with parameters. For example, if we change the ASCII class definition to:

```
public class ASCII : Attribute
{
        public string MyData;
        public ASCII(string MyDataIn)
        {
                MyData = MyDataIn;
        }
}
```

we can pass some data to the class by applying the attribute as:

```
[ASCII("Hello Attribute World")]
public class MyClass
{
}
```

Now when the GetCustomAttributes method is called it returns a single instance of the ASCII class with MyData set to Hello Attribute World.

In other words, calling the GetCustomAttributes method has resulted in the class constructor being used with the data provided by the ASCII attribute tag.

The tag is a call to the constructor and you can think of:

```
[ASCII("Hello Attribute World") ]
```

as being equivalent to:

```
new ASCII("Hello Attribute World");
```

being executed when you call GetCustomAttributes on any class that the attribute is applied to so returning an instance complete with whatever initialization the constructor has performed.

To see that you have indeed got an instance of the ASCII class complete with the string set by the constructor try:

```
ASCII[] attrs=(ASCII[]) typeof(MyClass).GetCustomAttributes(
                                    typeof(ASCII), false);
MessageBox.Show(attrs[0].MyData);
```

After casting the returned array to ASCII you can access all its public methods and properties. While this isn't the way that attributes are normally used, it is perfectly valid.

Initializing Fields

As well as using the constructor to initialize the instance, you can also use named parameters to initialize member variables. For example, if we add a public variable MoreData to the attribute class:

```
public class ASCII : Attribute
{
      public string MyData;
      public string MoreData;
      public ASCII(string MyDataIn)
      {
            MyData = MyDataIn;
      }
}
```

it can be initialized using:

```
[ASCII("Hello Attribute World", MoreData="SomeData")]
```

Now when GetCustomAttributes is called the instance is constructed as follows:

```
attrs[0]=new ASCII("Hello Attribute World");
attrs[0].MoreData = "SomeData";
```

Once again you can test this assertion by using a `MessageBox`:

```
ASCII[] attrs=(ASCII[]) typeof(MyClass).GetCustomAttributes(
                                    typeof(ASCII), false);
MessageBox.Show(attrs[0].MoreData);
```

where you will discover that the public string `MoreData` has indeed been set to "SomeData" by the attribute.

You should now be able to see the general principle:

- ◆ Any unnamed parameters used in the attribute are passed to the constructor in the order in which they are given.

- ◆ Any named parameters are used as initialization statements after the instance has been constructed.

Notice that all of the unnamed parameters have to come before the named parameters. For example, an attribute applied as:

```
[MyAttribute(a,b,c,... name1=A,name2=B...)]
```

results in:

```
MyAttribute MyInstance= new MyAttribute(a,b,c,...);
MyInstance.name1=A;
MyInstance.name2=B;
...
```

when the `GetCustomAttributes` method is used.

Notice also that named parameters are optional, if they are not supplied then the corresponding variable is left uninitialized.

It is also important to know that the type of parameter you can use is limited to the majority of the simple types, i.e. `int`, `long`, `float`, `string`, `System.Type`, `object`, a publicly accessible `enum` and a one-dimensional array of any allowable type.

You might think that as you can pass an object you can pass anything, but this isn't the case. There is an additional condition that restricts parameters to constants of the appropriate type. So, while you can have:

```
[ASCII("Hello Method",MyObject=1)]
```

and even:

```
[ASCII("Hello Method",MyObject="Hello")]
```

you can't have:

```
[ASCII("Hello Method", MyObject=new object())]
```

or anything like it.

Each time you request the details of an attribute a new object is instantiated no matter what class is involved. For example, if we go back to the simpler version of ASCII with a single parameter constructor, the following:

```
[ASCII("Hello Attribute World")]
public class MyClass
{
}

[ASCII("Hello Again")]
public class MyClass2
{
}
```

does indeed create distinct attribute instances as you can demonstrate:

```
ASCII[] attrs1=(ASCII[])typeof(MyClass).GetCustomAttributes(
                               typeof(ASCII), false);
ASCII[] attrs2=(ASCII[])typeof(MyClass2).GetCustomAttributes(
                               typeof(ASCII), false);
MessageBox.Show(attrs1[0].MyData);
MessageBox.Show(attrs2[0].MyData);
```

The result is two message boxes that correctly show each of the messages set by the attribute tags. However, you get two instances even if you call GetCustomAttributes a second time on the same class.

What isn't generally realized is that you can change attribute values fairly easily at run time. The reason is, of course, that the instances of the attribute classes that are created are perfectly normal objects and can be used without restriction. For example, we can get the object:

```
ASCII[] attrs1=(ASCII[])typeof(MyClass).GetCustomAttributes(
                               typeof(ASCII), false);
```

change the value of its public variable and show that it has changed:

```
attrs1[0].MyData="A New String";
MessageBox.Show(attrs1[0].MyData);
```

and finally create another instance and show that its value is unchanged:

```
ASCII[] attrs3=(ASCII[]) typeof(MyClass).GetCustomAttributes(
                               typeof(ASCII), false);
MessageBox.Show(attrs3[0].MyData);
```

Practical Attributes

Now that we have clarified the basic mechanism that is used to implement attributes we need to investigate some of the intricacies of using attributes in a real situation. The first thing to say is attributes can be applied to more than just a class. To restrict what an attribute can be applied to you need to apply

315

the `AttributeUsage` attribute to the class that is associated with your custom attribute - yes an attribute applied to your custom attribute! For example:

```
[AttributeUsage(AttributeTargets.Method)]
public  class ASCII : Attribute
```

restricts the `ASCII` attribute to being applied to methods only. If you try to apply it to anything else the compiler will generate an error message.

IntelliSense provides a list of `AttributeTargets` and you can OR targets together to produce a set of things that the attribute can be applied to, an example of this is given later.

Being able to tag other entities with attributes raises the question of how to access them at run time? The answer is that there are overloaded versions of `GetCustomAttributes` which return arrays of attributes associated with different types of entity. For example, `GetCustomAttributes(memberinfo)` will retrieve an array of attributes applied to the member specified by the `memberinfo` class.

To see how this works, first add a member function to `MyClass` and tag it with the `ASCII` attribute:

```
public class MyClass
{
        [ASCII("Hello Method")]
        public void MyMethod()
        {
        }
}
```

To retrieve attributes associated with a member we first have to retrieve its `memberinfo`. There are many ways of doing this, but in most cases specifying it by name is sufficient using the `GetMember` function:

```
System.Reflection.MemberInfo[] member =
                    typeof(MyClass).GetMember("MyMethod");
```

The `GetMember` function retrieves all members that match the name of the specified string which can include wildcard characters. In this case it should just return a `memberinfo` class corresponding to the unique `MyMethod` function.

To retrieve any attributes applied to the method we can use the usual:

```
Attribute[] attrs = Attribute.GetCustomAttributes(member[0]);
```

Or, if you just want the `ASCII` attributes that have been applied, we can use the alternative:

```
ASCII[] attrs = (ASCII[]) member[0].GetCustomAttributes(
                                    typeof(ASCII), false);
MessageBox.Show(attrs[0].MyData);
```

The `GetMember` function will return members of a range of different sorts – methods, properties etc.

If you want, you can be more specific and use functions such as `GetMethod` to return a single `MethodInfo` class that is specified by name and other information. For example:

```
System.Reflection.MethodInfo method =
                           typeof(MyClass).GetMethod("MyMethod");
ASCII[] attrs =
      (ASCII[]) method.GetCustomAttributes(typeof(ASCII), false);
```

There is also a `GetMethods` function which will return an array of methods that match a name that includes wildcard characters. You can return fields, properties, interfaces and so on and use the corresponding `GetCustomAttributes` to return an array of attributes applied to them.

Retrieving attributes is generally straightforward – use reflection to get the entity and then call `GetCustomAttributes`.

One slightly more complicated situation is when an attribute is applied to a parameter. In this case we have to first retrieve the method, then the parameter and then its attributes. To see this in action change the `ASCII` attribute to read:

```
[AttributeUsage(AttributeTargets.Method |
                                AttributeTargets.Parameter)]
public  class ASCII : Attribute
{
      public string MyData;
      public string MoreData;
      public ASCII(string MyDataIn)
      {
            MyData = MyDataIn;
      }
```

Notice that this is an example of OR-ing together parameters used in the constructor call.

The attribute can now be applied to methods and parameters:

```
public class MyClass
{
      [ASCII("Hello Method")]
      public void MyMethod(
            [ASCII("Hello MyParameter")] string MyParameter)
      {
      }
}
```

To retrieve the attribute we first need to get the method:

```
System.Reflection.MethodInfo method =
                        typeof(MyClass).GetMethod("MyMethod");
```

Then we need to get the parameters of the method:

```
System.Reflection.ParameterInfo[] pars= method.GetParameters();
```

Finally we can get and access the parameter attribute:

```
ASCII[] attrs = (ASCII[]) pars[0].GetCustomAttributes(
                                typeof(ASCII), false);
MessageBox.Show(attrs[0].MyData);
```

As well as controlling what an attribute can be applied to, you can also control how many times it can be applied and whether or not it is inherited using the `AttributeUsage` attribute. For example, if you change the ASCII class definition to:

```
[AttributeUsage(AttributeTargets.Method |
                        AttributeTargets.Parameter,
                        AllowMultiple=true,Inherited=true )]
public class ASCII : Attribute
```

you can place multiple attributes on a single entity and the attribute is inherited. For example, following:

```
[ASCII("Hello Method")]
[ASCII("Hello some more")]
public void MyMethod(string MyParameter)
{
}
```

`GetCustomAttributes` will return an array with two instances of `ASCII` with `MyData` set to the corresponding string.

Similarly, if you create a new class that inherits from `MyClass` the attributes are also inherited. For example:

```
public class MyClass3 : MyClass
{
}
```

has two `ASCII` attributes, exactly the same as `MyClass`.

You can, of course, forbid multiple attributes and stop attribute inheritance by setting `AllowMultiple` and `Inherited` to `false`.

Using Attributes

It is very difficult to find a convincing practical example that uses attributes that is general enough to convey the principles and ideas. If you look at the way attributes are used in C# and in the Framework you will soon discover that they have a limited application without extending the way that they behave to affect the compiler. Of course, using custom attributes you can't do this.

Some built-in attributes do give you a good idea of what they are good at without extra tricks. For example, the whole PInvoke and COM Interop marshaling of parameters is a perfect example. You apply marshaling attribute tags to the parameters of external methods you want to call and when you use them the Framework/CLR uses these attributes to decide how to transform managed data into the correct unmanaged data and vice versa.

What makes this a good use of attributes is that the marshaling has to be applied at the class level and once applied isn't going to be changed at the instance level. Moreover, the code that processes the instances can keep all of the mechanisms that load and respond to the attributes applied hidden from view. As far as the user of the attributes is concerned it's a matter of applying the attribute, then ignoring it in all the code they write, but when they use some supplied machinery the attribute makes it work correctly.

Consider for a moment the problem of assigning a format to the fields of a struct using a new attribute, Formattable. Implementing a rough sketch of such a facility reveals quite a lot about the difficulties inherent in doing a "good job" using attributes. The idea is simple, the implementation quickly becomes complicated. First we need a new attribute:

```
[AttributeUsage(AttributeTargets.Field,
                AllowMultiple = false,
                Inherited = false)]
public class Formattable : Attribute
{
        public string format;

        public Formatable(string _format)
        {
                format = _format;
        }
}
```

There is nothing new here, but it is worth saying that it would be better to implement the format string as a get/set property.

This attribute can now be applied to any field in any struct or class. Notice that you can restrict its application to, say, a field in a struct rather than a class.

Now that we have an attribute we can apply it:

```
public struct MyData
{
        public int notacost;
        [Formatable("Money")]
        public int cost;
}
```

Here we have a simple struct with two int fields one of which, cost, will hold a currency value and hence is tagged with the Formattable attribute set to Money.

Immediately we have a problem in that the user can enter any string they care to into the new attribute, not just the few we want to allow. One way of restricting the input to an attribute is to define an enum, for example:

```
public enum FormatType{Money,Percentage};
```

With this enum the attribute definition changes to:

```
[AttributeUsage(AttributeTargets.Field,
            AllowMultiple = false,
            Inherited = false)]
public class Formattable : Attribute
{
        public FormatType  format;
        public Formatable(FormatType _format)
        {
                format = _format ;
        }
}
```

and the struct becomes:

```
public struct MyData
{
        public int notacost;
        [Formatable(FormatType.Money)]
        public int cost;
}
```

Now the user really can only enter values that you provide.

The next task is to create some machinery to process the attribute. In this case we can assume that some sort of method has to be provided that displays the struct, taking notice of the attributes. We are going to write a display method that accepts a struct and formats each of its fields depending on the annotation.

The simplest way of providing this machinery is to introduce a `static` class – after all why should we need to create instances of this machinery?

```
public static class Formatter
{
```

The first problem is what to pass to the method that does the formatting? In principle we could pass any struct or class to the method and there really isn't a type-safe way of doing this without using generics and this would complicate the example. However, as long as we actually test the type passed to the method this should at least be run-time type-safe.

If you want to restrict what can be passed to structs you can, using:

```
static public void display(ValueType a)
```

Unfortunately this also allows simple types such as `int` and `long` to be passed so you need to add another test. The problem is that `struct` isn't a type, it's a keyword that creates a struct which inherits directly from `ValueType`, as do all simple types. This means you can't separate all structs from the rest of the `ValueTypes`. You can't even simply test to see if what has been passed in has fields to determine if it is a struct because simple types like `int` also have fields!

Moving on to provide the mechanism for inspecting and processing the attributes, the first step is to get all the fields:

```
System.Reflection.FieldInfo[] fields= a.GetType().GetFields();
```

Next we step through the array and process each field in turn:

```
foreach (System.Reflection.FieldInfo field in fields)
{
```

We need the array of `Formattable` attributes that have been applied and, in this case, we also need the value of the field:

```
Formatable[] formats=(Formatable[])field.
                     GetCustomAttributes(typeof(Formatable),false);
int temp = (int)field.GetValue(a);
```

Notice that we should also check that the type of the field is suitable for the formatting about to be applied, but this has been omitted for simplicity.

Now we can use the `Formattable` attribute object to determine what format of string to store in format:

```
string format="";
if (formats.Length!=0)
{
        if (formats[0].format==FormatType.Money)
        {
                format="C";
        }
}
```

Notice there can only be one `Formattable` object because of the:

```
AllowMultiple = false
```

Finally we can display the result and close the `foreach` loop, method and class:

```
        }
    MessageBox.Show(temp.ToString(format));
    }
}
```

Of course, in a real application we wouldn't just display the resulting format. It would be used in some way.

Now you can write:

```
MyData SomeData = new MyData();
SomeData.cost = 123;
SomeData.notacost = 456;
Formatter.display(SomeData);
```

The `cost` field, tagged as money format, will display with a currency symbol and the `notacost` field will display without a currency symbol.

Unfortunately as it stands the `display` method also accepts simple types so:

```
Formatter.display(1);
```

displays the two fields associated with a boxed int. There seems to be no elegant way of stopping this from happening. One solution would be to require the `Formattable` attribute to be applied to the entire struct before any of its fields are processed. That is, change the attribute to:

```
[AttributeUsage(AttributeTargets.Field|AttributeTargets.Struct,
                AllowMultiple = false,
                Inherited = false)]
public class Formattable: Attribute
```

you also need to add a constructor that takes no parameters and add a test that the passed-in parameter did indeed have a `Formattable` attribute before processing it.

The static method that implements the machinery would be better associated with the struct or, in general, the types to which it applies. That is, it should be a method of the type it is going to display the fields of. The extension method facility can be used to retrofit methods to classes that already exist. You can even add new methods to build in types such as `int` or `string`.

Unfortunately, the problem that structs inherit directly from `ValueType` makes it impossible to add an extension method to all structs and nothing else. You can easily add an extension method to a single named struct, but why bother? You might as well just add the method to the struct directly.

To add the display method to all value types you simple change its definition to:

```
static public void display(this, System.ValueType a)
```

That is, add the modifier this to the first parameter. Now you can call the display method using:

```
SomeData.display();
```

Now the display method has been added to every struct you create – powerful isn't it!

Unfortunately it has actually been added to every value type, so you can also write:

```
int i = 10;
i.display();
```

which is perhaps not what you intended. In this case it will display the two fields supported by a boxed int, i.e. the maximum and minimum values.

Postlude

Attributes are something that you probably won't use every day, but now that you know exactly how they work you can spot when the approach might be useful. There are alternatives to using attributes, but when they are appropriate they make a professional looking system for other programmers to make use of and customize the behavior of your classes.

Chapter 26

Bit Manipulation

Is C# a high-level or a low-level language? It doesn't really matter. All languages are low-level when you are thinking in terms of bits, and sometimes you just can't avoid thinking in bits.

There are all sorts of reasons why any language needs to get down to the level of the actual bits that make up any real program. Often it is forced on the programmer by the need to use legacy data or to work with raw data generated by another program or hardware device. In principle you can avoid it by introducing abstractions such as sets and so on, but at the end of the day it is usually simpler and more direct to work with the data as it is actually represented inside the machine.

This is often regrettable but mostly true.

Sooner or later you are going to have to solve a problem that comes down to working with the bit patterns that represent a variable's value.

So how should a high-level language handle such low-level work?

In the case of C# one important consideration is the need to stay in the realm of managed code. Of course, it is possible to descend to almost any level if you are happy with "unsafe" and PInvoke, but ideally C# should provide bit operations that are safe because they are part of managed code.

What is interesting about C# is that you can conclude that it isn't very good at low-level bit manipulation until you discover the `BitConverter` class and a few other, reasonably well-hidden, facilities.

Basic Operations

The basic bit manipulation operations that are provided can be confusing because of the availability of similar operators specialized to Boolean data types.

The bitwise operations are:

AND	&
OR	|
XOR (Exclusive Or)	^
NOT	~

These all work on integer data types and return the corresponding bitwise operation. For example:

```
int a = 0xF0, b = 0xFF;
int c = ~a & b;
```

computes NOT(a) AND b.

It is also worth introducing the "x" format specifier as used in 0xF0 to enter a hexadecimal format number. They don't work on floating point types or custom types unless you go to the trouble of overloading the operators. They do work on Booleans, however, and return just true or false according to the usual rules of the truth table.

There are also three logical operators that only work with Boolean:

AND	&&
OR	||
NOT	!

These only work with Boolean variables and return the same true or false results as the bitwise operators. The && and || operators are special because they are "lazy" evaluation operators. If you write:

```
bool x = false, y = true;
bool w = x & y;
bool v = x && y;
```

then w and v will have the same value. However, in the case of && the y variable will not be used at all because the fact that x is false means that the entire result has to be false no matter what values other variables have. In general, x&&y only evaluates y if x is true and x||y only evaluates y if x is false. This is not a question of efficiency, but allows for the possibility that evaluating y when the condition was already determined by x would cause an error of some sort. For example:

```
a = 0;
if (a != 0 & (b / a) < .1) { };
```

throws an exception because it attempts to perform the illegal divide by zero, whereas:

```
a = 0;
if (a != 0 && (b / a) < .1) { };
```

doesn't because the lazy evaluation avoids trying to divide when a is 0.

In addition to the bitwise logical operators C# also has a left- and right-shift operator. For example, a = a >> 8; shifts the contents eight bits to the right and a = a << 8; shifts the contents eight bits to the left. You can consider a left-shift to be an integer multiply by two and a right-shift to be a multiply by two. If the data type being shifted is a signed 32- or 64-bit type then an arithmetic right-shift is performed, i.e. new high-order bits are set to the sign bit. If the data type is an unsigned 32- or 64-bit type then a logical right shift is performed, i.e a zero bit is shifted into the high location.

If you want to perform logical shift on a signed type you can simply use an explicit cast. For example:

```
int a = -1;
int b = a >> 8;
```

performs an arithmetic shift right, but:

```
int c = (int) ((uint)  a >> 8);
```

performs a logical shift right, i.e. it shifts in zeros from the right.

All of the logical operators and the shifts work with 32- or 64-bit data types. In the case of the simple logical operations 16- and 8-bit data is automatically converted to 32-bit types and you need to use an explicit cast to recover the original data type, for example:

```
byte a = 0xFF, b=0xF0;
byte c = (byte)(a & b);
```

Things are just as simple with shifts, for example what is the result of:

```
Int16 a = 0xFF;
Int16 c = (Int16)((int)a << 8);
```

You will discover that the answer is 0xFF00.

There is also a problem with signed types. If you attempt to assign a hex value that represents a negative number, for example:

```
Int16 a = (Int16)0xFFFF;
```

you'll find it doesn't work.

If you want to force it to work then use:

```
Int16 a;
unchecked { a = (Int16)0xFFFF; }
```

where the variable declaration has now to be separate otherwise it would only be defined within the scope of the unchecked. To avoid this, use unsigned types as in:

```
UInt16 a = 0xFFFF;
UInt16 c = (UInt16)(a << 16);
```

You could argue that using unsigned types is the best way to represent bit patterns, but it is often necessary to perform bit manipulation on other data types simply because this is the object of the exercise.

You can use combinations of shifts and logical operators to create other types of shift including bit rotates. For example, a rotate left routine is fairly easy to create:

```
UInt16 RotateLeft(UInt16 data, int n){
      Int16 mask;
      unchecked{mask=(Int16)0x8000;}
      mask= (Int16)(mask  >> (n-1));
      String s = mask.ToString("X");
      UInt16 top = (UInt16)(data & mask);
      top = (UInt16) (top >> (16 - n));
      data = (UInt16)(data << n);
      data = (UInt16)(data | top);
      return data;
}
```

This works by first creating a mask with the top n bits set to 1 by using an arithmetic shift. Next we use the mask to extract the top n bits which we shift right to become the bottom n bits. Finally the shift left by n is performed and what were the top n bits are stored as the bottom n bits of the result. Of course, this could be written in a more compressed form by combining expressions, but the important question of how efficient this is could only be answered by benchmarking against alternative methods, such as performing a repeated shift and high to low bit transfer.

BitConverter

One of the most common reasons for having to resort to bit manipulation is that you have a raw stream of bytes and need to turn them into structured data. As the logical operations don't work for non-integral types, this is something of a problem if you want to convert bytes into floats, say. It is even not particularly easy to convert bytes into integral types. That is, the problem that you most often have to solve is that you have a stream of bytes and groups of bytes represent either floating point or integer values and you need to convert the stream into those types.

This is where the BitConverter class becomes important. It is intended to help you serialize an object to bytes and back again but this doesn't stop us using it for other purposes. The BitConverter has a GetBytes method that will convert any of the standard data type into a byte array and a specific To*Type* method that converts the same byte array back into the appropriate data type. So, for example:

```
double a=1.234;
byte[] data;
data=BitConverter.GetBytes(a);
```

returns an 8-byte array containing the bits that were stored in the 8-byte double. To reconstruct the double we use:

```
double b = BitConverter.ToDouble(data);
```

There are also two alternative forms of the To*Type* method that let you specify the location in the array of the data which is very useful when processing raw byte streams. The BitConverter class allows you to both generate and reconstruct data from byte streams, but it also gives you the opportunity to perform logical operations on a range of data types as a byte array and then restore the result.

It is important to realize that BitConverter is "little endian" which is something that non-Intel programmers don't take for granted. For example, what value is stored in x after this:

```
byte[] IntVal={0x00,0x01} ;
Int16 x = BitConverter.ToInt16(IntVal, 0);
```

If you think the answer is 1 then you are working in big endian format, i.e. the high-order byte comes first, but the answer on Intel-based machines is 256 because they are little endian and take the first byte as the low-order byte. Usually this isn't a problem once you know about it, but it can result in some messy byte switching if you are trying to work with little endian data.

String Problems

There is one other problem with using BitConverter and strings.

What do you think is stored in s in this case?

```
byte[] data={(byte)'A',(byte)'B',(byte)'C'};
String s = BitConverter.ToString(data);
```

You might think that it would be "ABC" but the answer is "41-53-4A", i.e. a string representation of the hexadecimal values stored in the byte array.

In short, `BitConverter` isn't much use converting raw bytes into strings. The only solution to this problem seems to be to use one of the "unsafe" string constructors that takes a pointer to a byte array:

```
unsafe String ToString(sbyte[] data){
        string s;
        fixed(sbyte* pdata=data) {
                s = new string(pdata) ;
        }
        return s;
}
```

To use this method you have to compile with "allow unsafe". If you now try:

```
sbyte[] data ={(sbyte)'A',(sbyte)'B',(sbyte)'C',0 };
string s = ToString(data);
```

you will see that the string "ABC" has been constructed from the raw byte array.

Postlude

Bit manipulation is something we try to avoid, but in some applications it is unavoidable due to the need to interact with raw data, or even raw hardware. In most cases you can do the job with safe code, but you still need to understand binary representation and all of the techniques involved in working with it. Occasionally you will still need to resort to unsafe code, but with care this can be made effectively safe.

Chapter 27

Advanced Structs

Structs are a fundamental data type in C# and most other modern programming languages. In C# structs are the value type equivalents of classes, which are reference types. In general, structs can have methods as well as properties and, with the exception of inheritance, they can be used in the same way as a class. Structs cannot inherit from another struct or another class. In this chapter we are going to ignore the object-oriented aspects of the struct and concentrate on it as a data type, i.e. we are going to focus on the struct as a data structure.

Data structures are inherently simple, but you might be surprised at how fast things can become more complicated. The problems mostly arise when you have to work with structures created in other languages, either saved and reloaded, sent over the wire or when calling native functions that are not part of C# or .NET.

You need to have a rough idea of how to call an API function using PInvoke and what marshaling is all about, which was covered in Chapter 25. Many of the techniques described in this chapter can be extended to any data type.

Layout

In many situations you can simply declare and use a struct without worrying about how it is implemented and specifically how its fields are laid out in memory. However, if you have to provide structs for consumption by other programs, or use such "foreign" structs, then memory layout matters. What do you think the size of the following struct is?

```
public struct struct1
{
        public byte a;      // 1 byte
        public int b;       // 4 bytes
        public short c;     // 2 bytes
        public byte d;      // 1 byte
}
```

A reasonable answer is 8 bytes, this being the sum of the field sizes.

If you actually investigate the size of the struct using:

```
int size = Marshal.SizeOf(test);
```

you will discover, in most cases, that the struct takes 12 bytes. The reason is that most CPUs work best with data stored in sizes larger than a single byte and aligned on particular address boundaries. Pentium-derived CPUs like their data in 16-byte chunks and like data to be aligned on address boundaries that are the same size as the data. So, for example, a 4-byte integer should be aligned on a 4-byte address boundary, i.e. the address should be of the form 4n-1. The exact details aren't important, you just need to be aware that such considerations will modify the layout from what you might expect.

What is important is that the compiler will add "padding" bytes to align the data within a struct. You can control the padding explicitly, but notice that some processors throw an exception if you use data that isn't aligned correctly. To control the layout of a struct you need to use InteropServices, so add:

```
using System.Runtime.InteropServices;
```

The struct's layout is controlled by a StructLayout attribute. For example:

```
[StructLayout(LayoutKind.Sequential)]
public struct struct1
{
        public byte a;      // 1 byte
        public int b;       // 4 bytes
        public short c;     // 2 bytes
        public byte d;      // 1 byte
}
```

forces the compiler to assign the struct sequentially as listed in the definition, which is what it does by default.

Other values of LayoutKind are Auto, which lets the compiler determine the layout, and Explicit, which lets the programmer specify the size of each field. Explicit is often used to create sequential memory layouts with no packing, but in most cases it is simpler to use the Pack field. This tells the compiler exactly how to size and align the data that makes up the fields. For example, if you specify Pack = 1 then the struct will be organized so that each field is on a byte boundary and can be read a byte at a time, i.e. no packing is necessary. If you change the definition of the struct to:

```
[StructLayout(LayoutKind.Sequential, Pack = 1)]
public struct struct1
```

you will discover that it is now 8 bytes in size, which corresponds to the fields being laid out in memory sequentially with no packing bytes. This is what you need to work with most of the structures defined in the Windows API and in C/C++.

In most cases you don't need to use other values of Pack, but if you do set Pack = 2 then you will find that the size of the struct is now 10 bytes because a byte is added to each of the byte fields to make the entire struct readable in 2-byte chunks. If you set Pack = 4 then the size increases to 12 bytes to allow the entire struct to be read in blocks of 4 bytes. After this nothing changes because the pack size is ignored once it is equal or larger to the alignment used for the CPU, which is 8 bytes for the Intel architecture.

The layout of the struct for different pack sizes can be seen in below:

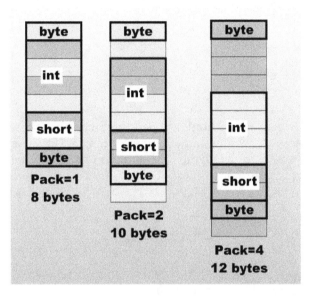

It is also worth mentioning that you can modify the way a struct is packed by simply reordering its fields. For example, by changing the field ordering to:

```
public struct struct1
{
        public byte a;  // 1 byte
        public byte d;  // 1 byte
        public short c; // 2 bytes
        public int b;   // 4 bytes
}
```

the struct doesn't need packing and occupies just 8 bytes without the need for any intervention.

Being Explicit

If you really do want to specify the space allocated to any particular field you can use Explicit. For example:

```
[StructLayout(LayoutKind.Explicit)]
public struct struct1
{
        [FieldOffset(0)]
        public byte a; // 1 byte
        [FieldOffset(1)]
        public int b;  // 4 bytes
        [FieldOffset(5)]
        public short c;// 2 bytes
        [FieldOffset(7)]
        public byte d; // 1 byte
}
```

produces an 8-byte struct without any padding bytes. In this sense it is equivalent to Pack = 1, which is much simpler to use. However, Explicit really does give you complete control should you need it. For example:

```
[StructLayout(LayoutKind.Explicit)]
public struct struct1
{
        [FieldOffset(0)]
        public byte a;  // 1 byte
        [FieldOffset(1)]
        public int b;    // 4 bytes
        [FieldOffset(10)]
        public short c; // 2 bytes
        [FieldOffset(14)]
        public byte d;  // 1 byte
}
```

produces a 16-byte struct with extra bytes following the b field.

A common use of an Explicit layout is to provide fixed length buffers for use in DLL calls, for example. You cannot simply declare a fixed-size array within a struct because initializing fields isn't permitted. That is:

```
public struct struct1
{
        public byte a;
        public int b;
        byte[] buffer = new byte[10];
        public short c;
        public byte d;
}
```

generates an error.

If you want a 10-byte buffer one way of doing it is:

```
[StructLayout(LayoutKind.Explicit)]
public struct struct1
{
        [FieldOffset(0)]
        public byte a;
        [FieldOffset(1)]
        public int b;
        [FieldOffset(5)]
        public short c;
        [FieldOffset(8)]
        public byte[] buffer;
        [FieldOffset(18)]
        public byte d;
}
```

This leaves a block of 10 bytes for the buffer at the end of the struct.

There are a number of interesting points in this declaration. The first is why use an offset of 8? The reason is that you can't start an array on an odd address boundary. If you use 7 you will see a run-time error informing you that the struct cannot be loaded because of an alignment problem. This is important because it means you can cause problems by using Explicit if you don't know what you are doing.

The second is that the entire struct has additional bytes added to the end to bring its size up to a multiple of 8 bytes. The compiler still gets involved with memory allocation. In practice, of course, any external structure that you are trying to convert to a C# struct should be correctly aligned and the problem shouldn't arise.

Finally it is worth noting that you can't refer to the 10-byte buffer using the array name, as in buffer[1] etc, because C# thinks that the buffer is unassigned. As you can't use the array and it causes an alignment problem, a much better way to declare the struct is:

```
[StructLayout(LayoutKind.Explicit)]
public struct struct1
{
        [FieldOffset(0)]
        public byte a;   // 1 byte
        [FieldOffset(1)]
        public int b;    // 4 bytes
        [FieldOffset(5)]
        public short c; // 2 bytes
        [FieldOffset(7)]
        public byte buffer;
        [FieldOffset(18)]
        public byte d;   // 1 byte
}
```

To access the 10-byte field you have to use pointer arithmetic on buffer, see the next chapter, which is of course considered "unsafe".

To allocate a fixed number of bytes to the last field in a struct you can use the Size= field in the StructLayout as in:

```
[StructLayout(LayoutKind.Explicit,Size= 64)]
```

After C# 2.0, which permitted fixed arrays within structs, the above construction is unnecessary, but it is still used in practice.

It is worth noting that fixed arrays essentially use the same mechanism, i.e. fixed size allocation and pointers, hence this too is unsafe. If you need the fixed size buffers within a call to a DLL then probably the best method is to use explicit marshaling for the arrays, which is considered "safe". Let's take a look at all three methods in use.

Calling the API

As an example of using structs with layout requirements we can use the EnumDisplayDevices function which is defined as:

```
BOOL EnumDisplayDevices(
        LPCTSTR lpDevice,// device name
        DWORD iDevNum, // display device
        PDISPLAY_DEVICE lpDisplayDevice, // device information
        DWORD dwFlags   // reserved
);
```

This is fairly easy to convert into a C# declaration:

```
[DllImport("User32.dll",CharSet=CharSet.Unicode)]
 extern static bool EnumDisplayDevices(
        string lpDevice,
        uint iDevNum,
        ref DISPLAY_DEVICE lpDisplayDevice,
        uint dwFlags);
```

The _DISPLAY_DEVICE structure is defined, in C, as:

```
typedef struct _DISPLAY_DEVICE {
        DWORD cb;
        WCHAR DeviceName[32];
        WCHAR DeviceString[128];
        DWORD StateFlags;
        WCHAR DeviceID[128];
        WCHAR DeviceKey[128];
} DISPLAY_DEVICE, *PDISPLAY_DEVICE;
```

It is clear that it contains four fixed-sized character arrays.

This can be translated into C# using an Explicit layout as:

```
[StructLayout(LayoutKind.Explicit,Pack = 1,Size=714)]
public struct DISPLAY_DEVICE
{
        [FieldOffset(0)]
        public int cb;
        [FieldOffset(4)]
        public  char DeviceName;
        [FieldOffset(68)]
        public char DeviceString;
        [FieldOffset(324)]
        public int StateFlags;
        [FieldOffset(328)]
        public  char DeviceID;
        [FieldOffset(584)]
        public  char DeviceKey;
}
```

Notice the use of Size= to specify the storage needed by the DeviceKey field.

When this is used in an actual call:

```
DISPLAY_DEVICE info = new DISPLAY_DEVICE();
info.cb = Marshal.SizeOf(info);
bool result = EnumDisplayDevices(null,0,ref info,0);
```

you can directly access the first characters in each of the buffers using the field variables. For example, DeviceString holds the first character of the device string buffer. If you want to get at the rest of the buffer you have to get a pointer to DeviceString and use pointer arithmetic to step through the array.

As long as you are using C# 2.0 or better then a simpler solution is to use a fixed array as in:

```
[StructLayout(LayoutKind.Sequential,
                          Pack = 1)]
public unsafe struct DISPLAY_DEVICE
{
        public int cb;
        public fixed char DeviceName[32];
        public fixed char DeviceString[128];
        public int StateFlags;
        public fixed char DeviceID[128];
        public fixed char DeviceKey[128];
}
```

Notice that now the struct has to be declared as unsafe, but now after the API call we can access the character arrays without using pointers. Pointers are still used behind the scenes, however, and any code that uses the arrays has to be marked as unsafe.

The third and final method is to use custom marshaling. Many C# programmers don't realize that marshaling isn't just about the way that the system types data for passing to DLLs but instead is an active process that copies and transforms the managed data. For example, if you choose to pass a reference to an array of typed elements then you can ask for it to be marshaled as a value array and the system will convert it into a fixed length buffer, and back to a managed array, without any extra effort on your part.

In this case all we have to do is add the `MarshalAs` attribute (see Chapter 24), specify the type and size of the arrays:

```
[StructLayout(LayoutKind.Sequential,Pack = 1,
                              CharSet = CharSet.Unicode)]
public struct DISPLAY_DEVICE
{
      public int cb;
      [MarshalAs(UnmanagedType.ByValArray,SizeConst=32)]
      public char[] DeviceName;
      [MarshalAs(UnmanagedType.ByValArray,SizeConst=128)]
      public char[] DeviceString;
      public int  StateFlags;
      [MarshalAs(UnmanagedType.ByValArray,SizeConst = 128)]
      public char[] DeviceID;
      [MarshalAs(UnmanagedType.ByValArray,SizeConst = 128)]
      public char[] DeviceKey;
}
```

What happens in this case is that, when you make the DLL call, the fields are marshaled by creating unmanaged buffers of the correct size within the copy of the struct that is to be passed to the DLL function. When the function returns, the unmanaged buffers are converted into managed `char` arrays and the field variables are set to reference them. As a result when the function is complete you will discover that the `struct` has `char` arrays of the correct size containing the data.

Clearly, as far as calling a DLL is concerned, the custom marshal is the best option as it produces safe code, although using `PInvoke` to call a DLL isn't really safe in any reasonable sense of the word.

Serializing Structs

Now that we have looked at the complicated question of how to control the memory layout of a struct, it is time to discover how to get at the bytes that make up a struct, i.e. how do we serialize a struct?

While there are many ways of doing this job, the most commonly encountered uses `Marshal.AllocHGlobal` to allocate an unmanaged buffer from the global heap. After this everything is achieved using memory transfer functions such as StructToPtr or Copy, for example:

```
public static byte[] RawSerialize(object anything)
{
        int rawsize = Marshal.SizeOf(anything);
        IntPtr buffer = Marshal.AllocHGlobal(rawsize);
        Marshal.StructureToPtr(anything,buffer, false);
        byte[] rawdata = new byte[rawsize];
        Marshal.Copy(buffer, rawdata, 0, rawsize);
        Marshal.FreeHGlobal(buffer);
        return rawdata;
}
```

In fact, there is no need to do so much bit moving as it is fairly easy to move the bytes in the struct directly to the byte array without the need for an intermediate buffer.

The key to this generally useful technique is the GCHandle object. This will return a garbage collection handle to any managed data type. If you ask for a "pinned" handle then the object will not be moved by the garbage collector and you can use the handle's AddrOfPinnedObject method to retrieve its starting address. For example the RawSerialise method can be rewritten:

```
public static byte[] RawSerialize(object anything)
{
        int rawsize = Marshal.SizeOf(anything);
        byte[] rawdata = new byte[rawsize];
        GCHandle handle = GCHandle.Alloc(rawdata,GCHandleType.Pinned);
        Marshal.StructureToPtr(anything,
                                handle.AddrOfPinnedObject(),
                                false);
        handle.Free();
        return rawdata;
}
```

This is both simpler and faster. You can use the same methods to deserialize data in a byte array into a struct, but rather than considering this example it is more instructive to examine the related problem of reading a struct from a stream.

Structs From Streams

A fairly common requirement is to read a struct, possibly written using some other language, into a C# struct. For example, suppose you need to read in a bitmap file which starts with a file header, followed by a bitmap header and then the bitmap data. The file header structure is easy to translate:

```
[StructLayout(LayoutKind.Sequential,Pack = 1)]
public struct BITMAPFILEHEADER
{
        public Int16 bfType;
        public Int32 bfSize;
        public Int16 bfReserved1;
        public Int16 bfReserved2;
        public Int32 bfOffBits;
};
```

A function that will read any structure available as a stream and return a struct can be written without the need for generics:

```
public object ReadStruct(FileStream fs,Type t)
{
        byte[] buffer = new byte[Marshal.SizeOf(t)];
        fs.Read(buffer,0,Marshal.SizeOf(t));
        GCHandle handle = GCHandle.Alloc(buffer,GCHandleType.Pinned);
        Object temp =
                Marshal.PtrToStructure(handle.AddrOfPinnedObject(), t);
        handle.Free();
        return temp;
}
```

You should recognize the use of the GCHandle object to enable the data to be transferred. The new feature is the use of a Type object to specify the type of the struct being read in. Unfortunately there is no way to use this to return an object of the specified type and so we need to use a cast when calling the function, as in:

```
FileStream fs = new FileStream(
                @"c:\1.bmp",
                FileMode.Open,
                FileAccess.Read);
BITMAPFILEHEADER bmFH =(BITMAPFILEHEADER) ReadStruct(fs,
                                                typeof(BITMAPFILEHEADER));
```

If we want to avoid the cast then we need to create a generic method. This is just a matter of introducing a type parameter <T> and then using it throughout the method as if it was the type of the struct:

```
public T ReadStruct <T> (FileStream fs)
{
        byte[] buffer = new byte[Marshal.SizeOf(typeof( T ))];
        fs.Read(buffer,0,Marshal.SizeOf(typeof(T)));
        GCHandle handle = GCHandle.Alloc(buffer,GCHandleType.Pinned);
        T temp = (T) Marshal.PtrToStructure(
                            handle.AddrOfPinnedObject(),
                            typeof(T));
        handle.Free();
        return temp;
}
```

Notice that now we have to cast the object returned by PtrToStructure to the type in the method rather than in the method call, which becomes:

```
BITMAPFILEHEADER bmFH =  ReadStruct <BITMAPFILEHEADER>(fs);
```

It is interesting to contemplate just how much better the generic method is than the method that needs the explicit cast.

Manual Marshaling

Marshaling works so well most of the time that there is a tendency to forget that it is doing anything at all. However, as soon as you hit something even slightly out of the ordinary, you might be surprised at what happens when it stops working. For example, some API calls need you to pass a pointer to a pointer to struct. You already know how to pass a pointer to a struct, it's just pass by reference using ref. This might lead you to believe that a simple modification will allow you to pass a pointer to that pointer, but things are more complicated than you might expect. Let's look at this one step at a time.

In the AVIFileCreateStream API call the last two parameters are passed as pointers to an IntPtr and a struct respectively:

```
[DllImport("avifil32.dll")]
extern static int AVIFileCreateStream(
      IntPtr pfile,
      ref IntPtr pavi,
      ref AVISTREAMINFO lParam);
```

To use this API call you would use:

```
result = AVIFileCreateStream(pFile, ref pStream, ref Sinfo);
```

At this point, given our earlier examples, it would appear easy to take over the marshaling of the pointer to the struct and do it manually. For example, what could be wrong with changing the declaration to:

```
[DllImport("avifil32.dll")]
extern static int AVIFileCreateStream(
        IntPtr pfile,
        ref IntPtr pavi,
        IntPtr lParam);
```

However, if you try to use it by passing the address of the pinned structure:

```
GCHandle handle = GCHandle.Alloc(Sinfo, GCHandleType.Pinned);
result = AVIFileCreateStream(pFile, ref pStream,
                                handle.AddrOfPinnedObject());
handle.Free();
```

the result is a run-time error:

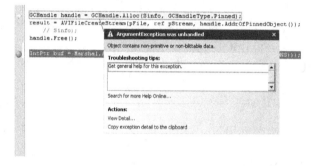

The reason is that while you are indeed passing a pointer to the start of the struct, that struct is in managed memory and unmanaged code cannot access it without generating a protection error.

What we are forgetting is that standard marshaling does much more for us than generate addresses to use as pointers. The default marshaling for all parameters passed by ref also makes a copy of the entire data in unmanaged memory before deriving a pointer. It then copies the unmanaged memory back to the managed type when the function ends.

It isn't difficult, and is indeed quite useful, to write a function that does the same job as default marshaling:

```
private IntPtr MarshalToPointer(object data)
{
        IntPtr buf = Marshal.AllocHGlobal(Marshal.SizeOf(data));
        Marshal.StructureToPtr(data, buf, false);
        return buf;
}
```

This simply returns an IntPtr to an area of the global heap that contains a copy of the data. The only problem with this function is that you have to remember to release the allocated heap memory after use. For example:

```
IntPtr lpstruct = MarshalToPointer(Sinfo);
result = AVIFileCreateStream(pFile,ref pStream,lpstruct);
Marshal.FreeHGlobal(lpstruct);
```

works exactly like default marshaling.

But don't forget that lpstruct is itself still being marshaled as a pass-by-value integer. To copy the result back to the struct, an additional function is required:

```
private object MarshalToStruct(IntPtr buf,Type t)
{
        return Marshal.PtrToStructure(buf, t);
}
```

Now that we have mastered the manual marshaling of a simple pointer to a struct, the next step is a pointer to a pointer to a struct. Surprisingly this requires nothing new because the struct-to-pointer function will actually convert any data type to an unmanaged pointer, including a pointer. The function AVISaveOptions is a suitable example as it needs two pointers to pointers as parameters:

```
[DllImport("avifil32.dll")]
extern static int AVISaveOptions(
      IntPtr hWnd,
      int uiFlags,
      int noStreams,
      IntPtr ppavi,
      IntPtr ppOptions);
```

In fact the ppavi parameter is a pointer to a handle, which is itself a pointer, and the ppOptions is a pointer to a pointer to a struct.

To call this function we first need the struct:

```
AVICOMPRESSOPTIONS opts = new AVICOMPRESSOPTIONS();
```

You can look up the definition of the structure in the standard AVI documentation.

Next we need the marshaled pointer to the struct:

```
IntPtr lpstruct = MarshalToPointer(opts);
```

and then the pointer to the pointer:

```
IntPtr lppstruct = MarshalToPointer(lpstruct);
```

followed by the pointer to the handle:

```
IntPtr lphandle = MarshalToPointer(pStream);
```

The call to the API function is now simple:

```
result = AVISaveOptions(
        m_hWnd,
        ICMF_CHOOSE_KEYFRAME |
        ICMF_CHOOSE_DATARATE,
        1,
        lphandle,
        lppstruct);
```

where the other parameters and constants aren't of any great interest to us and you can find more details in the API's documentation.

When the function completes, all that is left to do is transfer the data in the unmanaged buffer back into the managed struct:

```
opts = (AVICOMPRESSOPTIONS) MarshalToStruct(lpstruct,
                                    typeof(AVICOMPRESSOPTIONS));
```

You have to be careful to use the pointer to the struct and not the pointer to the pointer!

Finally we can free all of the unmanaged memory we used:

```
Marshal.FreeHGlobal(lpstruct);
Marshal.FreeHGlobal(lppstruct);
Marshal.FreeHGlobal(lphandle);
```

All this might seem complicated. Using pointers-to-pointers is never an easy thing to do and it is one of the reasons that C# makes sure that when you do use pointers you mark the code as unsafe. However, you might like to contemplate just how safe this sort of juggling is - and all without an unsafe block in sight. On the other hand the general principles are very simple. When you pass anything by ref to an API it has to be copied to unmanaged memory and the address of this memory is passed to the function. Normally default marshaling takes care of this and you can ignore it, but it still happens. If you need to go beyond what is provided by the marshaling attributes then you have to perform this copying explicitly.

Postlude

The layout of data in memory is something you can generally ignore unless you need to interface to the outside world. Mostly thing go simply, but what is easy or even natural in languages such as C and C++ is regarded as undesirable at best and often unsafe at worst. With some general techniques of working with memory and pointers, however, you can interface to almost anything.

Chapter 28

Pointers

In a modern language the argument is that you should never need to get down and dirty with pointers because to do so simply reveals that you are thinking at too primitive a level and in severe danger of meeting the real hardware that underpins everything. While this is true there are still times when reality pokes through the abstraction and you do have to interact with the hardware in ways that can only be achieved using pointers. In addition, there are all those wonderful C and C++ programs that use pointers and need to be converted to something more polished and safe.

In short, you certainly should know about pointers, even if hopefully you never actually make use of them in a real production application. If you do find that pointers are essential to something low-level that you are trying to implement then it is also important that you know how to implement them in as "safe" a way as possible.

Reference, Pointer and Address

First we need to clear up some confusion that exists between the three terms "reference", "pointer" and "address".

Starting with the most basic, "address" means the numerical address where something is stored. Most computer hardware assigns addresses using a simple incrementing scheme starting at some value and continuing to some other value, e.g. 0 to 1000, and each address corresponds to a memory location capable of storing some data with a given number of bits. This simple idea has become increasingly complicated as hardware has developed and with the introduction of hardware memory mapping. Now the address that data is stored at can change without the data being moved due to the use of address translation hardware. Even if the hardware doesn't get in the way, addresses change while an application is running because the operating system, or a garbage collection system, often moves things around to make things more efficient.

While once the address of something was a fixed and reliable way of accessing it, today it is surrounded by a range of problems.

The "pointer" is the step in abstracting the idea of an address. At its most basic a pointer is simply a variable that can be used to store the address of something. You can use a pointer to gain access to the data item pointed at, a process called "dereferencing". You can also subject the pointer to arithmetic operations that move its location in the "store". That is, if there are a number of objects stored one after the other in the address store you can perform pointer arithmetic to change the object that is pointed at. Pointer arithmetic is the reason that many programmers like pointers, but it is also the reason why pointers are dangerous.

A mistake in the pointer computation can result in it pointing somewhere it shouldn't and the whole system can crash as a result.

There really is no reason why a pointer shouldn't be abstracted away from the basic idea of an address, but in most cases pointers are just wrappers for machine addresses and this also raises the question of what happens if the system does something that changes the address of an object. More of this later.

Finally we reach the highest point of abstraction of the address idea in the form of a "reference". A reference is simply a reference to an item of data or an object. If this sounds like a pointer there is a sense in which this is true, but the key idea is that you can't manipulate a reference directly. That is, while there certainly is pointer arithmetic, there can be no reference arithmetic.

All you can do with a reference is to pass it to another user or dereference it and access the data that it references.

As in the case of abstract pointers there is no reason why a reference shouldn't be abstracted away from the underlying machine address, but in most cases, and C# in particular, a reference is just a wrapper for an address. In future implementations, however, a reference could be implemented as a handle or index to a table, to another table, to a resource index and so on, until finally the hardware converts the reference to the address of an actual data object.

The point is that while we all know that in C# a reference, and for that matter a pointer, is simply a wrapper for an address, this is a detail of implementation and not something you should rely on or make use of.

References Revisited

As discussed in Chapter 3, in C# we make use of references all the time in the form of variables that have been assigned any reference type. For example, if you create an instance of a class then the instance variable isn't an object but a reference to an object of the appropriate type. That is, after:

```
MyClass MyObject = new MyClass();
```

MyObject is a reference to an instance of MyClass. In practice it contains the address of the instance but, as already explained, you shouldn't rely on this form of implementation. You can think of MyObject as a sort of "safe pointer". It is safe because you can't do anything much with it. You can't manipulate a reference so that it points at some other object unless you assign a new reference to it:

```
MyClass MyObject2 = MyObject;
```

This stores a reference in MyObject2 to the same object that MyObject references. A raw pointer behaves in this way too but in this case it is a lower level concept and you are encouraged to think about the assignment as assigning pointers rather than anything to do with value versus reference semantics.

The difference between a reference and a value basically comes down to assignment semantics – does assignment produce a copy of the referenced data/object? If it does then we have value semantics. If it doesn't we have reference semantics. What gets duplicated in an assignment is the pointer/reference not the object.

You can argue, and it is a good argument, that all assignment is value assignment and the value of a reference variable is just a reference just as the value of a pointer is the address it stores.

That is the key difference isn't the way assignment works but what is being assigned and this is an abstraction from a pointer to a reference.

Many of the subtleties of reference semantics are simply a consequence of not admitting that a reference is nothing more than a pointer and the value of a pointer is something that acts like an address.

Pointers In C#

Pointers in C#' are a generalization of the reference type to include pointer arithmetic. In other words, a reference that you can do arithmetic with is a pointer. Pointers are so dangerous that they have to be quarantined within your code. First the entire project has to be marked as unsafe by using the Project Properties to set the "Build, Allow Unsafe Code" flag. Then any use of pointers has to be enclosed in an unsafe{} block to mark it out even more clearly.

You cannot create a pointer to anything you care to point at, only to a restricted subset of types that have a simpler way of using memory, so making pointer use slightly less tricky. Essentially you can only create a pointer to any simple value type, e.g. `int`, `float`, `char`, to an enum, to another pointer or to a struct that doesn't contain other managed types. So you can't have a pointer to an object, or to a delegate or to a reference. This is restrictive and basically amounts to not allowing pointers to anything that is created on the heap or is subject to dynamic memory management. However, you can have a pointer to a struct that contains simple value types and you can create pointers to arrays of simple value types. This is generally enough to allow pointers to be used to work with legacy implementations of data structures or to work with binary data structures that have been received over the network or from a file. You can also create pointers to functions using the `delegate*` type.

You can also have a pointer of type `void`, i.e. a pointer to an unknown type, but to be of any use in pointer arithmetic you need to cast a void pointer to a pointer to a given type. To declare a pointer type C# uses the C++-like syntax `type* variable;` where * is the dereferencing or indirection operator and is generally used in conjunction with the address-of-operator &, which as its name suggests, returns the address of a variable.

For example:

```
unsafe{
        int* pMyInt;
        int MyInt;
        pMyInt = &MyInt;
}
```

creates a pointer to an integer, i.e. `pMyInt` and stores the address of the integer `MyInt` in the pointer.

The first important thing to note is that a pointer does not inherit from an object and so there are no methods associated with it and no boxing and unboxing. For example, you can't use a `ToString()` method call to display the value of a pointer. What you can do, however, is to use a cast to convert a pointer to a more usual data type. So, to display the contents of the pointer you would use something like:

```
MessageBox.Show(((int)pMyInt).ToString());
```

Of course, this assumes that the current implementation of `int` is large enough to contain a pointer, i.e. a machine address. Notice that this is not dereferencing the pointer, but showing you the pointer's contents. Also notice that the way that machine represents an address comes into consideration and this is a reflection of the fact that pointers are a low-level construct.

The indirection operator returns the values stored at the address that a pointer is pointing at. For example:

```
MessageBox.Show((*pMyInt).ToString());
```

displays the current contents of MyInt, i.e. the value of whatever pMyInt is pointing at. That is, *pMyInt is an int.

The indirection operator and the address of the operator really are the inverse of one another. That is:

```
MessageBox.Show((*&MyInt).ToString());
```

just displays the content of MyInt.

A pointer can be null and applying the indirection operator in this case generates an exception. Obviously it makes no sense to use indirection on a void pointer - what would the data type of the result be? However, you can always cast a void pointer and then use indirection.

Notice that this process can produce complete nonsense. For example, consider:

```
void* pMyData = &MyInt;
MessageBox.Show((*(double*)pMyData).ToString());
```

This sets a void pointer to an integer, specifically a 32-bit integer, then casts it to a double pointer, i.e. double*, and finally uses the indirection operator to return the value so pointed at. If you try this out you will find that it works, but it is mostly nonsense because the original int was only 4 bytes of storage and the double is 8 bytes.

Where did the additional 4 bytes come from? The answer is that you have succeeded in reading data from a neighboring memory location, one that you normally would not be able to access. Of course, reading from a memory location that you don't understand is fairly safe, but who knows what effect writing to such a location is going to have?

This is the basic mechanism that malware uses to escape the confines of managed code or more simply to access memory it has no right to access and is the reason pointers are considered unsafe. For example, try:

```
int MyInt2 = 0;
int MyInt = 1234;
void* pMyData = &MyInt;
*(double*)pMyData = 123456.789;
MessageBox.Show(MyInt2.ToString());
```

You might be surprised to discover that the value of MyInt2 has changed and is no longer 0, even though it isn't assigned a new value within the program. The simple explanation is that MyInt2 is allocated storage alongside MyInt and when we assign an 8-byte value to MyInt the extra four bytes overwrite

MyInt2. This is clearly dangerous, unexpected and usually unwanted behavior and, as already mentioned but it cannot be said too often, results in code that is "unsafe".

One very common use of pointers is to get at the internals of a data type. For example, suppose you want to retrieve the four bytes that make up a 32-bit integer:

```
int MyInt = 123456789;
```

We can always use a void pointer to get the address of any variable:

```
void* MyPointer;
MyPointer = &MyInt;
```

Then we can cast it to a pointer to any of the standard types and use pointer arithmetic, in this case to a byte which is then converted to a char:

```
byte* pMyByte = (byte*)MyPointer;
char MyChar = (char)*(pMyByte + 3);
MessageBox.Show(MyChar.ToString());
```

The reason we don't go directly to a char pointer is that a char is two bytes in size and we are converting a 4-byte int to four ASCII byte characters rather than Unicode 2-byte characters.

In most cases there are managed ways of gaining access to the internal structure of the common data types using either the Convert or BitConvertor classes. In this case the GetBytes method of the BitConvertor can be used to convert the int to a byte array and then any of the bytes can be converted to a char using the Convert class:

```
Byte[] Bytes=BitConverter.GetBytes(MyInt);
MyChar = Convert.ToChar(Bytes[3]);
```

As long as there is a GetBytes method that will convert the data type into a byte array, you don't need to use pointers.

Multiple Indirection

If you think you have got the idea of indirection then it's time to put you to the test. The real mark of a pointer expert is being able to handle double, treble, and more, indirection. In theory this is easy.

For example:,

```
int** ppMyInt;
int* pMyInt;
int MyInt=1234;
pMyInt = &MyInt;
ppMyInt = &pMyInt;
MessageBox.Show((**ppMyInt).ToString());
```

In this case we declare a pointer to a pointer, i.e. `ppMyInt`, and use it to point at `pMyInt`.

To display the value pointed at by `pMyInt`, i.e. the value in `MyInt`, we have to use two levels of indirection as in `**ppMyInt`. In this case double indirection is fairly easy to follow but in real cases it can become very difficult to work out when you need a pointer or a pointer to a pointer and so on.

Pointers, Arrays and Fixed

There is a very close relationship between pointers and arrays, indeed you could say that pointers in languages such as C and C++ were introduced just so that it was possible to create arrays. In principle the address of the first element of an array can be used to find any element of an array, but things are a little more complicated. For example:

```
int[] MyArray = new int[10];
for (int i = 0; i < 10; i++) MyArray[i] = i;
int* pMyArray = &MyArray[0];
MessageBox.Show((*pMyArray).ToString());
```

should create a pointer to the first element of the array, but if you try it you will discover that you simply get an error to the effect that you can't take the address of an unfixed expression. The reason is that, while `MyArray[0]` is just an integer variable, the compiler knows that the array is a managed object and can be moved at any time. If you were to take the address of an array and then it moved, the address would be useless and the pointer would end up pointing to some other location. You can see the danger in a pointer not pointing at what you thought is was pointing at.

To make a meaningful array address you have to use the `fixed` keyword:

```
fixed(pointer declaration){
      instructions to be carried
      out while data is fixed
}
```

The `fixed` construction tells the compiler that the array or any data type in the pointer declaration should not change its location until the end of the fixed block. In other words, within the fixed block it is safe to use the pointer. For example:

```
fixed (int* pMyArray= &MyArray[0]){
 MessageBox.Show((*pMyArray).ToString());
}
```

will work and will display the contents of the first element of the array.

You can also use the array name as a shorthand for &MyArray[0] as in:

```
fixed (int* pMyArray= MyArray){
    MessageBox.Show((*pMyArray).ToString());
}
```

Notice that the pointer declared in the fixed statement goes out of scope when it ends, so you can't use pMyArray unless the array is fixed.

Pointer Arithmetic

If you want to access other array elements then you simply use pointer arithmetic as in:

```
fixed (int* pMyArray= MyArray){
    MessageBox.Show((*pMyArray+5).ToString());
}
```

which displays MyArray[5]. Notice that this is rather more subtle than you might think as adding 5 to the address of the start of the array actually adds 5 times the size of a single integer element. That is, the arithmetic operators have been overloaded to work in units of the size of the data type being pointed to. There is a sizeof operator which returns the size of any value type and this is used to work out what to add to a pointer. That is, pointer+5 is translated to:

```
pointer+5*sizeof(pointertype);
```

So, pointer+n doesn't mean "*add n to the address in pointer*", but "*move on n elements in the array*".

To complete the connection between arrays and pointers you can also use array indexing as a shortcut to dereferencing and pointer arithmetic. That is, pointer[5] is a synonym for *pointer+5:

```
fixed (int* pMyArray = &MyArray[0]){
    MessageBox.Show(pMyArray[5].ToString());
}
```

There is a restriction on the use of the fixed pointer in that it cannot be modified within the fixed statement. This isn't a problem as you can simply make a copy of it:

```
fixed (int* pMyArray= MyArray){
    int* ptemp = pMyArray;
    MessageBox.Show((*++ptemp).ToString());
}
```

which displays the contents of MyArray[1].

This sort of pointer manipulator works with multi-dimensional arrays, for example:

```
int[,] MyArray = new int[10,10];
fixed (int* pMyArray= &MyArray[0,0]){
        for (int i = 0; i < 100; i++){
                *(pMyArray + i) = i;
        }
}
```

This initializes a two-dimensional array by accessing it as a linear block of memory. Of course, the order in which the array is initialized depends on how it is stored in memory and I leave it to you to breakpoint the example and discover if it is stored in row or column order. It is this sort of trick, i.e. accessing a 2-D array as if it was a 1-D structure, that made, and still makes, pointers so attractive, to some developers.

Notice that you can initialize multiple pointers within a fixed statement as long as they are all of the same type. To initialize multiple pointers of different types you have to use nested `fixed` statements, one for each type.

Structs

It is time now to turn our attention to structs and pointers to structs. You might well imagine that if an array is something you have to fix before using pointers to it then you would certainly have to fix a struct in the same way. You don't have to because a `struct` is a value type and allocated on the stack. So you can use:

```
public struct MyStructType{
        public int x;
        public int y;
};
MyStructType MyStruct=new MyStructType();
MyStructType* pMyStruct = &MyStruct;
```

Now, how do you access a field using a pointer? You can use the fairly obvious:

```
(*pMyStruct).x = 1;
```

That is, dereference the pointer and use the usual dot selector. However, in a homage to the C++ usage you can also write:

```
pMyStruct->y = 2;
MessageBox.Show(pMyStruct->x.ToString());
```

Here the -> dereferences the pointer and selects the field in a single step.

Strings

It is usually said that you can't have a pointer to a string because a string is a managed object, but, just like an array, you can fix a string and then you can initialize a char pointer to the first character in the string. For example:

```
string MyString = "Hello pointer world";
fixed (char* pMyString = MyString){
    MessageBox.Show((*(pMyString + 6)).ToString());
}
```

creates a string in the usual way, fixes it and obtains a char pointer to its first char. Then we can perform pointer arithmetic to access the sixth character in the string.

Memory Allocation

As well as working with value types you can create your own primitive data types using the stack. The statement stackalloc *type*[n] allocates enough stack to store n copies of the stated data type and returns a pointer to the start of the allocation. You don't need to fix the storage as the stack isn't moved or garbage collected while the variables are in scope. You also don't have to remember to deallocate the memory because the stack is automatically cleaned up when the variables go out of scope, usually when the method that declared them returns. For example:

```
int* pMyArray = stackalloc int[100];
pMyArray[10] = 34;
MessageBox.Show(pMyArray[10].ToString());
```

allocates 100 integers, i.e. 400 bytes, on the stack and uses the pointer to store 34 in the four bytes starting at the 40th byte and then displays this value.

Notice that the use of the array indexing makes this look exactly like allocating and using a standard array. However, the block of memory really is just a block of memory that you can do what you like with. For example:

```
public struct MyStructType{
    public int x;
    public int y;
};
MyStructType* pMyDataBlock = stackalloc MyStructType[1];
pMyDataBlock->x = 34;
```

allocates a struct on the stack, but this is really just sizeof(MyStructType) which happens to be just two integers, i.e. 8 bytes.

We can use the pointer to the structure in the usual way to set or access a field. That is, we can use the block as if it was a struct, but if we want to we can just treat it as a block of 8 bytes and use it as some other data structure.

For example, if you want to treat the data as an array of `int` you can by casting the pointer:

```
*((int*)pMyDataBlock) = 36;
```

This expression is a little difficult to follow so a simpler multi-step version is:

```
int* pMyArray = (int*)pMyDataBlock;
pMyArray[0] = 36;
```

This casts a pointer to `int` then uses array indexing to access the first element of the array, which is the same as the x field of the struct. Notice that this correspondence depends on the way the struct is organized in memory and currently the C# compiler stores fields in the order in which they are declared – see also Chapter 27.

A range of attributes can be applied to ask the compiler to use particular memory layouts for a struct, see Chapter 27, but even then you are making use of details of implementation that could change and make your program invalid.

Function Pointers

Most of the time delegates are sufficient as a way of passing functions around in a program, but you can also use a pointer to a function. You create a pointer to a function in the way you would expect using the address operator, but you also have to specify the parameter and return types:

```
delegate*<int,void> pFunc=&myFunction;
```

The need for the parameter and return types to be specified is mainly to resolve any problems with function overloading.

Having specified a pointer to void `myFunction(int)`, you can call `myFunction(int)` using `pFunc(42)`. Notice that no dereferencing is needed because when you call a function the address is automatically used. You can pass a function pointer as a parameter. For example:

```
void myFunction2(delegate*<int,void> myParam){
      myParam(42);
}
```

and make use of it as:

```
myFunction2(pFunc);
```

Notice that `myFunction` can only be called in an unsafe context as it has an `unsafe` parameter. You can also use a calling convention specifier, but only `managed` or `unmanaged` and `unmanaged` can be any of `Cdecl`, `Stdcall`, `Thiscall` and `Fastcall`. You cannot perform pointer arithmetic on a function pointer.

Postlude

You might be excited to learn all about pointers but, as you might have detected, they are not really a good idea. C and C++ programmers moving to C# tend to think in terms of pointers and hence like the facility, but in practice you almost never need them. If you need to do a quick conversion of a C/C++ program that uses pointers then it might be acceptable to use C# pointers to get things moving, but it should be considered a stopgap measure until you can implement the ideas without pointers.

About the only time pointers might be necessary is in making use of API calls within the PInvoke subsystem. Even here there are usually alternatives and often passing by reference solves even pointer-to-pointer problems. Things do get more difficult when you need to pass a pointer to a block of memory and in this case you might have to use a fixed array or allocate memory on the stack and pass it directly to the API call. In most cases you don't need to use pointers when implementing an algorithm in C# from scratch

Index

Other Books by Mike James

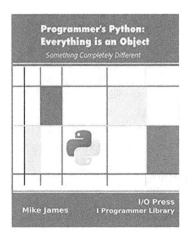

Programmer's Python:
Everything is an Object
Mike James
ISBN: 978-1871962581

This book sets out to explain the deeper logic in the approach that Python 3 takes to classes and objects. The subject is roughly speaking everything to do with the way Python implements objects. That is, in order of sophistication, metaclass; class; object; attribute; and all of the other facilities such as functions, methods and the many "magic methods" that Python uses to make it all work.

This is a fairly advanced book in the sense that you are expected to know basic Python. However, it tries to explain the ideas using the simplest examples possible. As long as you can write a Python program, and you have an idea what object-oriented programming is about, it should all be

JavaScript Jems:
The Amazing Parts
Mike James
ISBN: 978-1871962420

This book is a "meditation" on the features that make JavaScript stand apart from other languages and make it special in terms of having admirable qualities. Each Jem is intended to be an enjoyable read for any JavaScript programmer showing the language in a new light. These are referred to as "Jems". It's not a word you will find in the dictionary, but it is used in the same sense as its homophone "Gem" as "something prized for its beauty and value".

Here we have a collection of twenty jems about features that have their advantages and disadvantages over their counterparts in other languages.

The Programmer's Guide To Theory:
Great ideas explained
Mike James
ISBN: 978-1871962437

Computer science, specifically the theory of computation, deserves to be better known even among non-computer scientists. The reason is simply that it is full of profound thoughts and ideas. It contains some paradoxes that reveal the limits of human knowledge. It provides ways to reason about information and randomness that are understandable without the need to resort to abstract math.

This is not an academic textbook, but could be the precursor to reading an academic textbook.

The Programmer's Guide To Kotlin
Second Edition
Mike James
ISBN: 978-1871962703

Kotlin experienced a surge of popularity when Google made it a first-class language for Android development and gradually it has found its way into many domains as an object-oriented language that is fun and flexible in its approach. It is an interesting language because it is 100% runtime compatible with Java while being easier to use. Using Kotlin will make programming simpler and your programs better, and this is why you need to learn Kotlin.

This book introduces Kotlin to programmers. You don't have to be an expert in Java or any other language, but you do need to know the basics of programming and using objects. As with all languages Kotlin has some subtle areas where an understanding of how things work makes all the difference and this second edition pay close attention to these gotchas and has a completely new chapter on Coroutines, which is perhaps the Kotlin feature with the most pitfalls and the least documentation. After reading this book all is made clear and workable.